Civilized Rebels

Civilized Rebels compares in depth four very well-known literary and political figures, who all opposed arrogant regimes and became prisoners. Through comparative biographies of Oscar Wilde, Jean Améry, Nelson Mandela and Aung San Suu Kyi, it explores the long-term process of the retreat of the West from global power since the late nineteenth century, relating this to the decline and fall of the British Empire and the trauma surrounding Brexit. Drawing on rich empirical materials to examine themes of forced displacement, war, poverty, imprisonment and the threat of humiliation, the book reveals how these highly civilized rebels penetrated their opponents' mind-sets, while also providing a sophisticated analysis of how their struggles fitted into the larger world picture. Methodologically and theoretically innovative, and written in a lively and accessible style, *Civilized Rebels* will appeal to scholars across a range of disciplines, with interests in globalization, historical international relations, postcolonial and subaltern studies, comparative biographical studies, European studies, the sociology of emotions and historical sociology.

Dennis Smith is Emeritus Professor of Sociology at Loughborough University, UK. He is the author of *The Rise of Historical Sociology, Globalization: The Hidden Agenda*, and *Conflict and Compromise: Class Formation in English Society 1830–1914*.

Global Connections

Series Editor: Robert Holton, Trinity College, Dublin

Global Connections builds on the multi-dimensional and continuously expanding interest in globalization, focusing on "connectedness" and providing accessible, concrete studies across a broad range of areas such as social and cultural life, and economic, political and technological activities. Interdisciplinary in approach, the series moves beyond abstract generalities and stereotypes: "Global" is considered in the broadest sense of the word, embracing connections between different nations, regions and localities, including activities that are trans-national, and trans-local in scope; "connections" refers to movements of people, ideas, resources, and all forms of communication as well as the opportunities and constraints faced in making, engaging with, and sometimes resisting globalization.

For a full list of titles in this series, please visit www.routledge.com/series/ASHSER1306

Titles in the series include:

Global Culture
Consciousness and Connectivity
Roland Robertson and Didem Buhari-Gulmez

Eurocentrism at the Margins
Encounters, Critics and Going Beyond
Lutfi Sunar

Glocal Pharma
International Brands and the Imagination of Local Masculinity
Ericka Johnson and Ebba Sjögren

The Socio-Political Practice of Human Rights
Between the Universal and the Particular
Kiran Kaur Grewal

The Global Repositioning of Japanese Religions
An Integrated Approach
Ugo Dessì

Civilized Rebels
An Inside Story of the West's Retreat from Global Power

Dennis Smith

LONDON AND NEW YORK

First published 2018
by Routledge
2 Park Square, Milton Park, Abingdon, Oxon OX14 4RN

and by Routledge
711 Third Avenue, New York, NY 10017

Routledge is an imprint of the Taylor & Francis Group, an informa business

© 2018 Dennis Smith

The right of Dennis Smith to be identified as author of this work has been asserted by him in accordance with sections 77 and 78 of the Copyright, Designs and Patents Act 1988.

All rights reserved. No part of this book may be reprinted or reproduced or utilised in any form or by any electronic, mechanical, or other means, now known or hereafter invented, including photocopying and recording, or in any information storage or retrieval system, without permission in writing from the publishers.

Trademark notice: Product or corporate names may be trademarks or registered trademarks, and are used only for identification and explanation without intent to infringe.

British Library Cataloguing in Publication Data
A catalogue record for this book is available from the British Library

Library of Congress Cataloging in Publication Data
Names: Smith, Dennis, 1945- author.
Title: Civilized rebels : an inside story of the West's retreat from global power / Dennis Smith.
Description: Abingdon, Oxon ; NewYork, NY : Routledge, 2018. | Includes bibliographical references and index.
Identifiers: LCCN 2017050374 | ISBN 9780815393160 (hbk) | ISBN 9780815393177 (pbk) | ISBN 9781351189316 (ebk)
Subjects: LCSH: Dissenters--Case studies. | Radicals--Case studies. | Political prisoners--Case studies. | Imperialism. | Balance of power. | International relations.
Classification: LCC HN49.R33 S65 2018 | DDC 303.48/4--dc23
LC record available at https://lccn.loc.gov/2017050374

ISBN: 978-0-8153-9316-0 (hbk)
ISBN: 978-0-8153-9317-7 (pbk)
ISBN: 978-1-351-18931-6 (ebk)

Typeset in Times New Roman
by Taylor & Francis Books

Contents

	Preface	vi
	Acknowledgements	x
1	Rebels and regimes	1
2	Oscar Wilde	33
3	Jean Améry	61
4	Nelson Mandela	87
5	Aung San Suu Kyi	115
6	Confronting humiliation	151
7	The big picture	176
	Index	195

Preface

What happens if you put together an Irish wit, a Jewish intellectual, an African prince and a Burmese politician with a flower in her hair? As my son pointed out, in a classic stand-up comedy routine they would all be walking into a bar. Maybe they should have done just that. It might have saved them a lot of trouble. But suppose you don't get shown the bar menu. What if you are thrown into the cellar and beaten unmercifully? Or worse? We are talking about the kind of thing that has happened to millions of people, including Oscar Wilde, Jean Améry (born Hans Mayer), Nelson Mandela and Aung San Suu Kyi.

How do people respond if that sort of thing happens to them, if they get pushed down and kicked out? How do they cope when unwelcome, degrading displacement stares them in the face? That issue is worth exploring, especially since the West is gradually losing its previous position of overwhelming global power. Does it fear the prospect of going down in the world? The balance of power and wealth is shifting towards China, India and the countries of South and Southeast Asia. Does this threaten the West? What might it lose? What is its future? We explore these questions historically and comparatively, searching for the big picture without losing sight of individual men and women seeking pathways across shifting sands.

Wilde, Améry, Mandela and Suu Kyi are at the centre of this story, which takes us from the transatlantic West in the late nineteenth century to Southeast Asia in the early twenty-first century. These are all deeply controversial figures. They have all aroused both admiration and disgust. Their images reflected in public opinion's mirror have undergone sharp revision as unfolding events, shifting values and changing political agendas have offered new perspectives.

Oscar Wilde and Nelson Mandela became heroes and martyrs in the public mind but only after each had endured a ghastly, stinking apprenticeship as a hate figure: one a despicable queer corrupting all he touched, the other a dangerous terrorist threatening all decent people.

Aung San Suu Kyi's reputation has travelled in the opposite direction. For almost three decades beginning in 1988 she was the hero challenging Burma's cruel military regime, the martyr condemned to near-solitary house arrest for a total of fifteen years, the victim of two assassination attempts. But by 2018

Suu Kyi's image as a Burmese leader was covered from head to foot in rotten eggs and foul ordure. By that time her character had been spat upon, her honour and reliability questioned, and her effigy kicked and beaten in the press and social media from Malaysia to Maryland.

Jean Améry was kicked, beaten and worse by professional torturers. He was an Austrian concentration camp survivor who elbowed aside the notion that Jews should take a high-minded philosophical approach to the experience of utter humiliation meted out by the Nazis. He blasted his audience with the most vivid and penetrating account he could provide of his suffering flesh and tormented mind, both in Auschwitz and since his release. Améry explored the history and highways of Europe to explain his own predicament, and ours, in the postwar West.

Améry traces the West's passage since 1918 from decaying imperialism through militant populism to corporate capitalism. He also scouts out the tracks taken by displaced and humiliated people as they search for revenge, reconciliation or, as a last resort, release from pain through self-destruction. Améry achieved substantial positive recognition during the last few decades of his life but he never felt properly appreciated. His work provides an invaluable resource for this book's argument.

My object is not to praise or to condemn any of these four rebels. Instead, I want to make sense of what they said and did by exploring these cases, looking both inwards and outwards. Exploring inwards, biographical evidence and the reports of close associates provide a basis for controlled speculation about the emotions, values, perceptions and commitments that influenced our rebels' actions. Exploring outwards involves careful comparative and historical analysis of familial, regional, national and global configurations.

How do the 'inner' personal dynamics driving Wilde, Améry, Mandela and Suu Kyi relate to the broader socio-political and cultural settings in which they operated and to the long-term socio-historical processes of which their lives were a part? In particular, I am trying to understand how the political and cultural interventions of our rebels are related to four streams of historical development.

How did the words and actions for which they are most famous or notorious stem from and drive forward their lives and careers?

What part did these rebels play in the unfolding fates of the oppressive regimes they confronted?

Taken together, what do these four rebel careers tell us about the British Empire's long struggle against decline, disintegration and defeat, a struggle that pitched it, in turn, against the French Third Republic, Nazi Germany, Imperial Japan and, more recently, the United States whose overwhelming economic strength and military power displaced British strategic influence across Eurasia?

Finally, how does the decline of the British Empire relate to the retreat of the West from global domination? This has been underway since at least the end of the Cold War. It has become increasingly evident in the early twenty-first century. We can hear its quickening footsteps: the terrorist attacks on New York and Washington in 2001; the great economic crash of 2008; Britain's Brexit vote in 2016; Donald Trump's election as US president in the same year; and the inauguration of China's Belt and Road Forum in 2017, celebrating Beijing's massive infrastructure initiative, carrying its business and diplomatic thrust westwards across Eurasia and the Indian Ocean. After half a millennium of relatively unimpeded advance, the tidal drift has shifted direction against the West, which is learning to assimilate unpleasant feelings of potential threat and loss.

My own interest in threat and loss started young. It was stimulated by real life bomb stories our parents told my brother, sister and me in Nottingham shortly after World War II. They would reminisce about near misses and unlucky neighbours during air raids in Nottingham as well as Liverpool where my father had relatives. He was there in 1940 one night when a large bomb devastated houses on the other side of the street. Next morning the postman delivered his call-up papers through a hole in the house wall made by the blast.

During the 1950s I had more immediate worries; especially, the Deenie gang. These were half-mythical primitive rebels, tough lads, and also tough girls, since this was an equal opportunity gang. Their home territory was inter-war terraced housing at the edge of nearby Broxtowe. They supposedly spent their time planning to beat the living daylights out of us, the softer kids on Bilborough's new postwar council estate. The Deenies were urban marcher lords, guarding the frontier between established denizens and incoming outsiders. Now and then, some of us walking home from school would get picked off like straggling gazelles. Our core response strategy was flight.

A more intellectual stimulus hit me during my undergraduate years. It was J.H. Plumb's very positive review in the *New York Times* of Barrington Moore's *Social Origins of Dictatorship and Democracy* in 1966. The historian Jack Plumb was my unsparing college tutor at Christ's College, Cambridge, and his opinion mattered to me. So I read Moore's book and learned about the radical potential of declining classes threatened with extinction, especially the aristocracy and peasantry confronted with the rise of manufacturing cities, powerful trading corporations and urban citizens talking about freedom and equality.

My doctoral thesis, which I completed at Leicester University while a lecturer there, scouted out other lives on the downward slope. It was published as *Conflict and Compromise. Class Formation in English Society 1830–1914* (Routledge 2016, 2nd edn). I compared two struggles in mid and late Victorian England. One took place in and around Birmingham. It was the rearguard action, led by lords and archdeacons from the surrounding landed estates and market towns, against aggressive, reforming, big-city manufacturers like the upstart Joseph Chamberlain who also figures in this present book at a later point in his career.

The other struggle was focused on Sheffield, self-proclaimed capital of South Yorkshire, fringed by the glorious Peak District. I explored the violent resistance Sheffield's tightly organized cutlery trades mounted against advancing mechanization and the rise of Big Steel in Brightside and Attercliffe. This work features several such crucial contests, hard-fought in politics, industry, education and the professions, between the authoritarian and exclusionist tendency in English society and the powerful contrary push for greater equality and fuller participation.

This present book is closely related to two others. The first is *Conflict and Compromise*, just described. The second work is *Globalization. The Hidden Agenda* (Polity Press 2006). This captured my developing take on the dynamics of globalization and imperialism. It ranged across the past half millennium, making empirical comparisons and using them to fashion a fresh theoretical perspective, one balancing the supposedly liberating effects of globalization against its capacity to trigger humiliation. All three books in this trilogy focus on a struggle that is central to modern world history and our shared future. It is between the urge to repress and exclude, and the countervailing demand for liberation and a fuller human life. *Conflict and Compromise* traces these currents in the stormy cities of the English provinces in the Victorian age. *Globalization: The Hidden Agenda* absorbs the deep shock of the American invasion of Iraq in 2003 by locating its humiliations in a geo-historical context, reaching back to Hammurabi. *Civilized Rebels* provides a link between the other two works. It takes soundings from the depth of degradation and the heights of courage displayed as the elephantine British Empire shuddered before World War I, sank to its knees in the interwar decades, and finally collapsed after World War II.

Acknowledgements

After over half a decade of research on this particular project, driven by curiosity, I am grateful for the encouragement and tolerance of my colleagues and family. The sociology group in the Department of Social Sciences at Loughborough University, where I am an emeritus professor, asked me to give a public lecture a few years ago. That was when I put this fascinating quartet of rebels together for the first time. I thank all my departmental colleagues for all their comments, often constructive, then and since. The Auto/Biography Study Group of the British Sociological Association has allowed me to try out parts of my developing argument over the past few years. Jenny Byrne and Michael Ebdon shepherded me through this very enjoyable challenge. This group is refreshingly warm and supportive. More recently, I have been delighted to spend some weeks visiting the Department of Historical Sociology at Charles University in Prague, making presentations on the themes of this book and other topics. Professor Jiri Subrt has been a brilliant host and all members of the network of scholars associated with this unique department have made me feel very welcome.

I have learned a very great deal from the many members of the international community of social scientists, historians and other specialists I have met in recent years. To these must be added the scholars whose research is listed in the bibliography and cited in the notes as well as the journalists and commentators whose skills provide us with their first draft of history. I hope I have not misrepresented or misinterpreted their important work. Where and if this has happened I apologize. Any errors are mine alone.

While thinking about and working on the themes of this book I have spent time in South Africa, Switzerland, the United States, Canada, Mexico, Brussels, Austria, Turkey, Russia, Lebanon, Cyprus, Greece, Ireland, and a number of other EU member states including Slovenia, Croatia, Poland, the Czech Republic, Denmark, Sweden, Norway, Germany, France, Spain, Portugal, Italy and, unsurprisingly, the UK, including Scotland during the independence referendum in 2014. I have not been to Burma (Myanmar) but I have visited its powerful close neighbours, China and India, including Kashmir, as well as South Korea and Singapore. Wherever I could I have spoken to non-academics as well as academics. I do not mention any names here because life is tough in many places. I appreciate all the insights I gained from many people.

My frankest critics while writing this book have been home-based. Who else but family and family friends would check draft after draft of chapters for clarity and reader friendliness? I was able to draw with gratitude on the shrewd insights of a choreographer (Dr Sue Smith), a research sociologist (Dr Penny Smith) and a comedy show promoter (Ed Smith), when permitted by their children: Poppy, Finn, Bonny, Phoebe, Benjamin, Florence, Indigo, Manny and Nico. My wife Tanya read everything but tempered her critiques with the knowledge that I would probably change most of it anyway. Our friend Fiona Campbell paid me the compliment of usually enjoying what I wrote, which was nice. The two cats were totally indifferent and are in no way responsible for the final result. I suppose I am.

Finally, I owe a great deal to Professor Robert Holton of the Hawke Research Institute, University of South Australia, for his strong support, to Neil Jordan, senior editor at Routledge, to Alice Salt the editorial assistant, to my copy editor, Liz Nichols and to Kevin Selmes, the production editor.

1 Rebels and regimes

The road to Brexit

Expect the unexpected: that is surely our motto for the twenty-first century. For example, the great Andromedid meteor shower made a surprise appearance in December 2011.[1] Did you see it? The last spectacular Andromedid display before that happened in 1885. You probably missed that one, too. The sky was full of shooting stars on the 28th November 1885. That same day General Harry North Dalrymple Prendergast VC landed at Mandalay, meaning business. He had sailed up the Irrawaddy river with his Burma Expeditionary Force. He was armed with a clutch of new-fangled Maxim guns. These weapons had been invented two years previously. They could fire six hundred rounds a minute.[2] This gave them considerable persuasive capacity. They won arguments, quickly.

By the end of the day, Prendergast had loaded the Burmese royal family into bullock carts and sent them on a steamer down the river into permanent exile. From that time until the Japanese invaded in 1942 Burma was British. Soon after Prendergast's arrival, the king's revered white elephant, symbol of his sovereignty, fell down dead and was dragged without ceremony out of the palace gates. This gave a strong hint to the Burmese about how little they and their way of life would be respected.

Do keep a close eye on your white elephants. Other people tend not to respect them as much as you do. As we all know, elephants are enormously resourceful, take up large amounts of space, need a lot of food, deposit great piles of dung, and it is best not to get too close when they give up the ghost and keel over. So it was with the British Empire.

Those huge beasts with waving trunks and flapping ears supposedly never forget. In a similar way, being unable to accept past glories were over was the elephantine curse of the post-imperial British. They found it hard to forget. Within living memory their island had ruled over the modern world's biggest global empire. Then suddenly, after World War II, it was gone. This wasn't the first such humiliation. After 1776 the precious, hard-won American colonies fought themselves free from British rule with French help. But on that occasion Britain's recovery was rapid, turbo-charged by spectacular industrial growth. A second British Empire was carved out during the nineteenth century. The Indian Raj was the jewel in its crown. But the jewel unclipped itself in 1947. The rest soon followed.

How could that have happened? After all, who won the war? What went wrong? As Oscar Wilde's Lady Bracknell might have put it: 'To lose one empire may be regarded as a misfortune but to lose both looks like carelessness'.[3] To misquote the historian J R Seeley, losing half the world in a fit of absence of mind would be bad enough.[4] But letting Britain's empire fall from its bankrupt hands because the British could not afford to run it was intolerably worse; totally humiliating. After World War II Britain was too poor to pursue its imperialist ambitions. Losing the British Empire was a great calamity, difficult to get over. The resulting trauma sometimes led to extreme or eccentric behaviour.

A major example of this was the disastrous Suez adventure in 1956. Another instance, minor but spectacular in its own way, occurred in January 2017 when the British Foreign Secretary, Boris Johnson, made an official visit to Burma's most sacred space, the Shwedagon Pagoda in Yangon. The occasion inspired him. He began to recite out loud Rudyard Kipling's nostalgic imperialist poem about 'the road to Mandalay', published in 1892.[5] The British Ambassador immediately got very jumpy. 'Come you back, you British soldier', intoned the Foreign Secretary, an evocative but provocative line. Was the minister really contemplating, even fancifully, a restoration of British colonial rule? At this point the ambassador reminded the man responsible for British foreign policy that he was being recorded. What the minister was doing was 'not a good idea'; 'not appropriate'. Luckily, the ambassador's words staunched this flow of post-imperial nostalgia. The Foreign Secretary's stopped reciting Kipling but *sotto voce* muttered 'good stuff.'[6]

Civilized Rebels is about the British Empire's decline, collapse and aftermath. This includes Britain's troubled relationship with Ireland, and its desperate confrontations with the Third Reich and Imperial Japan. We investigate the miserable legacy the British left behind in South Africa and Burma, which disrupted and delayed those nations' still incomplete liberation from autocratic, oppressive and neglectful rulers. Not least, we examine Britain's restless and resentful search for a satisfactory post-imperial identity. This took that country first into the Common Market and then, over four decades later, into a prolonged trauma over Brexit, Britain's projected withdrawal from the European Union.

We examine contrasting perspectives on the gradual disintegration of British imperial influence. These take us to late Victorian Dublin and London, Vienna in the 1930s, Antwerp, Brussels and Johannesburg in the 1940s, early twenty-first-century Yangon and Mandalay, and present-day Britain. On the way, we see dramatic confrontations between well-known insurgents and the regimes they challenged. We interrogate the lives of four formidable rebels who smarted under oppression's lash but fought on. They all knew what they were fighting for, and studied their enemies closely.[7]

These rebels are Oscar Wilde (1854–1900), Jean Améry (1912–78), Nelson Mandela (1918–2013) and Aung San Suu Kyi (born 1945): two avant-garde writers and two insurgent politicians: three men and one woman; two Europeans, one African and one Asian. Between them, our rebels saw the British Empire from the inside (Wilde) and the outside (Améry), at its height (Wilde) and on its last legs (Mandela, Suu Kyi). Two of them endured its painful aftermath in Africa (Mandela) and Asia (Suu Kyi). The regimes these insurgent spirits faced were based, respectively, in late Victorian Britain, Hitler's Germany, South Africa under *apartheid*, and Burma, sometimes known as Myanmar, under military dictatorship.[8]

By comparing these cases we can triangulate the British Empire's decline. This takes us from its highpoint in the 1860s and 1870s to its struggle for survival against Hitler's Germany and Imperial Japan in the 1940s. From British colonialism's malign aftermath in postwar Africa and Asia through to the existential threats posed by Brexit[9] to the empire's residual core, the United Kingdom itself. A ghost labelled the Commonwealth still shimmered across the world's oceans in the early twenty-first century. But imperial Britain had shrivelled to a few scattered islands and peninsulas, many of them tax havens, plus the United Kingdom itself, already shorn of Ireland and faced with possibly losing yet another nation, Scotland. Unexpectedly, in 2016 the British narrowly voted in a referendum to leave the European Union (EU), the UK's global anchoring point for nearly half a century.

At the centre of this inquiry are the links between three major geo-historical shifts currently under way: Britain's retreat from Europe, the West's retreat from global power, and, entwined with both, the British Empire's retreat from ruling the waves. Making sense of each retreat will help us understand the other two.

Our four rebels are not the only victims of abusive threats and violent oppression designed to intimidate and diminish them. Nor are they the only ones to react strongly, driven by anger, fear, sorrow or disgust. Many people are chronically vulnerable to humiliating forced displacement – being pushed down, elbowed aside, and kicked out – at several levels of social activity and political life. The poor, weak and stigmatized are habitual victims, individually and collectively. Defeat and degradation also threaten the powerful, whether good, bad or ugly. Reforming leaders promoting justice and democracy, metropolitan cliques controlling colonial empires, and fascist or neo-fascist dictatorships are all vulnerable.

In fact, people scattered across entire nations or continents may be moved to collective grief or rage as their fortunes change. Populist movements, right and left, drawing large crowds have recently sprung up across North America, Europe and in neighbouring Russia and Turkey. Brexit is part of a wider rebellion from below now rumbling in the West, both through the European Union, and in the United States. What does it all mean?

We can trace, here and there, the interplay of mood and motive back and forth between different levels, individual, group, nation and world, over historical time and geographical space. This is what this book does. In fact, the biographies of our four rebels, taken together, transport us from the north Atlantic seaboard in the 1850s to the Pacific Rim at the present day. These rebel careers are interwoven with the British Empire's struggles as it confronts intransigent Irish, insubordinate Boers, and insurgent Burmese, fights off the Third Reich and Imperial Japan, and tries to maintain international credibility after World War II.

We begin with Wilde (born 1854) and Améry (born 1912) as the Empire wrestles rivals in Paris, Berlin and Washington. The narrative then shifts to Mandela (born 1918) and Suu Kyi (born 1945). British rulers in South Africa and Burma disarmed indigenous power structures and stripped out natural resources, but were finally forced to leave when their authority, confidence and credit failed. The effects of British imperialism's lengthy aftermath in Africa and Asia became entangled with the end of the Cold War, the collapse of the Soviet Union, and the rise of China and India. Before imperialism died, characters such as Mahatma Gandhi (1869–1948) and Jan Christian Smuts (1870–1950), both highly inventive lawyers with very big ideas, moved across continents, competing to shape what might replace it.[10] But in the 1930s they were both shoved aside by rougher types with more brutal attitudes.

Did colonial methods and fascist techniques have a degree of elective affinity?[11] This would be an oversimplification, requiring refinement from recent work by the likes of Walter Mignolo.[12] However, imperialist influences may be traced flowing from India, Africa and Australasia to Nazi Germany, and then returning to Africa, inspiring *apartheid*. A subplot brought the inhumane repression of Imperial Japan to the postwar military regime in Burma. In both Burma and South Africa the outcomes after World War II included neo-fascist regimes and prolonged internal conflict. Mandela and Suu Kyi took up the task of confronting autocracy and fighting for human rights, with real but limited success.

The global and historical perspective adopted here may help us make sense of Suu Kyi's response to the Rohingya crisis during 2016–17 which grievously disappointed people throughout the world. Democracy Burma-style was, at least during those years, a mixture of xenophobic populism and state repression. Suu Kyi's party, the National League for Democracy, gained a parliamentary majority in 2015 because it allowed citizens to express their resentment of the military's neglect of the people's material needs. But this resentment was tempered by popular fear of the military's capacity to damage or silence its critics. This was combined with overwhelming enthusiasm for the violent campaign against Muslim 'outsiders' mounted by Burma's senior generals and extremist factions within Burma's highly influential Buddhist monasteries.

Evidence does exist that indirectly, behind the scenes and in very constricted circumstances, Suu Kyi had been trying to put life into a peace process within the troubled Rakhine state. But her political influence within Burma would probably have been greatly reduced if she had directly and openly opposed the military's campaign against the Rohingya. Her record since becoming Burma's State Counsellor reveals neither a saint nor a martyr but a pragmatic politician who has been working to try and realize, as far as possible, the vision inherited from her father of a democratic Burma that incorporates and respects all those that live there.

That is why we need to try to understand, as far as we can, why the Rohingya crisis left Suu Kyi looking helpless, speechless and even complicit. What happened?

This exercise in comparative biography is also an investigation of emotional dynamics and shifting political cultures played out in people's lives and conduct over generations. We are concerned with the making and unmaking of colonial domination, military dictatorship, totalitarian despotism and racialized oppression, often in times of violent conflict. These structural shifts are closely related to the West's gradual retreat from global power over the past century and a half. This still unfinished historical process has already been punctuated by two world wars, several civil wars, numerous massacres and countless other outrages. This perilous transition will run far into the future.

Looking back we see how closely Wilde and Améry inspected the mechanisms of force and fraud that drove British imperialism across the world and fuelled Nazi oppression in Europe. Between them they describe not only the Nietzschean delight of exerting absolute mastery but also the horror of being threatened by overwhelming force or trickery. We are shown different forms of resignation and revolt deployed by potential fall guys. This leads to another issue. How do the world's peoples cope with the destructive impact of acts of humiliation, sometimes deliberately targeted and bureaucratically organized, acts that disrupt the lives of individuals, families, communities and nations, turning them into resentful victims? Humiliated people may take revenge when they can, unless they see equally or more effective alternatives.

These responses are part of larger dynamics, liable to shape history in ways that move beyond human control. One way to explore these dynamics is to improve our understanding of how populations respond to the degradations brought by brutalization, neglect and deprivation. Analysing these struggles between rebels and regimes helps us to understand the range of ways that individuals, groups and institutions respond to threatened humiliation. These responses may be seen across the different levels mentioned: from individuals to nations and even global regions such as Europe and the West as a whole.

There is yet another nugget to be unearthed from the people and situations examined here, specifically from Améry's brilliant intelligence, in both senses of that word. Based on intense personal experience and sustained reflection, Améry analyses the dynamics of suicide. He argues that in many cases it is a last-ditch assertion of the victim's wish to become an effective agent, to take back control from a world that is becoming overwhelming. This gives us valuable insight into the meaning of Brexit.

The British Empire and the West

Before going further, we should get the British Empire and the West into perspective as historical objects. The heart of the West lies, historically, within a broad zone that extends around Aachen in the Rhineland, where Charlemagne (742–814 CE) was buried, then southwards towards Rome itself, haunt of emperors, poets and popes. In the late Middle Ages, a term such as Christendom might have been used for this region and other lands beyond, with Heaven and Hell included on the map when depicting it. Those latter neighbourhoods are generally absent from modern Western cartography, making way for more secular delights and horrors. In any case, over subsequent centuries the early West of the Apennines and Rhine valley broadened out in many directions: into Scandinavia and the Nordic regions, across the North American continent, and eastwards in the direction of Asia.

The West dealt with in this book is Europe and North America. There are complications. The term West normally implies some notion of East. The West has summoned up at least three Easts.[13] One is the supposedly vast and mysterious Orient, a wondrous 'other' that by the time of Voltaire (1694–1778) had become identified with the Ottoman Empire, whose territorial heartland very roughly coincides with modern-day Turkey. That empire fell apart by 1918. The next East was the Soviet Union, depicted in horror comic terms by its Western opponents long after its most monstrous phase had passed. The Soviet Union collapsed between 1989 and 1991. The Turks and the Russians have, in effect, been treated as half in, half out members of the Western club. Most recently, a third East has arisen, the People's Republic of China. This was never a member of the Western club, nor wished to be. The Beijing regime cultivated memories of China's so-called century of humiliation from the 1840s to the 1940s while, at the same time, laughing off Western colonialism with the remark that even an elephant gets fleas.[14]

The West's social identity and sense of itself have gradually transformed over several phases of existence.[15] The challenge is to discern the long-term processes expressed through its shorter-term shifts and starts. The West is the dynamic outcome of the bonds, divisions, aspirations, aversions, capabilities and vulnerabilities of all its people, not just those that live there permanently but also those that go out into the world beyond. One persisting characteristic has furnished large parts of Europe with a long-term strategic advantage. This has been a combination of two factors: on the one hand, political fragmentation and socio-cultural diversity; on the other hand, a broadly shared overarching framework for human conduct inherited from the medieval Church and its successors. This politico-cultural context has allowed the inhabitants of city-states, independent princedoms, and later, sovereign national states to trade, compete, experiment and innovate with relative freedom.

Add in other factors such as greed, ambition, intermittent persecution and a shortage of sufficient land and other resources to satisfy those that wanted them. One result was outward migration, often into other peoples' space, cutting through resistance with a mix of force, fire and fear, spreading terror and inducing compliance. During the ninth and tenth centuries the Vikings had already made themselves familiar with the lands and seas between Byzantium, Newfoundland and Novgorod. In the eleventh and twelfth centuries their descendants, the Normans, forced their way into Cyprus and Sicily, and onward into the Middle East, helping to found Crusader kingdoms in the Levant. By the fifteenth century the most dramatic crusading action was on the Iberian peninsula, pushing Islamic peoples and rulers back towards North Africa. This thrust continued, in diverse directions, on and off, for another four centuries: from the Iberian conquest of Latin America in the late fifteenth and sixteenth centuries to the European scramble for Africa in the nineteenth and early twentieth centuries.[16]

This sustained effort was driven by arrogance, zeal, daring, desperation and, sometimes, egocentricity on a grand scale. The forward thrust and heavy lifting that cumulatively established the West's strong global position was carried out by soldiers, sailors, traders, preachers, engineers and others from Portugal and Spain, Italy and Germany before and after their nineteenth-century unification, the Low Countries, now the Netherlands and Belgium, France, Britain, Russia and many other such places. Strength, conquest, glory and personal advantage were the watchwords of all Europe's empires, like most empires before and since. Much of the work was resolutely ignoble and gruesome but it was effective. European imperialism was a strict and cruel governess imposing discipline in the global nursery of modernization, making it profitable for the aggressive new masters from the West. Europeans brutally asserted their will on slaves, serfs and debt-entrapped peasants in Asia, Africa and America as well as within Europe itself. They turned their will, adrenalin, muscle power and firepower into lasting authority. They wielded the whips, hanged the resisters, and imposed their own rules, boundaries and hierarchies. This was the labour of many generations, directed by adventurers whose origins ranged from Glasgow to Genoa and beyond.

The United States was a beneficiary of these historical labours. It has been the West's leading power for approximately three-quarters of a century. But the West itself was well established as the world's most aggressively dynamic global region by the mid eighteenth century, before the United States was even a twinkle in the eyes of the Founding Fathers and, indeed, Founding Mothers. As everybody knows, those venerable parents got it together in 1776. At that time, the principal face, although not the only one, that the West presented to the world was British, stereotypically rosy-cheeked naval officers and pasty-faced sailors. This remained the situation, give or take the odd beard or moustache, for nearly two centuries, up to World War II.

There was always competition. The British ventured out from a West mapped out as a network of political and commercial capitals. This network was centred on Europe but soon included New York and other major North American urban centres. Cities such as London, Liverpool, Paris, Madrid,

Lisbon, Amsterdam, Berlin, Vienna, St Petersburg and Constantinople contended to lift themselves up the relevant pecking order, whether commercial, diplomatic or dynastic. By the end of the nineteenth century the West's imperial masters considered themselves the world's civilized peoples, superior beings with responsibilities for, and rights over, less advanced peoples that could be saved or improved. Those beyond saving or improving might, perhaps, have to be cleared away, especially if they were in the wrong place.[17]

The Ottoman Empire, run by a Muslim dynasty, had its headquarters on the European continent at Constantinople (Istanbul) and was drawn into Europe's network of alliances during these centuries. Notoriously, it became known as the sick man of Europe. This resounding gong was handed round to others later, including Britain. Constantinople was always vulnerable to being labelled by competing powers as delinquent, defective or both. Compare St Petersburg on the western coast of Russia near the Baltic Sea. This city, Russia's capital since 1717, was a confident participant in Europe's diplomatic and military contests. It had strong credentials. Russia's religion, Orthodox Christianity, and its Cyrillic alphabet, named after a monk called Cyril, both originated in Greece, the traditional progenitor of Western civilization. The buildings of St Petersburg were extravagantly classical and constructed on a grand scale. This was megaphone architecture, underscoring membership and identity; also found in Vienna, another capital on the edge of things, defending Southern Europe's borders.

Russia drove its frontiers east and south, deep into Central Asia and Siberia. Meanwhile, the British forced their way into India and then Burma, keeping a close eye on the French in next-door Siam, later Thailand. By 1870 France had once again become a republic, a little below the salt. In 1877 Benjamin Disraeli turned Britain's monarch into the Empress of India. Britain and Russia were the high-status big league players of the mid and late nineteenth-century West. Like a restless red setter, Germany tried to push its nose in. It was a family affair. Relations soured before World War I but Czar Nicolas II in his Winter Palace was first cousin to King George V in Buckingham Palace and Kaiser Wilhelm II in his *Berliner Schloss*. In 1918 the Russian capital moved to Moscow, far enough away from the western frontier to exhaust a Napoleon or a Hitler but close enough to share with Europe the same cultural cosmos, recognizable in music, literature, art, ballet and the contest between political ideologies.

But this cosy picture of competitive slaughter and slavery sanctified by incense and unction makes the life of the West seem far too untroubled. In fact, no sooner had Britain secured mastery of the world's seas than the pushback from below began. It came in two mighty shoves: one on the West's periphery in 1776 and one at its centre in 1789. The American Revolution gave practical force to two great anti-imperialist ideas: the free citizen and the sovereign people. The French Revolution gave birth to a nation in arms with the mission of bringing freedom and enlightenment to the world. Both revolutions challenged the dynastic imperialism of Europe's aristocracies and monarchies.

Alexis de Tocqueville (1806–59) recognized the incompatibility between aristocracy and democracy.[18] It was a highly contentious issue in France for several decades before an enduring democratic political structure emerged with the Third Republic (1870–1940). Americans, northerners and southerners, spent decades sniping at each other then four years fighting a full-scale civil war (1861–5) over issues of freedom, equality and independence for states and citizens. By contrast, the British somehow managed to be on both sides of these issues at once. They incorporated the aggressive, expansive spirit of citizenship and national sovereignty, which helped to supercharge their explosive industrial growth. But at the same time Britain retained its aristocracy, monarchy and imperialist urge, and by the 1870s had secured its grip on India.

In 1920 the British Empire encompassed over one fifth of the world's territory and population. Its relative global weight was roughly similar to China's today. Between the mid-nineteenth century and World War I, the railways, the electric telegraph, steamships, and other space and time shrinking technologies held the British Empire together and globalized the modern world. Many populations across the globe first learned the practical meaning of modernity by dealing with the British. During the following century, from the 1920s to the present, the British Empire reluctantly relaxed its grip and by the early twenty-first century, it had long passed away. But modern states were still playing on an international pitch substantially marked out by Britain or coalitions led by Britain.[19]

Between the two world wars the West had a paradoxical aspect. It paraded its imperial grandeur but was profoundly fragmented. The United States remained in relative diplomatic isolation while Europe split into conflicting parts, setting imperial London against Nazi Berlin and fascist Italy, and Soviet Moscow against all those three. When Spain went to war with itself, its civil conflict provided a testing ground for Europe's contenders.

But during those inter-war decades the British Empire remained prominent as a major institutional conduit and symbolic mediator between the West and the world. Its principal competitors in grandeur had been toppled: notably in Moscow, Vienna, Berlin and Constantinople. The British monarchy was left almost alone on this sparse horizon, trying to adapt. Anachronistically, the Emperor of India was titular head of one of the world's leading urban-industrial democracies. Small wonder the 1916 Dublin uprising against the British, and the Irish revolt more generally, made a big impact as far as Burma. De Valera was a hero to Suu Kyi's rebellious father. That reflection takes us back once more to our four rebels and the regimes they opposed.

The road to Mandalay

During the late nineteenth century the British Empire faced a threefold challenge from Ireland. There was the violence of Fenian bombers in English cities, the disruptive manoeuverings of the Irish Parliamentary Party led by Charles

Stewart Parnell, and the sustained and subversive assault on the imperial establishment's cultural, political and moral assumptions being made by the first of our rebels, the Anglo-Irishman, Oscar Wilde.

The second regime was Hitler's Third Reich (1933–45). The Nazis initially drew inspiration from the British Empire but later became its deadliest enemy.[20] Jean Améry, an Austrian Jew spent much of his rebellious life engaged in resistance against the Nazis, suffering in their concentration camps, and expressing implacable resentment against his tormentors. The two other regimes grew in socio-political soil previously tended by the British. One was the *apartheid* state in South Africa (1948–94) whose most prominent opponent was Nelson Mandela. The final case was the military dictatorship in Burma (1962–2010), opposed by Aung San Suu Kyi, born in 1945, following her return from exile in 1988. All four rebels suffered imprisonment: Wilde in British jails, Améry in Nazi concentration camps, Mandela on an island off the South African coast, and Suu Kyi under house arrest in the middle of Burma's biggest city.

Oscar Wilde was convicted of gross indecency under section 11 of the Criminal Law Amendment Act of 1885. His punishment was two years hard labour served between 1895 and 1897 in Pentonville, Wandsworth and, most famously, in Reading Gaol where he wrote *De Profundis*, a long letter to his lover, Lord Alfred Douglas.

Jean Améry was arrested in 1943 as an anti-Nazi resistance worker in Belgium. He was tortured by the Belgian secret police. When they discovered Améry was Jewish, he was sent to Auschwitz. Only 615 of 23,000 Jews from Belgium survived such an experience: less than three per cent. Améry was one of them.[21]

Nelson Mandela was found guilty of sabotage in 1964 and subsequently spent twenty-seven years in various prisons, including Robben Island, along with other political detainees. Finally, in 1989 Aung San Suu Kyi was found guilty of conduct 'likely to undermine the community peace and stability' of Burma, an offence under article 10a of the law to 'safeguard the state against the dangers of those desiring to cause subversive acts.' Apart from short spells in prison, Suu Kyi spent fifteen years under house arrest, living in near solitude in her family home in the middle of Yangon.[22]

Comparing our four rebels' prison experiences and their lifelong struggles against oppression gives us clues about how humiliation threatens to corrode lives, imposing a brutal reordering of statuses, and a forced recasting of personal and group identities. Those at the receiving end are faced with questions. Do we hold our ground and reject attempts to humiliate us – or try to escape? Do we build up our strength to protect our interests effectively – or settle for a symbolic revenge that protects our honour even if it leaves us weak and vulnerable? Do we try to harm those we believe are victimizing us – or try to remove the causes of humiliation by increasing mutual understanding, sympathy and interdependence among all concerned? These four prisoners responded in very dissimilar ways to their incarceration and other abusive treatment they received during their lives. Comparing those lives we see how individuals may try to divert, diffuse or diminish the hostile beam of humiliation.

Fortunately, our rebel prisoners are all acute observers, brilliant performers and adventurous explorers. Oscar Wilde left his alienated homeland of Ireland to scout out the heights and ravines of London's corrupt high society where anxieties about imperial decline had already taken hold. A century later, the British Empire was virtually gone. Jean Améry analyses the angry and bereft Britain of the 1960s as an outside observer from his base in Brussels. He saw the British in the international context shaped by the destructive impact of Nazism and the rise of the post-war West.

Finally, Mandela and Suu Kyi endured, in different ways, the post-colonial aftermath in Africa and Southeast Asia. The British government helped create a political climate in South Africa that offered little resistance to the *apartheid* regime. The Afrikaner leaders who introduced that system in 1948 had, in many cases, responded enthusiastically to Hitler during the 1930s. By contrast, in 1947 the British left Burma embroiled in a civil war that lasted until a military junta came to power in 1962, and flared up, intermittently, thereafter. Burma's new rulers had a taste for quasi-fascist authoritarianism and disdain for the sufferings of others. This reflected the influence of the Japanese military instructors who trained the senior officers of the fledgling Burmese army in the early 1940s

These rebellious prisoners had complicated relationships with their public reputation. To some they were charismatic idols; to others, a disgusting queer, a dirty Jew, an uppity Black and a scandalous woman. In fact, all four were immensely resourceful, flexible and determined. They had the advantage of rich and complex cultural backgrounds. They were all, in a word, formidable. Oscar Wilde, Dublin-born in 1854, was a blistering rocket of a man, charming and outrageous. His startling hair, inquiring gaze, and impressive bulk were shocking to encounter. Wilde ditched his Irish brogue on the road between Trinity College Dublin and Magdalen College, Oxford. Not content with being a brilliant Oxford scholar Wilde rapidly turned himself into a blazing transatlantic celebrity. In 1882, aged twenty-eight, he donned a big hat, dressed up like a dandy, and wowed his way through America's railroad halts, dispensing wit and wisdom on the lecture circuit. Returning to Europe, Wilde swept like a storm through salons, restaurants and reception rooms in London and Paris.

During his lifetime, Oscar Wilde's notoriety and shock value grew: Storm Oscar became Hurricane Oscar. Prison, illness and, finally, death all slowed him down. But Wilde's sensational life and brilliant writings ranging from the visionary essay 'The Soul of Man under Socialism'[23] to the hilarious play *The Importance of Being Earnest* made his posthumous fame global.[24] Wilde was always diverting, usually amusing, often unsettling, and sometimes very disturbing. Above all, he was a subtle critic of London Society, the cream of a socio-political establishment that controlled a global empire but was losing confidence in its own authority.

Wilde's political and moral objections to the imperial elite had been sharpened by a childhood amongst the lively and insecure Irish-born Protestant elite in Dublin. As Terry Eagleton puts it, the Anglo-Irish lived 'at the hub of one civilization' but as 'outcasts from another'.[25] Many identified strongly with the Irish people against the Ascendancy, as those governing Ireland on behalf of the British crown were known. Wilde's mother once called for armed revolution in Ireland. Wilde wrote two early plays about anarchist assassins. Later, he mocked English upper-class cynicism and hypocrisy, above all in his theatrical comedies staged in the early 1890s.

Behind the glamour and smears Oscar Wilde was much more than an outrageous extrovert with a sideline in scandalous sexual behaviour. He was a practiced border dweller, drawing on both his English and Irish identities, hovering between Anglicanism and Catholicism, and skipping between the homosexual and heterosexual worlds of London and Oxford. He was a first-class scholar, an acute critical commentator, a formidable debater, a skilled charmer, and a raconteur able to fine-tune his delivery according to his audiences, which ranged from his young sons to middle-aged royalty. Not least, he was: a supporter of Irish Home Rule; a friend of anarchists, socialists and feminists; and a dedicated cultural saboteur determined to undermine the British imperial establishment's self-confidence and self-righteousness.

Next comes Jean Améry. In his photographs Améry looks wrapped up in some project that consumes him but makes him anxious. Above his brow stretches a dome-like forehead lined with amusement, anxiety, anger and ambition. Below that brow are piercing half-closed eyes, a defiant long nose, a strong chin, and a mouth shaped by sardonic smiles and chain-smoked cigarettes. Not easy to forget. Jean Améry sounds French but, as we know, he was an Austrian of Jewish origins, born Hans Mayer. He adopted his new name after the war, at the age of forty-three. Améry's best-known work is *At the Mind's Limits*.[26] This classic meditation on Auschwitz is a towering presence in Holocaust literature but in real life Améry soon felt trapped within its pages. He wanted more. Améry hungered to be a great novelist like Thomas Mann (1875–1955), dealing with the whole human condition.

In 1943 Améry was captured, tortured and consigned to Auschwitz. His carefully nurtured cultural inheritance shrivelled up. There was no poetry behind those electrified fences: 'No bridge led from death in Auschwitz to *Death in Venice*.'.[27] Austria was his birthplace, Belgium his adopted post-war home. Améry became thoroughly familiar with multiple places of domicile for body and mind, from Alpine caves to city cafes. He was the child of a devoutly Catholic mother and a secularized Jewish father. These diverse assets gave him strength and resilience. Often on the run, he got good practice in putting on the face required for survival, whether nonchalant or eager. Jean Améry was able to evoke in a highly articulate way the experience undergone by victims of Nazi torture. But he was also: a consummate explorer of popular postwar Western political and literary culture; an acute observer of Britain's malaise as the empire slipped from its grasp; a perceptive analyst of mood, situation and significance, and a daring exponent of the human urge to assert sovereignty at all costs.

Thirdly, we turn to Nelson Mandela: grey headed, with high cheekbones and a sympathetic smile. His message was profoundly humanitarian. In old age he advised everyone to 'place human solidarity, the concern for the other, at the centre of the values by which you live.'[28] In his twenties and thirties Mandela radiated arrogance, ambition, charm and good looks. He was a living contradiction of *apartheid*'s stereotype of indigenous Africans. He devoted his life to destroying the system that legalized racial discrimination and exploitation.

Mandela was both a country boy and a city slicker. He learned to discern the wants, strengths and weaknesses of others, first when training as a traditional African counsellor and later as a specialist in the *apartheid* state's legal system. Mandela understood the mindset of the Afrikaner police chief, the Methodist missionary, the African village chief and the township dweller. He was: a leading member of African royalty in the Transkei; a high-flying lawyer trained in first-class English educational institutions; a warrior for human rights; and a self-sacrificing hero who brought apparently irreconcilable political forces together in South Africa. Mandela became a global icon but shrewdly realized that the harsh atmosphere of South African politics would tarnish his reputation if he stayed in power too long.

Our final guest in these pages is Aung San Suu Kyi, born in 1945, and well known for her steely bright eyes, long slender neck and dark hair, often bedecked with flowers. Her father, General Aung San (1915–47), founded the modern nation of Burma. He led the fight for independence from the British who had invaded Burma during the nineteenth century. Aung San was assassinated in 1947. Instability and civil war soon followed. After fifteen years of intermittent chaos the Burmese military took over political control in 1962. By then Aung San Suu Kyi was living abroad as she did for nearly three decades.

Abroad Suu Kyi acquired a prestigious higher education, multiple degrees, a publication record, an influential international network, a British husband, and two children. She watched international diplomats at work and play, and married an anthropologist. She wrote a comparative study of Burmese and Indian intellectual traditions, and had deep sympathy for Japanese life and culture. Suu Kyi could play between Burmese and Western lifestyles and cultural assumptions. She drew strength from Buddhism while also understanding Anglo-Saxon Christianity. Suu Kyi's ambition was to carry forward her father's unfinished work. Above all, she wanted to reconcile Burma's warring ethnic minorities in the nation's borderlands. Suu Kyi retained the demeanour and voice of an Oxford don's wife, which she was for many years. However, she was a Burmese patriot before she was a transatlantic liberal. Her family had bred rebels since at least 1885 when British soldiers sailed up the Irrawaddy and took the watery road to Mandalay.

Educated dissidents

These are highly civilized rebels. Being civilized has at least two meanings. One relates to behaviour and attitude, the other to being well versed in the high culture of a major civilization. Oscar Wilde was a brilliant Greek scholar, an Oxford prizewinner, and a highly regarded literary critic and practitioner.[29] For his part, Jean Améry did not complete his baccalaureate but became thoroughly engaged with German *Kultur*. Like Wilde, Améry valued culture highly but wanted to shape it, not subordinate his personality to it. Mandela's schooling at an elite Methodist High School was followed by a university degree in law that included Latin. On Robben Island he once played Creon in an inmates' performance of *Antigone*.[30] Suu Kyi also trained at a Methodist High School and later acquired a degree in Philosophy, Politics and Economics at St. Hugh's College, Oxford.

A second meaning of being civilized is being able to exercise rational self-control in a balanced and even way, maintaining objectivity while staying open to one's own and other peoples' feelings. Being civilized in this sense may be compatible with a range of moral perspectives and emotional tendencies. It is, for example, possible to be a civilized assassin who puts her understanding of the proposed victim's emotional state to effective use in carrying out her mission. Not, perhaps, a pleasant thought but here is a nicer one. Some uses of the word 'civilized' in this second sense may overlap with a more morally elevated notion of being civilized. This entails recognizing the human needs of others and responding generously to them as if they were our own, doing this with a caring rather than a controlling intention. In practice such attitudes are liable to come and go over time in the case of any individual or group although they may become institutionalized and strongly internalized in some cases.

But here the criteria are the minimal ones of exercising rational self control, being balanced, level headed, objective and calculating, and remaining, so to speak, in touch with one's own feelings and those of others but not, in the main, being overwhelmed by them. These are the strengths of, for example, the courtier, the counsellor and the diplomat. Oscar Wilde employed such skills to build up an extensive network of acquaintances in metropolitan high society in London, Paris and New York. He mastered the appropriate styles and etiquette, not least so he could sometimes deliberately break the rules. As a young man, Améry transferred with relative ease from the rough and jaunty culture of an Austrian provincial town to the smoother, sharper ambience of Vienna's intellectual circles. Later, he adapted to the self-discipline and careful self-presentation required to maximize survival chances in Auschwitz, an arena whose rulers were ready to execute offenders for the slightest slip up. In three very different contexts Améry quickly learned to fit in while trying to improve his chances of success or, more fundamentally, staying alive.

The young Nelson Mandela trained to be a counsellor and courtier in the household of Thembuland's traditional hereditary ruler, his close relative.[31]

Subsequently, he reconfigured his skills to navigate the South African law courts, initially as a defence counsel, later as a defendant. On Robben Island Mandela became leader and spokesperson of the ANC prisoners, moderating conflicts between competing interests. Finally, from the age of eight Suu Kyi was also in a household where she acquired poise, charm, and careful detachment. Her mother, Khin Kyi, served as a government minister (1953–60) and then became Burma's Ambassador to India, (1960–67), accompanied by Suu Kyi.

Primitive rebels, past and present, influenced the campaigns of these civilized rebels, indirectly at least. In his book *Primitive Rebels*, Eric Hobsbawm used this term to mean insurgents who engaged in '"archaic" forms of social agitation'[32] such as banditry, rural secret societies, millenarian peasant movements, waves of religious enthusiasm, and rioting urban mobs. All our civilized rebels had links, direct or indirect, with primitive rebels of this kind. Consider, for example, *The Fall of Feudalism in Ireland*,[33] written by Michael Davitt (1846–1906), a political ally of Charles Stewart Parnell, leader of the Irish Home Rule party in Westminster. Davitt's book claimed that bandits, *tories* and outlaws in eighteenth-century Ireland were direct precursors of his own Land League agitation. Davitt opposed alien landlords exploiting Irish agriculturalists and stealing their land. Oscar Wilde supported Parnell and corresponded with Davitt in the late 1890s. Both had experience of English prisons.[34]

Améry served on the fringes of the Belgian anti-Nazi resistance.[35] Even more than Wilde, his links to primitive rebels were mediated through historical tradition and literature. A key transmitter was, surely, the Jewish community in Hohenems, his father's birthplace. This town is situated close to Austria's border with Switzerland, the mountainous refuge of heretical radicals such as Huldrich Zwingli (1484–1531) in Zurich and Jean Calvin (1509–64) in Geneva.[36] Just over thirty miles from Hohenems is Gossau, a Swiss town that saw a large popular uprising during the French revolutionary years. Also close by is Altstätten; home of Johann Ludwig Ambühl (1750–1800) who popularized the story of the fourteenth-century rebel William Tell, promoting him as the great Swiss national hero, a theme later taken up by Friedrich Schiller (1759–1805), Améry's first great literary love.

Mandela and Suu Kyi were more directly influenced by the recent activities of primitive rebels. The indigenous people of South Africa were in revolt against colonial rule throughout the late nineteenth and early twentieth centuries; for example, the Transkei millenarian movement led by Wellington Buthelezi during the 1920s.[37] Govan Mbeki (1910–2001), a leading activist in the African National Congress (ANC), recorded the early struggles of indigenous Africans against European colonialists in his books *South Africa: The Peasants' Revolt* and *The Struggle for Liberation in South Africa*.[38] He wove these events into the larger story of the liberation struggle that culminated in the defeat of *apartheid*.

Mbeki served in Robben Island with Mandela. His books describe many examples of rebellious behaviour in the Transkei such as boycotts, tearing down fences across traditional common land, and protest meetings of African peasants in the mountainous terrain of East Pondoland during 1960. Mbeki was the ANC's Michael Davitt. Mandela came from a less radical rural tradition. Even in jail he relished the responsibilities that came his way as part of the Transkei's traditional rural hierarchy.

Banditry and rural resistance were even more common in Burma than South Africa. In 1960 only 19 per cent of Burma's population were urbanized, compared to 47 per cent of city dwellers in South Africa. By 2016 Burma's cities had still attracted only 35 per cent of the national population while 65 per cent of South Africans were urbanites.[39] In Burma a vast zone of mountains and forests curves around the more highly urbanized central Irrawaddy plain, stretching to the nation's frontiers in the west, north and east. Highly independent ethnic nations, frequently militant, occupy this dangerous ground.

Primitive rebels have played very different roles in South Africa and Burma. From the 1960s the Burmese military government fought a long war on many fronts against borderland militias, vainly trying to undermine their solidarity and beat them into submission. By contrast, the *apartheid* regime tried to cultivate and strengthen the pre-industrial tribal structures of African peasant communities. It wanted to confine as many Africans as possible to the rural areas, living on inferior land within Bantustans where chiefs would exercise their traditional authority within guidelines set by the national government.

The ANC leadership planned to turn South Africa into a rapidly industrializing, urbanizing socialist society. Ironically, that was also the official goal of the military dictatorship controlling Burma's national government after 1962. However, unlike the ANC, the Burmese generals could not depend on the population voting for them. So they dispensed with democracy and relied instead on fear and force. During its six decades in government the military regime failed to modernize Burma's industrial economy. Inconveniently, a large proportion of Burma's natural resources, such as teak, jade, rubies, copper, tin, antimony, zinc, tungsten and hydropower potential, is located in the rebellious frontier zones along with about a third of Burma's population. Just as significant are opium production and a thriving drug trade, especially on the borders with Thailand and China.

The history of Burma has been greatly influenced by the drug trade's prevalence in the so-called golden triangle where Burma, Thailand and China meet. In this area primitive rebels were in close touch with those growing and trafficking opium. Neither wished to see the forests and mountains pacified by the central state. The so-called opium wars with China (1839–42 and 1856–60) showed Britain's determination to claim a large stake in this commerce. Occupying Burmese territory during and after the 1820s gave them increased leverage. The British alleviated the problem of rebellious forest-dwellers by recruiting many into the British army, especially from the Karen people. The British encountered another type of primitive rebel among the dominant Burman people of the Irrawaday plain and delta. Gangs of *dacoits* (armed robbers) led by bandit chiefs harassed the British troops that had captured Mandalay and expelled the Burmese royal family in 1885. One of those rumbustious captains of mayhem, a local hero, was an ancestor of Aung San Suu Kyi, born a little over half a century later.

Demanding attention

Let us catch sight of our four civilized rebels as they make their decisive breakthroughs into popular consciousness. We can observe Oscar Wilde on his first really big opening night on Saturday 20th February 1892. By this time Wilde, author of the scandalous novel *The Picture of Dorian Gray*[40] and the anarchist tract 'The Soul of Man under Socialism',[41] was flying dangerously high. He seemed to be challenging the very foundations of social behaviour, sexual morality and political stability. Was Wilde becoming a man to be afraid of rather than laughed at? This question was hanging in the air as his debut as playwright in London's fashionable West End took place in early 1892 at St. James's Theatre.

Lady Windermere's Fan was a cleverly plotted melodrama about a marital crisis within a noble household. Its plot exposed a string of lies, threats and self-deceptions. The house of Windermere swept towards social disaster only to swerve away at the last moment. Following the final curtain a man in his late thirties sauntered onto the stage. Wilde was an impressive sight: six foot three inches high, with a languorous posture belying his incipient stoutness. For the occasion he wore a green carnation and was smoking a cigarette, both teasing gestures.

According to George Alexander, manager of St James's Theatre and the producer of *Lady Windermere's Fan*, Wilde told the audience he had 'enjoyed this evening *immensely*', watching the actors perform his '*delightful* play'. He thought the audience's appreciation has been 'most intelligent' and congratulated them on the '*great* success' of their performance. It persuaded him they thought '*almost* as highly' of the play as he did himself (italics in the original). Alexander's report of Wilde's curtain speech implies shocking arrogance. This was the Oscar Wilde journalists had learned to recognize and expect.

But compare another version of Wilde's curtain address, given by the theatre critic of the *Boston Evening Transcript*. This American newspaper was presumably less entangled in the cultural politics of London Society so perhaps more objective and detached. According to this report, Wilde was scrupulously polite. He thanked the audience for the honour of being invited to speak, and expressed at length his warm appreciation to the theatre management, the actors and all involved. He concluded by saying he was 'pleased to believe that you like the piece almost as much as I do myself'. In other words, Wilde balanced humorous self-congratulation with mock self-deprecation.[42]

Alexander's taunting spin was designed to play well with the London press. Perhaps it inspired the cartoon entitled 'Fancy Portrait' that appeared in *Punch* magazine on 5th March 1892, two weeks after the opening night.[43]

This shows Wilde in evening dress casually resting his elbow on a Greek pedestal. A sheaf of papers labelled 'speech' protrudes from his trouser pocket. Lady Windermere's fan is suspended from his left hand. Smoke billows from the cigarette in his mouth as he rests his other hand on his cheek. The words 'puff...puff...puff' float amidst the smoke, carrying a sexual connotation, then as now. Below the cartoon is a quote from the *Daily Telegraph* criticizing Wilde for smoking, and the cartoonist's mimicking comment: 'Quite too-too perfickly ridiculous.'

This is a coded attack on Wilde's supposed political motives and cultural intentions. The cartoon shows that Wilde's elbow has pushed William Shakespeare's bust off the pedestal. It lies in the dust beside the works of Irish-born but English-bred playwright, Richard Sheridan, an old-Harrovian, a Whig MP for over thirty years, and long-term owner of Drury Lane Theatre. Pride of place on Wilde's pedestal goes to the younger Alexander Dumas, the French dramatist whose plays Wilde admired. Down on the floor are some tiny mannequins, the actors who performed Wilde's play. Each bears the label 'puppet' and all are attached to strings stretching down from Wilde's casually extended left hand. This cartoon was crafted in the spirit of the Maxim gun. It blasted quick-fire bullets at Wilde's sexuality, his supposedly controlling spirit, his allegedly unpatriotic love for the culture of England's traditional rival, France, and, by implication, his interfering and inappropriate attacks on the English establishment and its cultural icons. Why such venom? Wilde had satirized the late nineteenth-century English *zeitgeist* in a vivid way. He knew it well and despised it. His excellent understanding of English high society made him a dangerous sniper. *Punch*, a conservative magazine, was keen to smoke him out.

If Wilde's notoriety made him vulnerable, Jean Améry's anonymity helped save him. He learned discretion in the presence of murderers. He knew how to melt into the background. Being able to read German handwriting got Améry an office job at Auschwitz. Two decades after his release in 1945, he put aside discretion and spoke out. On Monday 19th October 1964, Améry struck a resounding bell intended to bruise German ears. Améry's arena was a hushed studio in Stuttgart belonging to Southwest German Radio. His main audience was in the Swabian region that lies between Stuttgart and Munich, capital of Bavaria.

The sound of Améry's disembodied message coming across the airwaves surely discomforted many cosily carpeted Swabian homes. It turned those relaxed lounges into the scene of a ghostly séance. By 1964 Adolf Eichmann (1906–62) had been tried and executed, Günter Grass (1927–2015) had dramatized the neuroses of the German majority, and Hannah Arendt (1906–75) had exposed the dangers of complying with the deceptively banal routines of a murderous bureaucracy. The Israelis had asserted the righteousness of the victims' cause and the inexorable character of justice.[44] But who would depict the experience of the victim? Enter Améry.

Imagine a truly demonic Dickens using his ghosts to take Scrooge, his German audience, on a thoroughly hellish journey.[45] Améry transported his listeners to a place where the smell of burning human fat was normal; where thieves, bullies and kapos (trustee prisoners) ruled; where every day 'university professors, lawyers, librarians, economists and mathematicians'[46] did rough manual labour till they broke down and were sent to the gas chambers; where prisoners were hanged for a trifle on roll call, and died daily on all sides. It was a place where everyone learned to recognize the prisoner who was finished, who became 'a bundle of physical functions in its last convulsions' (9); where encountering heaped-up corpses was routine; and where prisoners debated the least painful way to die: the gas chamber, a blow to the skull from a guard, or suicide by running into the electrified barbed wire?

Améry wanted his German audience to know that he had been deeply damaged, and they should accept the blame. He insisted that, despite the contrary impression apparently given by ex-prisoners such as Primo Levi (1919–87), in the camps aesthetic antennae and intellectual sensitivities were disabled.[47] Poetry was powerless, philosophy redundant. What counted for survival was street knowledge, not Shakespeare or Hölderlin. Intellectuals were hobbled by their very respect for institutional authority, leaving them unable to lie and cheat effectively as a means of surviving. In Auschwitz metaphysics was displaced by cynicism. Survivors lost their joy in intellectual speculation, shed their old arrogance. Améry emerged shorn of his old pre-war idealism, no longer understanding the world but perceiving it with greater clarity.

Turning to Nelson Mandela, like Oscar Wilde he gave some of his best performances in a theatrical setting, in his case the courtroom. On Monday 20th April 1964, six months before Améry's radio talk, Mandela stood up in the dock at the Supreme Court in Pretoria in the early days of the Rivonia Trial. In Rivonia, a suburb of Johannesburg, Mandela and others had met in a secret hideout to plan a violent underground resistance campaign. The nub of the defence case was that no plans for sabotage had been adopted, nor any specific preparations made. This technical defence would allow the court to avoid imposing the death penalty if it chose.

The day was saved by international pressure, political caution, and Mandela's ability to convey the nobility of the not-quite saboteurs' intentions. His quiet words and calm demeanour marked him out as a hero prepared to be a martyr. Clever courtroom tactics secured Mandela an uninterrupted four-hour slot. Substantial parts of the speech made it into the newspapers, both in South Africa and overseas. Mandela told a story of unremitting struggle for basic human rights against an implacable government. He said his cooperation with communists was equivalent to Churchill's wartime alliance with the Soviet Union. The legal and judicial apparatus of *apartheid* had denied Mandela the dignity and freedom to which every person was entitled, defining him as less than a full human being. It enchained him with pass laws and imposed bans denying him public space. By turning him into an outlaw, it had forced him into a warlike condition. Such an argument put *apartheid* itself on trial for subverting the humanity of its victims.[48]

The slow, steady beat of Mandela's long exposition gradually led up to the time bomb which exploded in his last few words, spoken directly to the judge. He declared that he had cherished democracy, equality and harmony as an ideal to live for but 'if needs be, it is an ideal for which I am prepared to die'.[49] According to the defendants' chief attorney, Joel Joffe, Mandela's concluding words were followed by half a minute's complete silence in the courtroom, 'like the silence after a play, before thunderous applause'.[50] There was no applause, but it was certainly a career-defining moment. Instead of turning Mandela into a martyr, the regime decided to keep him hidden away, and hopefully forgotten, for many decades. Did some far-sighted members of the regime suspect they might need Mandela one day, to help protect them from vengeful African anger?

Finally, we come to Aung San Suu Kyi in 1988, caring for her dying mother in the Burmese capital Yangon[51] during a popular uprising. Ne Win, president since 1962, told a televised meeting on 23rd July 1988 that he proposed having a national referendum on possibly moving to a multi-party democracy. He also announced his resignation. Soon afterwards, Suu Kyi got in touch with the main opposition leaders, some of them old hands, including ex-military. She refused to proclaim herself leader of the movement for democracy at that point but shrewdly suggested they use her house as a base and centre for information exchange. Then on 23rd August Suu Kyi told the regime she intended to make a speech and asked for martial law to be waived so people could attend. She got her way.

Three days later on Friday 26th August 1988 over half a million people gathered before the main Buddhist temple in Burma, the enormous Shwedagon Pagoda. On the platform were leading figures in the democracy movement and a line of students guarding them. Among the crowd were hundreds of monks in maroon robes. The atmosphere was humid and hazy. The government had distributed several copies of leaflets full of personal attacks on Suu Kyi and her English husband.

In perfect colloquial Burmese Suu Kyi said the rally had been called to inform 'the whole world of the will of the people.' She asked for unity and discipline and demanded a multi-party democratic government.[52] Suu Kyi coolly asserted her right to speak for the entire Burmese nation, addressing the whole world. She insisted that being married to a foreigner and living abroad had never interfered with her patriotic devotion to her country. Her family knew how complex and difficult Burmese politics were but she could not 'as my father's daughter' stand aside from Burma's 'second struggle for national independence.' Her father, Aung San, had worked for democracy, freedom and peace. He wanted the armed forces to serve a united nation, not be hated by the people

Suu Kyi attacked no-one but spoke up for unity, discipline, trust, honour and dignity by all key groups, including the military. Her speech ended with a call for elections as soon as possible. Above Suu Kyi's right shoulder was a huge poster of her father's face, young and handsome. This produced a distinctive reversal of the Dorian Gray effect. In Oscar's Wilde's famous story, Dorian Gray's portrait ages but Dorian keeps his youthful looks. Suu Kyi's father, Aung San, had died in 1947, over forty years before, while in his early thirties. Since 1947 Burma's government had grown much older and uglier. Ne Win, Aung San's old colleague and rival, still a power behind the scenes, was nearly eighty years old. But here was Aung San's picture brought vividly back to life in the shape of his daughter, Suu Kyi, still in her early forties. She looked very much like him.

Inside story

It is time to join the dots. As the start of our story in the late nineteenth century we find Lord Salisbury, soon to be prime minister, warning that Irish home rule might lead to the disintegration of the British Empire. By 2016 Scottish first minister Nicola Sturgeon is warning that Brexit might lead to national independence for Scotland and the break-up of the United Kingdom.[53] These four rebellious lives – Wilde, Améry, Mandela and Suu Kyi – track the British Empire as it tests its strength against subjects and rivals, and later suffers decline, retreat and collapse. They illuminate crucial turning points in the global career of European imperialism and, subsequently, the making of a post-imperial, and, increasingly, post-Western world. We get a grandstand view of some key sites of political struggle because each rebel bursts upon the scene at a strategically important historical moment in a key geopolitical location.

Wilde witnessed British imperialism at a time when military victories and defeats fed a mass popular press ministering to an expanding democratic electorate. He was born during the Crimean War (1853–6), part of the so-called great game played between the British and Russian empires for mastery in Eurasia. He died during the Boer War (1899–1902), a bloody episode in the deadly scramble between Europeans competing for African possessions.[54] The lives of Améry and Mandela span two great recessions and two world wars, followed by the Cold War. Améry's life began during the twilight of the Hapsburg dynasty, two years before the start of World War I. Mandela was born the year that war ended, thirty years before *apartheid* was imposed. When Améry committed suicide in 1978 the United States was still adjusting to defeat in Vietnam. By the time that Mandela's life support was switched off thirty-five years later, the Cold War was long over and *apartheid* had been officially dead for nearly two decades. The West, and South Africa, were still reeling from the credit crunch and sovereign debt crisis of 2007–8.

Aung San Suu Kyi was born three weeks before atomic bombs were dropped on Hiroshima and Nagasaki. She is now caught up in the latest round of the new great game for control of Eurasia. The principal competitors are no longer Britain and Russia. Instead, the game is mainly being played between the United States and Burma's immediate northeastern neighbour, the People's Republic of China.

22 *Rebels and regimes*

That is the broader context for this inside story. It is an inside story in three ways. We see these rebels opposing overbearing regimes *from inside* the societies those regimes dominated. We observe the different ways they handled time spent *inside* various kinds of prison, each with its distinctive horrors. Not least, we catch glimpses of the emotional turbulence they experienced in their own lives, the *internal* struggles they each endured.

Notes

1 'The return of a great 19th century meteor shower', *Scientific American*, 19th October 2012 at https://www.scientificamerican.com/article/return-of-a-great-19th-century-meteor-shower/ (accessed on 3rd September 2017).
2 See Chivers 2010, ch.3; Thant Myint-U 2007; Vibart 1914.
3 Lady Bracknell is, of course, the most famous character in Oscar Wilde's most famous play. All three, the author, the play and the character, figure prominently in the next chapter.
4 'We seem, as is it were, to have conquered and peopled half the world in a fit of absence of mind'. Seeley 1883, 10.
5 'Mandalay' was published in Kipling 1892.
6 https://www.theguardian.com/politics/video/2017/sep/30/boris-johnson-caught-on-camera-reciting-kipling-poem-in-burmese-temple-video
7 For other work by this writer that locates creative thinkers and political activists in their comparative historical context see, for example, Smith 1978; Smith 1982a; Smith 1983; Smith 1984a; Smith 1984b; Smith 1988; Smith 1990a; Smith 1990b; Smith 1991; Smith 1992; Smith 1998a; Smith 1998b; Smith 1999a; Smith 1999b; Smith 2000; Smith 2001a; Smith 2001b; Smith 2002; Smith 2004; Smith 2009a; Smith 2009b; Smith 2012b; Smith 2013; Smith 2014c; Smith 2016a; Smith 2016b; Smith 2016c; Smith 2016d; Smith 2017a; Smith 2017b; Smith forthcoming.
8 Burma was officially renamed Myanmar in 1989. Following Suu Kyi's comments in April 2016 Burma will normally be used here for convenience. See Aung San Suu Kyi, 'You can call my country Myanmar or Burma'; 22nd April 2016, *The Independent* at http://www.independent.ie/world-news/asia-pacific/aung-san-suu-kyi-you-can-call-my-country-myanmar-or-burma-34651556.html (accessed 20th August 2016).
9 Brexit is the shorthand term that came into use referring to the project of the United Kingdom leaving the European Union (EU). The referendum was held on 23rd June 2016 with 52 per cent of the electorate voting to leave the EU and 48 per cent voting to stay, on a 72 per cent turnout.

More generally, see also the following. *On Oscar Wilde*: Ellmann 1988; Eltis 1996; Friedman 2014; Wilde 2013. *On Jean Améry*: Améry 1980a; Améry 1999; Heidelberger-Leonard 2010; Zolkos 2011. *On Nelson Mandela*: Bundy 2015; Lodge 2006; Mandela 2002; Mandela 2003a. *On Aung San Suu Kyi*: Aung San Suu Kyi 1991a; Clements 2008; Lintner 2011; Lintner 2011. *On mid and late Victorian Britain*: Collini 1991; Jones 1971; Smith 2016a; Webb 1980. *On Ireland*: Bartlett 2010; Connolly 2011; Foster 1990; Whelehan 2012. *On the Third Reich*: Bukey 2001; Evans 2009; Gehl 1963; Lorenz and Weinberger 1994. *On South Africa*: Johnson 2015b; Plaut and Holden 2012; Thompson and Berat 2014; Welsh 2000. *On Burma (Myanmar)*: Larkin 2010; Lintner 1994; Rogers 2012; Thant Myint-U 2007a. *On Imperial Japanese army*: Drea 2016; Yenne 2014; *On USA, USSR and Cold War*: Walker 1994. *On China*: Bin Wong 1997; Bond 1991; Spence 1991. *On Ottoman Empire*: McMeekin 2015; Reynolds 2011;Wheatcroft 1995. *On the European Union* (EU): Cockfield 1994; Duchêne 1980; Middlemas 1995; Milward 1992. *On tax*

havens: Palan 2003; Shaxson 2012. *On populism*: Mishra 2017; Luce 2017. *On civilized behaviour, civilizations and civilizing processes*: Elias 1983; Elias 2000; Smith 2001. *On European imperialism*: Bartov and Weitz 2013; Belich 2009; Calder 1981; Darwin 2007; Gerwarth and Manela 2014; James 1997; Lieven 2002. *On the British Empire:* Barr 2012; Brendon 2008; Cain and Hopkins 2002; Darwin 1988; Darwin 1991; Darwin 2009; Darwin 2013; Ferguson 2004; Gallagher and Robinson 1953; Gott 2012; Howe 1993; Hyam 2006; Packenham 1992; Price 2008.
10 See Baxter 2017.
11 Goethe 1809; Weber 2002; Arendt 1973.
12 Mignolo 2011.
13 None of these is aligned in any simple way with the 'East' and 'West' cited by Gramsci in his visionary perspective. See Forgacs 2000, esp. 222ff; Anderson 2017.
   On the West's complex relations with its various Easts see, for example, the following: Ahmed 2003; Ahmed 2013; Bayly 2004; Bayly and Harper 2008; Blum 2014; Bobbitt 2002; Bobbitt 2008; Brzezinski 1997; Brzezinski 2004; Brzezinski 2012; Buruma and Margalit 2004; Chakrabarty 2000; Cooper 2003; Dietrich 2017; Donnison 2005; Emmott 2017; Ferguson 2004; Ferguson 2009; Gerges 2012; Hanson 2001; Ishihara 1991; Jacques 2009; Kagan 2003; Kupchan 2002; Kupchan 2012; Mahbubani 2005; Mahbubani 2008; Mahbubani 2009; Mishra 2013; Morris 2010; Ong 1999; Ong 2006; Pettis 2013; Pomeranz 2000; Rachman 2016; Rashid 2009; Rashid 2012; Rothkopf 2012; Rothkopf 2014; Stiglitz and Bilmes 2008; Said 1978; Said 1994; Simpendorfer 2009; Smith 2006a; Studwell 2014; Subramanian 2011; Urban 2015.
14 Zeng Wang 2012.
15 Other perspectives are available. For some parallels between Southeast Asia and elsewhere, including the West, see Lieberman 1984; Lieberman 1999; Lieberman 2003; Lieberman 2009. On Ottoman, Balkan, Levantine and Middle Eastern issues see, for example, Fisk 2006; Inalcik and Quataert 1994; Mansel 2011; Wheatcroft 1995; Wheatcroft 2003; Wheatcroft 2009; West 1993. For contrasting global perspectives see Fontana 2011; Osterhammel 2014; Ponting 2001.
16 Geoffrey Parker has provided a unique global analysis of the seventeenth-century climatic, economic and political crisis. Parker 2013.
17 For a classic expression of these attitudes see the eight-volume *Harmondsworth History of the World* edited by Arthur Mee, an industrious journalist who located the British Empire on a cosmo-historical grid shaped by his understanding of Darwin and the Bible. Mee, Hammerton and Innes 1907.
18 See Smith 1990.
19 See; for example; Barr 2012; Hopkirk 2006; Pakenham 1992.
20 For evidence see Arendt 1973, 185–222; Strobl 2000.
21 Heidelberger-Leonard 2010, 72.
22 Howland 2015; Dlamini 1984; Wilde 2013; '5;000 days in captivity: The world's most famous political prisoner and a dismal landmark'; 4th July 2009; *The Independent* at http://www.independent.co.uk/news/world/asia/5000-days-in-captivity-the-worlds-most-famous-political-prisoner-and-a-dismal-landmark-1731998.html (accessed 24th August 2016).
23 Wilde 1891b.
24 First performed in 1895. For Wilde's plays see Wilde 1994.
25 Eagleton 1999, 51.
26 Améry 1980a.
27 Améry 1980a, 16.
28 https://www.nelsonmandela.org/news/entry/nelson-mandelas-speeches-in-2008 (accessed 6th July 2016).
29 Ross 2014; Smith and Helfand 1989; Wright 2008.
30 Mandela 2003a, 182–3.

24 *Rebels and regimes*

31 Thembuland (birthplace of Nelson Mandela) and Pondoland (birthplace of Winnie Mandela) are areas within the Eastern Cape in South Africa.
32 Hobsbawm 1959, 1.
33 Davitt 2015; originally 1904.
34 Davitt 1890; Davitt 2015; Holland and Hart-Davis 2000, 348; 870–1.
35 For memoirs of Belgian resistance fighters; see Bodson 1994; De Ridder Files 1991.
36 See http://history-switzerland.geschichte-schweiz.ch/swiss-revolution-helvetic-republic-1798.html (accessed 13th September 2016).
37 Beinart and Bundy 1987, e.g 251–5.
38 Mbeki 1964; Mbeki 1992.
39 http://data.worldbank.org/indicator/SP.URB.TOTL.IN.ZS (accessed 6th January 2018).
40 Wilde 2011.
41 Wilde 1891b.
42 Ellmann 1988, 346; Fryer 2014, 69.
43 https://www.britannica.com/media/full/327607/154753 (accessed 6th July 2016).
44 See Arendt 1963; Grass 2010; Grass 2008.
45 Dickens 2003.
46 Améry 1980a, 4.
47 Levi 1987; Levi 1988.
48 Sitze 2014, 150–61.
49 Mandela 2002, 54.
50 Joffe 2014, 160.
51 Rangoon has been known as Yangon since 1989.
52 'Speech to a Mass Rally at the Shwedagon Pagoda; 26 August 1988; Aung San Suu Kyi' at www.burmalibrary.org/docs3/Shwedagon-ocr.doc; and https://www.youtube.com/watch?v=gJV7fw577wk (accessed 6th July 2016). Also Wintle 2007, 3–8; 253–64; Popham 2011, 46–58.
53 'Brexit: Nicola Sturgeon says second Scottish independence vote "highly likely"'; 24th June 2016; *BBC News*; at http://www.bbc.co.uk/news/uk-scotland-scotland-politics-36621030 (accessed 14th April 2017).
54 Hopkirk 2006; Pakenham 1992.

Bibliography

Ahmed, A. (2003). *Islam Under Siege*. Cambridge: Polity Press.
Ahmed, A. (2013). *The Thistle and the Drone. How America's War on Terror became a Global War on Tribal Islam*. Washington, DC: Brookings Institute Press.
Améry, J. (1980a). *At the Mind's Limits. Contemplations by a Survivor on Auschwitz and its Realities*. Bloomington, IN: Indiana University Press; originally published in 1966 in German as *Jenseits von Schuld und Sühne (Beyond Crime and Punishment)*. München: Szczesny.
Améry, J. (1999). *On Suicide. A Discourse on Voluntary Death*. Bloomington and Indianapolis: Indiana University Press; originally published in 1976 in German as *Hand an Sich legen. Diskurs über den Freitod*. Stuttgart: Klett-Cotta.
Anderson, P. (2017). *The Antinomies of Antoni Gramsci*. London: Verso.
Arendt, H. (1963). *Eichmann in Jerusalem. A Report on the Banality of Evil*. London: Viking Press.
Arendt, H. (1973). *The Origins of Totalitarianism*. San Diego, CA: Harcourt Brace & Company; originally published in 1951.

Aung San Suu Kyi. (1991a). *Freedom from Fear and Other Writings.* Edited with an introduction by Michael Aris. London: Penguin Books.
Bartlett, T. (2010). *Ireland. A History.* Cambridge: Cambridge University Press.
Barr, J. (2012). *A Line in the Sand: Britain, France and the struggle that shaped the Middle East.* London: Simon and Schuster.
Bartov, O. and Weitz, E.D. (eds) (2013). *Shatterzone of Empires. Coexistence and Violence in the German, Hapsburg, Russian, and Ottoman Borderlands.* Indianapolis, IN: Indiana University Press.
Baxter, P. (2017). *Gandhi, Smuts and Race in the British Empire. Of Passive and Violent Resistance.* Barnsley: Pen and Sword Books.
Bayly, C.A. (2004). *The Birth of the Modern World 1780–1914. Global Connections and Comparisons.* Oxford: Blackwell.
Bayly, C.A. and Harper, T. (2008). *Forgotten Wars: The End of Britain's Asian Empire.* London: Penguin.
Beinart, W. and Bundy, C. (1987). *Hidden Struggles in Rural South Africa.* London: James Currey.
Belich, J. (2009). *Replenishing the Earth. The Settler Revolution and the Rise of the Anglo-World, 1783–1939.* Oxford: Oxford University.
Bin Wong, R. (1997). *China Transformed. Historical Change and the Limits of European Experience.* Ithaca, NY: Cornell University Press.
Blum, W. (2014). *Killing Hope. US Military and CIA Interventions Since World War II.* London: Zed Books.
Bobbitt, P. (2002). *The Shield of Achilles. War, Peace and the Course of History.* New York, NY: Alfred A Knopf.
Bobbitt, P. (2008). *Terror and Consent. The Wars for the Twenty-first Century.* London: Penguin.
Bodson, H. (1994). *Agent for the Resistance. A Belgian Saboteur in World War II.* College Station: Texas T&M University Press.
Bond, M.H. (1991). *Beyond the Chinese Face. Insights from Psychology.* Oxford: Oxford University Press.
Brendon, P. (2008). *The Decline and Fall of the British Empire 1781–1997.* London: Vintage.
Brzezinski, Z. (1997). *The Grand Chessboard. American Primacy and its Geostrategic Imperatives.* New York, NY: Basic Books.
Brzezinski, Z. (2004). *The Choice. Global Domination or Global Leadership.* New York, NY: Basic Books.
Brzezinski, Z. (2012). *Strategic Vision. America and the Crisis of Global Power.* New York, NY: Basic Books.
Bukey, E.B. (2001). *Hitler's Austria: Popular Sentiment in the Nazi Era, 1938–1945.* Chapel Hill, NC: University of North Carolina Press.
Bundy, C. (2015). *Nelson Mandela.* Stroud: The History Press.
Buruma, I. and Margalit, A. (2004). *Occidentalism.* London: Atlantic Books.
Cain, P.J. and Hopkins, A.G. (2002). *British Imperialism 1688–2000.* Harlow: Longman.
Calder, A. (1981). *Revolutionary Empire. The Rise of the English-Speaking Empires from the Fifteenth Century to the 1780s.* New York: E.P. Dutton.
Chakrabarty, D. (2000). *Provincializing Europe. Postcolonial Thought and Historical Difference.* Princeton, NJ: Princeton University Press.
Chivers, C.J. (2010). *The Gun.* London: Simon & Schuster.

Clements, A. (2008). *The Voice of Hope. Aung San Suu Kyi. Conversations with Aung San Suu Kyi*. London: Rider Books.

Cockfield, A. (Lord Cockfield) (1994). *The European Union. Creating the Single Market*. London: Wiley Chancery Law.

Collini, S. (1991). *Public Moralists. Political Thought and Intellectual Life in Britain 1850–1930*. Oxford: Oxford University Press.

Connolly, S.J. (2011). *The Oxford Companion to Irish History*. Oxford: Oxford University Press.

Cooper, R. (2003). *The Breaking of Nations. Order and Chaos in the Twenty-first Century*. London: Atlantic Books.

Darwin, J. (1988) *Britain and Decolonisation. The Retreat from Empire in the Post-War World*. London: Palgrave.

Darwin, J. (1991). *The End of the British Empire*. London: Basil Blackwell.

Darwin, J. (2007). *After Tamerlane. The Global History of Empire*. London: Allen Lane.

Darwin, J. (2009). *The Empire Project. The Rise and Fall of the British World System 1830–1970*. Cambridge: Cambridge University Press.

Darwin, J. (2013). *Unfinished Empire. The Global Expansion of Britain*. London: Penguin.

Davitt, M. (1890). 'The Report of the Parnell Commission', *Nineteenth Century*, March, 357–383.

Davitt, M. (2015). *The Fall of Feudalism in Ireland: Or the Story of the Land League Revolution* (Classic Reprint). Charleston, SC: Forgotten Books; originally published in 1904.

De Ridder Files, Y. (1991). *The Quest for Freedom. A Story of Belgian Resistance in World War II*. Santa Barbara, CA: The Narrative Press.

Dickens, C. (2003). *A Christmas Carol and Other Christmas Writings*. London: Penguin Classics, 27–118; originally published in 1843.

Dietrich, C.R.W. (2017). *Oil Revolution: Anti-Colonial Elites, Sovereign Rights, and the Economic Culture of Decolonization*. Cambridge: Cambridge University Press.

Dlamini, M. (1984). *Hell Hole. Robben Island*, Nottingham: Spokesman.

Donnison, D.V. (2005). *Last of the Guardians: A Story of Burma, Britain and a Family*. Newtown: Superscript.

Drea, E.J. (2016). *Japan's Imperial Army: Its Rise and Fall, 1853–1945*. Lawrence, KS: University Press of Kansas.

Duchêne, F. (1980). *Jean Monnet. The First Statesman of Interdependence*. London: W.W. Norton.

Eagleton, T. (1999). *Scholars and Rebels in Nineteenth-Century Ireland*. Oxford: Blackwell.

Elias, N. (1983). *The Court Society*. Oxford: Blackwell.

Elias, N. (2000). *The Civilizing Process*. Oxford: Wiley-Blackwell.

Ellmann, R. (1988). *Oscar Wilde*. London: Penguin.

Eltis, S. (1996). *Revising Wilde: Society and Subversion in the Plays of Oscar Wilde*. Oxford: Clarendon Press.

Emmott, B. (2017). *The Fate of the West. The Battle to Save the World's Most Successful Political Idea*. London: Profile Books.

Evans, R.J. (2009). *The Third Reich at War. How the Nazis Led Germany from Conquest to Disaster*. London: Penguin.

Ferguson, N. (2004). *Empire. How Britain Made the Modern World*. London: Penguin.
Ferguson, N. (2009). *Colossus. The Rise and Fall of the American Empire*. London: Penguin.
Fisk, R. (2006). *The Great War for Civilisation. The Conquest of the Middle East*. London: HarperCollins.
Fontana, J. (2011*)*. *Por El Bien del Imperio. Una Historia del Mundo Desde 1945*. Barcelona: Ediciones de Pasado y Presente.
Forgacs, D. (ed.) (2000). *The Gramsci Reader. Selected Writings 1916–1935*. New York, NY: New York University Press.
Foster, R. (1990). *Modern Ireland 1600–1972*. London: Penguin.
Friedman, D.M. (2014). *Wilde in America. Oscar Wilde and the Invention of Modern Celebrity*. New York: W.W. Norton.
Fryer, J. (2014). *Wilde*. London: Thistle Publishing.
Gallagher, J. and Robinson, R. (1953). 'The Imperialism of Free Trade', *Economic History Review*, 2nd series, 6, 1, 1–15.
Gehl, J. (1963). *Austria, Germany, and the Anschluss, 1931–1938*. Evesham, UK: Greenwood Press.
Gerges, F.A. (2012). *Obama and the Middle East. The End of America's Moment?* New York, NY: Palgrave Macmillan.
Gerwarth, R. and Manela, E. (2014). *Empires At War 1911–1923*. Oxford: Oxford University Press.
Goethe, J.W. (1809). *Die Wahlverwandtschaften* (Elective Affinities). Berlin: J.G. Cottaische Buchhandlung.
Gott, R. (2012). *Britain's Empire. Resistance, Repression and Revolt*. London: Verso.
Grass, G. (2008). *Peeling the Onion*. London: Vintage Books.
Grass, G. (2010). *The Tin Drum*. London: Vintage Books.
Hanson, V.D. (2001). *Why the West Has Won. Carnage and Culture from Salamis to Vietnam*. London: Faber and Faber.
Heidelberger-Leonard, I. (2010). *The Philosopher of Auschwitz. Jean Améry and Living with the Holocaust*. London and New York: I.B. Taurus.
Hobsbawm, E. (1959). *Primitive Rebels*. London: Norton.
Holland, M. and Hart-Davis, R. (eds) (2000). *The Complete Letters of Oscar Wilde*. London: Fourth Estate.
Hopkirk, P. (2006). *The Great Game. On Secret Service in High Asia*. London: John Murray.
Howe, S. (1993). *Anti-Colonialism and British Politics: The Left and the End of Empire 1918–1964*. Oxford: Clarendon Press.
Howland, J. (2015). 'Intellectuals at Auschwitz: Jean Améry and Primo Levi on the Mind and its Limits', *Holocaust Genocide Studies* (Winter) 29, 3, 353–373.
Hyam, R. (2006). *Britain's Declining Empire. The Road to Decolonisation, 1918–68*. Cambridge: Cambridge University Press.
Inalcik, H. and Quataert, D. (eds) (1994). *The Economic and Social History of the Ottoman Empire 1300–1914*. 2 vols. Cambridge: Cambridge University Press.
Ishihara, S. (1991). *The Japan That Can Say No*. New York, NY: Simon & Shuster.
Jacques, M. (2009). *When China Rules the World. The Rise of the Middle Kingdom and the End of the Western World*. London: Allen Lane.
James, L. (1997). *Raj. The Making and Unmaking of British India*. London: Little, Brown.
Joffe, J. (2014). *The State vs. Nelson Mandela. The Trial that Changed South Africa*. London: Oneworld Publications.

Johnson, R.W. (2015b). *How Long Will South Africa Survive?* London: C. Hurst.
Jones, G.S. (1971). *Outcast London. A Study of the Relationship between Classes in Victorian Society.* Oxford: Oxford University Press.
Kagan, R. (2003). *Of Paradise and Power. America and Europe in the New World Order.* New York, NY: Alfred A Knopf.
Kipling, R. (1892). *Barrack-Room Ballads and other Verses.* London: Methuen.
Kupchan, C. (2002). *The End of the American Era. US Foreign Policy and the Geopolitics of the Twenty-first Century.* New York: Alfred A Knopf.
Kupchan, C. (2012). *No One's World. The West, the Rising East and the Coming Global Turn.* Oxford: Oxford University Press
Kwarteng, K. (2012). *Ghosts of Empire: Britain's Legacies in the Modern World.* London: Bloomsbury Paperbacks.
Larkin, E. (2010). *Everything is Broken. A Tale of Catastrophe in Burma.* London: Penguin.
Levi, P. (1987). *If This is a Man and The Truce.* London: Abacus.
Levi, P. (1988). *The Drowned and the Saved.* London: Abacus.
Lieberman, V. (1984). *Burmese Administrative Cycles: Anarchy and Conquest, c. 1580–1760.* Princeton, NJ: Princeton University Press.
Lieberman, V. (1999). *Beyond Binary Histories. Re-imagining Eurasia to c. 1830.* Ann Arbor, MI: University of Michigan Press.
Lieberman, V. (2003). *Strange Parallels. Southeast Asia in Global Context, c. 800–1830. Vol 1. Integration on the Mainland.* Cambridge: Cambridge University Press.
Lieberman, V. (2009). *Strange Parallels. Southeast Asia in Global Context, c. 800–1830. Vol 1. Mainland Mirrors. Europe, China, South Asia, and the Islands.* Cambridge: Cambridge University Press.
Lieven, D. (2002). *Empire. The Russian Empire and its Rivals from the Sixteenth Century to the Present.* London: Pimlico.
Lintner, B. (1994). *Burma in Revolt. Opium and Insurgency since 1948.* Chiang Mai, Thailand: Silkworm Books.
Linter, B. (2011). *Aung San Suu Kyi and Burma's Struggle for Democracy.* Chiang Mai, Thailand: Silkworm Books.
Lodge, T. (2006). *Mandela. A Critical Life.* Oxford: Oxford University Press.
Lorenz, D.C.G. and Weinberger, G. (eds) (1994). *Insiders and Outsiders. Jewish and Gentile Culture in Germany and Austria.* Detroit, MI: Wayne State University Press.
Louis, W.R. (ed.) (1998–9). *Oxford History of the British Empire*, 5 vols. Oxford: Oxford University Press.
Luce, E. (2017). *The Retreat of Western Liberalism.* London: Little, Brown.
Mahbubani, K. (2005). *Beyond the Age of Innocence. Rebuilding Trust between America and the World.* New York, NY: Publicaffairs.
Mahbubani, K. (2008). *The New Asian Hemisphere. The Irresistible Shift of Global Power to the East.* New York, NY: Publicaffairs.
Mahbubani, K. (2009). *Can Asians Think?* London: MarshallCavendish Editions; originally published in 1998.
Mandela, N. (2002). *Long Walk to Freedom. The Autobiography of Nelson Mandela. Volume One. 1918–1962.* London: Abacus.
Mandela, N. (2003a). *Long Walk to Freedom. The Autobiography of Nelson Mandela. Volume Two. 1962–1994.* London: Abacus.
Mandela, N. (2003b). *Nelson Mandela in his Own Words. From Freedom to the Future.* Edited by K. Asmal, D. Chidester and W. James, London: Abacus.

Mansel, P. (2011) *Levant. Splendour and Catastrophe on the Mediterranean.* London: John Murray.

Mbeki, G. (1964). *South Africa: The Peasants' Revolt.* London: Penguin Books.

Mbeki, G. (1992). *The Struggle for Liberation in South Africa: A Short History.* Cape Town: David Philip.

Mee, A., Hammerton, J.A. and A.D. Innes (eds) (1907). *Harmsworth History of the World*, 8 vols. London: The Carmelite Press.

Middlemas, K. (1995). *Orchestrating Europe. The Informal Politics of the European Union 1973–95.* London: Fontana Press.

Mignolo, W. (2011). *The Darker Side of Western Modernity. Global Futures, Decolonial Options.* Durham, NC: Duke University Press.

Milward, A.S. (1992). *The European Rescue of the Nation-State.* London: Routledge.

Mishra, P. (2013), *From the Ruins of Empire. The Revolt against the West and the Remaking of Asia.* London: Penguin.

Mishra, P. (2017). *The Age of Anger. A History of the Present.* London: Little, Brown.

McMeekin, S. (2015). *The Ottoman Endgame. War, Revolution and the Making of the Modern Middle East, 1908–1923.* London: Penguin.

Morris, I. (2010). *Why the West Rules – For Now. The Patterns of History and What they Reveal about the Future.* London: Profile Books.

Ong, A. (1999). *Flexible Citizenship. The Cultural Logics of Transnationality.* London: Duke University Press.

Ong, A. (2006). *Neoliberalism as Exception. Mutations in Citizenship and Sovereignty.* London: Duke University Press.

Osterhammel, J. (2014). *The Transformation of the World. A Global History of the Nineteenth Century.* Princeton, NJ: Princeton University Press.

Pakenham, T. (1992). *The Scramble for Africa.* London: Abacus.

Palan, R. (2003). *The Offshore World. Sovereign Markets, Virtual Place, and Nomad Millionaires.* Ithaca, NY: Cornell University Press.

Parker, G.N. (2013). *Global Crisis. War, Climate Change and Catastrophe in the Seventeenth Century.* New Haven CT: Yale University Press.

Pettis, M. (2013). *The Great Rebalancing. Trade, Conflict, and the Perilous Road Ahead for the World Economy.* Princeteon, NJ: Princeton University Press.

Plaut, M. and Holden, P. (2012). *Who Rules South Africa?* London: Biteback Publishing.

Pomeranz, K. (2000). *The Great Divergence. China, Europe, and the Making of the Modern World Economy.* Princeton, NJ: Princeton University Press.

Ponting, C. (2001). *World History. A New Perspective.* London: Pimlico.

Popham, P. (2011). *The Lady and the Peacock. The Life of Aung San Suu Kyi.* London: Rider Books.

Price, R. (2008). *Making Empire. Colonial Encounters and the Creation of Imperial Rule in Nineteenth-Century Africa.* Cambridge: Cambridge University Press.

Rachman, G. (2016). *Easternisation. War and Peace in the Asian Century.* London: The Bodley Head.

Rashid, A. (2009). *Descent into Chaos. The World's Most Unstable Region and the Threat to Global Security.* London: Penguin.

Rashid, A. (2012). *Pakistan on the Brink. The Future of Pakistan, Afghanistan and the West.* London: Penguin.

Reynolds, M.A. (2011). *Shattering Empires. The Clash and Collapse of the Ottoman and Russian Empires 1908–1918.* Cambridge: Cambridge University Press.

Rogers, B. (2012). *Burma. A Nation at the Crossroads*. London: Rider.
Ross, I. (2014). *Oscar Wilde and Ancient Greece*. Cambridge: Cambridge University Press.
Rothkopf, D. (2012). *Power, Inc. The Epic Rivalry between Big Business and Government and the Reckoning that Lies Ahead*. New York, NY: Farrar, Straus and Giroux.
Rothkopf, D. (2014). *National Insecurity. American Leadership in an Age of Fear*. New York, NY: Publicaffairs.
Said, E. (1978). *Orientalism*. New York, NY: Pantheon.
Said, E. (1994). *Culture and Imperialism*. London: Vintage Books.
Seeley, J.R. (1883). *The Expansion of England*. Cambridge: Cambridge University Press.
Shaxson, N. (2012). *Treasure Islands. Tax Havens and the Men who Stole the World*. London: Vintage Books.
Simpendorfer, B. (2009). *The New Silk Road. How a Rising Arab World is Turning Away from the West and Rediscovering China*. London: Palgrave Macmillan.
Sitze, A. (2014). 'Mandela and the Law' in R. Barnard (ed.) *The Cambridge Companion to Nelson Mandela*. Cambridge: Cambridge University Press, 131–161.
Smith, D. (1978). 'Social Development, the State and Education: A Structural Analysis of Francis Adams's *History of the Elementary School Contest in England*', *Prose Studies*, 1, 1, 19–36.
Smith, D. (1982a). '"Put Not Your Trust in Princes" – A Commentary on Anthony Giddens and the Absolutist State', *Theory, Culture and Society*, 1, 2, 93–99.
Smith, D. (1983). *Barrington Moore: Violence, Morality and Political Change*. London: Macmillan.
Smith, D. (1984a). 'Method and Morality in the Work of Barrington Moore', *Theory and Society*, 13, 151–176.
Smith, D. (1984b). 'Discovering Facts and Values: The Historical Sociology of Barrington Moore' in T. Skocpol (ed.) *Vision and Method in Historical Sociology*. Cambridge: Cambridge University Press, 313–355.
Smith, D. (1988). *The Chicago School. A Liberal Critique of Capitalism*. London: Macmillan.
Smith, D. (1990a). *Capitalist Democracy on Trial. The Transatlantic Debate from Tocqueville to the Present*. London: Routledge.
Smith, D. (1990b). 'Organisation and Class: Burawoy in Birmingham' in Stewart R. Clegg (ed.) *Organization Theory and Class Analysis. New Approaches and New Issues*. Berlin and New York: Walter de Gruyter, 367–387.
Smith, D. (1991). *The Rise of Historical Sociology*. Cambridge: Polity.
Smith, D. (1992a). 'Modernity, Postmodernity and the New Middle Ages', *Sociological Review*, 40, 4, 754–771.
Smith, D. (1998a). 'Zygmunt Bauman. How to be a Successful Outsider', *Theory, Culture and Society*, 15, 1, 39–45.
Smith, D. (1998b). 'Anthony Giddens and the Liberal Tradition', *British Journal of Sociology*, December, 49, 4, 660–669.
Smith, D. (1999a). *Zygmunt Bauman. Prophet of Postmodernity*. Cambridge: Polity.
Smith, D. (1999b). 'The Civilizing Process and The History of Sexuality: Comparing Michel Foucault and Norbert Elias', *Theory and Society*, 28, 1, 79–100.
Smith, D. (2000). 'The Prisoner and the Fisherman. A Comparison between Michel Foucault and Norbert Elias' in A. Triebel, H. Kuzmics and R. Blomert (eds) *Zivilisationtheorie in der Balanz*. Opladen: Leske and Budrich, 143–161.

Smith, D. (2001a). *Norbert Elias and Modern Social Theory.* London: Sage.
Smith, D. (2001b). 'Organizations and Humiliation: Looking Beyond Elias', *Organization,* 8, 3, 537–560.
Smith, D. (2002). 'The Humiliating Power of Organizations: A Typology and a Case Study' in A. van Iterson, T. Newton, W. Mastenbroek and D. Smith (eds) *The Civilized Organisation.* Amsterdam: Benjamin, 41–57.
Smith, D. (2004). 'Historical Social Theory' in Harrington, A. (ed.) *Modern Social Theory.* Oxford: Oxford University Press, 132–153.
Smith, D. (2006a). *Globalization. The Hidden Agenda.* Cambridge: Polity.
Smith, D. (2009a). [with Anja Jorgensen]. 'The Chicago School of Sociology. Survival in the Urban Jungle' in M.H. Jacobsen (ed.) *Encountering the Everyday. An Introduction to the Sociologies of the Unnoticed.* Basingstoke: Palgrave Macmillan, 45–68.
Smith, D. (2009b). 'In Conversation with Dennis Smith. An Interview with Karen O'Reilly', *ISA E-Bulletin,* 13, July, 151–171.
Smith, D. (2012b). 'Norbert Elias and The Court Society' in Marcello Fantoni (ed.) *Europa delle Corti/The Court in Europe.* Rome: Bulzoni Editore, 415–435.
Smith, D. (2013). 'Forced Social Displacement: The 'Inside Stories' of Oscar Wilde, Jean Améry, Nelson Mandela and Aung San Suu Kyi' in Nicolas Demertsiz (ed.) *Emotions in Politics.* London: Palgrave-Macmillan, 60–83.
Smith, D. (2014b). 'Englishness and the Liberal Inheritance after 1886' in R. Colls and P. Dodd (eds) *Englishness. Politics and Culture 1880–1920.* London: Bloomsbury, 2nd edition, 279–306.
Smith, D. (2016a). *Conflict and Compromise. Class Formation in English Society 1830–1914. A Comparative Study of Birmingham and Sheffield.* London: Routledge.
Smith, D. (2016b.) 'The Return of Big Historical Sociology' in R. Schroeder (ed.). *Global Powers. Michael Mann's Anatomy of the Twentieth Century and Beyond.* Cambridge: Cambridge University Press, 39–61.
Smith, D. (2016c). 'Barrington Moore' in *International Encyclopedia of the Social and Behavioral Sciences,* 2nd edition, 768–774.
Smith, D. (2016d). 'Coping with Captivity. The Social Phenomenon of Humiliation Explored Through Prisoners' Dilemmas' in E. Halas (ed.) *Life-World, Intersubjectivity and Culture. Contemporary Dilemmas.* Warsaw: Peter Lang, 147–165.
Smith, D. (2017a). 'The Fateful Adventures of the Good Soldier Bauman. An Appreciation of Zygmunt Bauman (1925–2017)', *Historical Sociology* (Prague), I, 9–18.
Smith, D. (2017b) 'Exploring Modernity's Hidden Agenda in Europe. The Complementary Contributions of Zygmunt Bauman and Ernest Gellner' in M.H. Jacobsen (ed.) *Beyond Bauman. Critical Engagements and Creative Excursions.* London: Routledge, 163–181.
Smith, D. (forthcoming). 'Norbert Elias: Surrealism, Shock and the Civilizing Process' in Walter Pape and Jiri Subrt (eds) *The Cultural Space of Central Europe in the 20th and 21st century: Intellectuals, Identities and Ideas.* Berlin: De Gruyter.
Smith, P.E. and Helfand, M.S. (1989). *Oscar Wilde's Oxford Notebooks. A Portrait in the Making.* New York and Oxford: Oxford University Press.
Spence, J.D. (1991). *The Search for Modern China.* New York, NY: Norton.
Stiglitz, J. (2010). *Freefall. Free Markets and the Sinking of the Global Economy.* London: Penguin Books.
Stiglitz, J. and Bilmes, L. (2008). *The Three Trillion Dollar War. The True Cost of the Iraq Conflict.* London: Allen Lane.

Strobl, G. (2000). *The Germanic Isle: Nazi Perceptions of Britain*. Cambridge: Cambridge University Press.

Studwell, J. (2014). *How Asia Works. Success and Failure in the World's Most Dynamic Region*. London: Profile Books.

Subramanian, A. (2011). *Eclipse. Living in the Shadow of China's Economic Dominance*. Washington, DC: PHE Press.

Thant Myint-U (2007a). *The River of Lost Footsteps. A Personal History of Burma*. London: Faber and Faber.

Thompson, L. and Berat, L. (2014). *A History of South Africa*. New Haven and London: Yale University Press.

Urban, M. (2015). *The Edge. Is the Military Dominance of the West Coming to an End?* London: Little, Brown.

Vibart, H.M. (1914). *The Life of General Sir Harry N.D. Prendergast: R.E., V.C., G.C.B. (The Happy Warrior)*. London: Eveleigh Nash.

Walker, M. (1994). *The Cold War and the Making of the Modern World*. London: Vintage.

Webb, B. (1980). *My Apprenticeship*. Cambridge: Cambridge University Press; originally published in 1926.

Weber, M. (2002). *The Protestant Ethic and the 'Spirit' of Capitalism and Other Writings*. London: Penguin; originally published in 1905.

Welsh, F. (2000). *A History of South Africa*. London: HarperCollins.

West, R. (1993). *Black Lamb and Grey Falcon. A Journey Through Yugoslavia*. Edinburgh: Canongate Press; first published in 1942.

Wheatcroft, A. (1995). *The Ottomans. Dissolving Images*. London: Penguin Books.

Wheatcroft, A. (2003). *Infidels. A History of the Conflict Between Christendom and Islam*. London: Viking.

Wheatcroft, A. (2009). *The Enemy at the Gate. Habsburgs, Ottomans and the Battle for Europe*. London: Pimlico.

Whelehan, N. (2012). *The Dynamiters: Irish Nationalism and Political Violence in the Wider World, 1867–1900*. Cambridge: Cambridge University Press.

Wilde, O. (1891b). 'The Soul of Man under Socialism', *Fortnightly Review*, 49, Feb 1891, 292–319.

Wilde, O. (1994). *The Complete Plays, Poems, Novels and Stories of Oscar Wilde*. London: Parragon.

Wilde, O. (2011). *The Picture of Dorian Gray. An Annotated, Uncensored Edition*, edited by Nicholas Frankel. Cambridge, MA and London: The Belknap Press; originally published in 1891.

Wilde, O. (2013). *De Profundis and Other Prison Writings*. London: Penguin.

Wintle, J. (2007). *Perfect Hostage. Aung San Suu Kyi, Burma and the Generals*. London: Arrow Books.

Wright, T. (2008). *Oscar's Books*. London: Chatto and Windus.

Yenne, B. (2014). *The Imperial Japanese Army. The Invincible Years 1941–2*. Oxford: Osprey Publishing.

Zeng Wang (2012). *Never Forget National Humiliation. Historical Memory in Chinese Politics and Foreign Relations*. New York, NY: Columbia University Press.

Zolkos, M. (ed.) (2011). *On Jean Améry. Philosophy of Catastrophe*. Lanham, MD: Lexington Books.

2 Oscar Wilde

Wilde ambitions

On 16th January 1892 Oscar Wilde, aged 38, appeared at the Westminster Police Court. It was shortly before the opening night of *Lady Windermere's Fan* in the West End. Oscar Wilde was not on trial. On the contrary, he was treated with deference, sitting with counsel by invitation of the magistrate. Wilde was there to wield influence as a distinguished gentleman and a well-connected celebrity. His object of concern that day was the accused, John Barlas (1860–1914), dishevelled and disturbed, highly-strung and unpredictable. Wilde had known Barlas since university. His challenge that day was to prevent his friend from being committed to a lunatic asylum.

Barlas was the son of a Scottish merchant who had traded in Rangoon (Yangon), Burma.[1] This city had fallen into British hands during the second Anglo-Burmese war (1852–3). Barlas senior died in 1861. His widow came home to Glasgow and got young John educated at Merchant Taylors' school in London. From there Barlas went on to New College, Oxford, studied a bit of law, and worked briefly as an assistant master at Cheltenham Grammar School. Barlas's wife was also born in Rangoon. His father-in-law, a Bengal lancer, was the grandson of Lord Horatio Nelson's sister. Barlas's brother-in-law, Thomas Arthur Harkness Davies (1857–1942), was also a military stalwart. He served with the Devonshire regiment in Afghanistan, Burma, South Africa, Ireland and France. This man, heavy with medals, came to be universally known as Uncle Tom.

Heaven knows what Uncle Tom thought of John Barlas. After university, Barlas devoted himself to anarchist politics, aesthetic poetry and adventurous social relationships. He became violent and unhinged, left his wife, and set up house with a London prostitute. On New Year's Eve, Barlas took his revolver to Westminster Bridge next to the Houses of Parliament. He fired three shots towards the Speaker's House. A nearby policeman arrested him. Barlas told him he was an anarchist and wanted to show his contempt for the House of Commons. Initially, he intended shooting the policeman but thought it would be a pity to kill an honest man. To rescue Barlas from his folly Wilde posted a bond of £200 together with Henry Hyde Champion (1859–1928), an ex-army officer and a well-heeled socialist.[2] Barlas was allowed to go free and later wrote to express his thanks. Wilde generously replied that Barlas and he were both 'poets and dreamers'.[3]

The whole event illustrates Wilde's exciting but precarious situation. He was living at the centre of a whirling force field where four social networks intersected: bohemian artists and writers, radical political activists, the upper ranks of high society and the *demi-monde*, a zone of dangerous excitement driven by desperation, deception, drugs and ready money.[4] Wilde had been a married man since 1884, and was a father twice over. However, by the late 1880s he was focusing his attention on attractive young men. Wilde, like Barlas, was an occasional visitor to the Rhymers' Club, founded in 1890 by W.B. Yeats. It met in places like the Olde Cheshire Cheese on Fleet Street or the notoriously *louche* Café Royal where strong drink and other intoxicants could be taken in relaxed settings.

The Rhymers' favoured themes were beauty, eroticism and transgression. Their decadent spirit found its way into Wilde's *The Picture of Dorian Gray*,[5] a tale of excess and immorality. Wilde depicted these scenes with the aesthetic sensitivities of a poet, not the didactic tone of a moralist. Like Barlas, Wilde had anarchist sympathies. His paper on 'The Soul of Man under Socialism'[6] demanded universal access to culture, attacked socio-economic inequality, and recommended the abolition of private property. Wilde treated the politically unthinkable as perfectly reasonable. His fascination with anarchism was more than intellectual. One dinner guest at his Tite Street home in Chelsea was Sergei Stepniak (1851–95), the revolutionary who assassinated the head of the Russian secret police in 1878. Stepniak migrated to London but danger lurked, even there. One day, strolling to meet a fellow Russian anarchist in Shepherd's Bush, he crossed the railway line near Woodstock Road, ignored a warning whistle, and was struck by a train with fatal results; a Tolstoyan demise.[7]

Like Stepniak, Wilde ignored warning whistles and left himself vulnerable. For example, in 1891 he went to a meeting of an exclusive literary coterie at Crabbet Park, seat of Wilfrid Scawan Blunt (1840–1922), a high-born English opponent of British imperialism. Blunt had served a prison sentence for his pro-Irish political activism and stood for parliament on that issue while still behind bars. Another attendee was George Curzon (1859–1925), later Viceroy of India, another Oxford contemporary of Wilde's. New visitors to the Crabbet Club had their merits and demerits debated in open forum. Curzon roundly humiliated Wilde for his 'little weaknesses' portrayed in *The Picture of Dorian Gray*. But Curzon was hardly scandal-free.[8] An even riskier swing through the upper branches of Society carried Wilde into the arms of the son of the fearsome Marquess of Queensberry. Wilde met Lord Alfred Douglas (1870–1945) through the Rhymers' Club. The relationship offered him new vistas. Led on by Douglas, Wilde acquired a new habit: enjoying the rough trade of rent boys. In the event, it was Wilde's adventures with 'Bosie' Douglas that finally sent him crashing down.[9]

But we have not yet encountered the deep roots of Wilde's rebellious inclinations. To discover them we must go to Ireland. Wilde's statue in Dublin's Merrion Square, erected in 1997, depicts him in a flamboyant pose. It is widely known as 'the quare in the square'. Oscar Wilde is not easily ignored but the Irish have done their best. Dubliners have only recently begun to accept Oscar Wilde as maybe one of their own. In fact, the importance of Wilde cannot be detached from his Irish origins and Ireland's history. Ireland suffered centuries of exploitation and oppression at the hands of the English state, going back to at least the eleventh century. Extra bitterness was introduced in the sixteenth century when Henry VIII took the English Church out of Papal control while Ireland remained staunchly Catholic. Periodically, forces serving the English crown crossed the Irish Sea to hammer down this rebellious population.

One decisive encounter in 1690 ended in victory for the Protestant King William III (William of Orange) at the Battle of the Boyne. William imposed an Anglo-Irish class of large landowners. This settler establishment had its own parliament in Dublin. However, the Anglo-Irish squirearchy became increasingly marginal during the nineteenth century. In 1798 a group of Protestant gentleman formed the United Irishmen and rose up against the crown. They were inspired by the French and American revolutions, which rejected monarchical despotism. Irish people in many parts of the country took the opportunity to rise up against London. Faced with this revolt just fifteen years after losing its American colonies, the British state responded decisively. After that it was downhill for the squirearchy. In 1800 the separate Irish parliament was abolished and the kingdoms of England and Ireland were legally united. By the 1870s the Protestant Church in Ireland had also lost its privileged position.

Influence shifted from the Anglo-Irish estate owners into other hands: the Roman Catholic priesthood; the larger Irish farmers, overwhelmingly Catholic, many owning their land; and, of course, Westminster, Whitehall and Buckingham Palace, represented by Dublin Castle, the Royal Irish Constabulary, and resident magistrates. By the late nineteenth century, ambitious members of Anglo-Irish families faced the challenge of avoiding boredom and feeling useless. There was more than one way to tackle this challenge.[10] Take, for example, Charles Stewart Parnell (1846–91), a prominent landowner in County Wicklow. He was wealthy, handsome, self-confident, respected by his Irish tenants, a distant descendant of the Tudor dynasty, and a good friend of the local Roman Catholic hierarchy. Parnell used these assets to become leader of the parliamentary movement demanding Home Rule for Ireland, seeking virtual political independence from England. He built up a strong contingent of MPs at Westminster.

Parnell's movement expressed Irish resentment towards the English political class, intensified by the devastating Irish famine of the 1840s. Whitehall did very little to help, claiming it could not interfere with the forces of nature or the laws of political economy. Some even saw starvation and emigration as ways of cutting the Irish problem down to size. Many people thought the

English callously left the Irish to die or fend for themselves. Hunger, desperation and bitterness continued long after the famine's worst years. Parnell had strong links with radical republicans such as Michael Davitt, who was prominent in the tenants' movement to reduce their rents and increase their rights. This resulted in the so-called Irish land war from the 1860s to the early 1880s.[11]

Edward Carson (1854–1935), an Anglo-Irish Dubliner, took a different approach. He rose to the top of the legal profession in England. By 1911 Carson was a prominent dissident, leader of the Ulster Unionists and diametrically opposed to the Irish Home Rule movement. These diehard Protestant loyalists had strong links to the British Army and the Conservative Party. Carson's supporters were as bitter and determined as Davitt's followers. They were prepared to take up arms rather than be separated from the United Kingdom. Oscar Wilde, who completely disagreed, was Carson's contemporary. They met in their college years and perhaps before that; a maid once recalled them playing together as infants, making sand castles on the beach. They were to meet again in 1895.

Another Anglo-Irish Dubliner was Bram Stoker (1847–1912) who followed yet another path. He moved to London and for over a quarter of a century worked closely with the celebrated actor Henry Irving, acting as his business manager at the Lyceum Theatre. Stoker had a parallel existence as a writer of Gothic novels, notably *Dracula* (1897).

Wilde had affinities with both Parnell the politician, whom he actively supported, and Stoker the writer, whose future wife he once amorously pursued.[12] From the cradle onwards Wilde's parents steered him towards high culture and radical politics. His mission was to make his mark and do something worthy and memorable. Elder brother Willie qualified for the law but became a journalist. He was a devotee of public houses, no high flyer, and failed to net a rich wife, despite some near misses. This put added pressure on Oscar.

Wilde's mother Jane Wilde (1821–96), a passionate poet with the pen name of Speranza, was a prominent supporter of the Irish rebellion of 1848. When Wilde toured America in 1882 he was welcomed in Irish communities as 'the son of Speranza,' Wilde's father, who married Jane in 1851, was the eye surgeon Sir William Wilde (1815–76). He spent his free time recording the archaeology, landscape, folklore and famines of his native land. He was both a natural scientist and a social scientist. Sir William earned his knighthood in 1864 for analysing mortality trends from the Irish Census. This task gave him vivid evidence of the human cost of the Great Famine that took a million lives in the late 1840s. The Wilde house in Dublin's fashionable Merrion Square was a nest of radicalism: a comfortable one with six live-in servants. Speranza held frequent soirées. Local celebrities, up-and-coming artists, writers and politicians would meet and talk. The hostess would dress in spectacular style. Oscar learned at a very early age how to stand out in the competitive circles of smart society.[13]

Wilde's parents were highly wilful. Like their son in later life, they sailed close to the wind, hugging the line between respectable living and scandalous behaviour, and sometimes crossing it. Jane once denounced herself in open court, trying to get arrested for sedition. Her husband fathered illegitimate children, before and after his marriage. He once faced unproven accusations that he had made improper advances to a female patient.[14] Dublin high society enjoyed scandals but was also fairly tolerant. People knew more about each other than in London.[15] Under the influence of these early years, Oscar may have felt less need or inclination to hide his later indiscretions. In any case, Oscar deeply respected and admired both his parents, especially his mother.

Wilde's sense of personal style was refined further at Trinity College, Dublin where he became a student in 1871, sharing a room with Willie for part of his time there. Wilde studied Greek, practised poetry, and pretended to paint. His principal mentor, John Pentland Mahaffey (1839–1919), specialized in the field of charming arrogance. When Wilde won a highly sought-after scholarship in classics at Magdalen College in 1873, Mahaffey saucily remarked: 'You're not quite clever enough for us here, Oscar. Better run up to Oxford'. Which is what he did. Wilde got his revenge when reviewing Mahaffey's published work in later years.[16]

When Wilde crossed the Irish Sea to England he arrived in a worried country. At first sight this seems counter-intuitive. Since losing the American colonies, the British had enjoyed a winning streak: burning down the American White House in 1812, defeating Napoleon at the battle of Waterloo in 1815, and picking up additional colonies in Africa and Asia at the Congress of Vienna (1815). Later, tasty pickings were added to the imperial larder, sometimes in instalments. In South Africa, for example, the Cape Colony was grabbed first. Natal and the Transvaal were added later. Burma was acquired bit by bit in three short wars. The British gradually forced their way into China during the so-called opium wars. British colonies were widely dispersed across the globe. So much that in 1884 Britain took the lead in introducing international time zones.[17] But British rule was fiercely contested. India burst into flame in 1857. The Maoris took up arms in the 1860s. The Zulus erupted in 1879. Conflicts multiplied. The imperial realm was forever in danger of being pulled apart by rebellious subjects or foreign enemies.

The sun never set on Britain's ever-expanding global empire. Nor did the cement. Tempting prizes glinted on every horizon. But so did the rifles and helmets of jealous rivals. These included Britain's ancient enemies, Russia and France, along with the United States and the German Empire, new kids on the global block. By the 1870s the United States was fast recovering from its recent civil war, and the Prussian king was master of a large newly unified realm in Europe. Would Britain measure up? Could the Empire be turned into Greater Britain? A lot depended on the spontaneous loyalty of 'Anglo-Saxons' overseas in Canada, Australia, New Zealand and, hopefully, South Africa. But the American colonies had already pulled away. What was to stop the others doing the same?

Also, the world's still unclaimed land with all its hidden treasure mainly lay in hot and disease-ridden parts of Africa and Asia. Victorians asked: how could white-skinned English people possibly live in such places? Charles H Pearson fed these fears in *National Life and Character. A Forecast*.[18] He argued that the 'white races' lacked the manly vigour needed to maintain their rule in the world's tropical climates.[19] The signs were not good: debilitating urban slums, calls for democratic socialism, and new plays, novels and poems toying with the fashionable delights of degeneracy. The British establishment could feel the ground shifting beneath its feet. Rudyard Kipling (1865–1936) disliked the prickly social atmosphere he found in upper class London. He arrived from India in 1889 and tried to fit in but found he could not.[20]

The British government had its hands full spending money, spilling blood, taking on the Afghans, holding on to the Sudan, forcing its way into Burma, subduing the Zulus, and capturing the gold and diamond riches of South Africa's Witwatersrand. Add to these British anxieties just one more: Ireland. Wilde came from one of the oldest and most troublesome parts of the empire. During the 1880s, a key decade in Wilde's blossoming career, the Fenians were bombing on the British mainland while Parnell's people were disrupting business in Westminster.[21] Ireland elbowed itself to the top of the political agenda just when the last thing the British government needed was trouble on its very doorstep. Imagine a sheet stretched out over a large and delicious imperial picnic to protect it from hungry wasps buzzing around. The edges are being strenuously tugged to cover food recently added. Then suddenly the sheet starts to split in the very middle. That split was the highly unwelcome Irish question. Such was the English socio-political scene into which Oscar Wilde, an androgynous aesthete from Dublin, was trying to insert himself.

Wilde's foppish exterior cloaked a formidable brain. He regularly teased then wowed his examiners. He had plenty on his mind. In his Oxford days Wilde hovered at several brinks, enjoying three contests taking place within himself: between the earthly delights of Greek art and the spiritual comforts of Roman religion; between the moralizing of John Ruskin (1819–1900), professor of fine art, and the flirtatious hedonism of Walter Pater (1839–94), a fellow of Brasenose College; and, not least, between the engaging wit of clever women and the smooth shoulders of beautiful young men.[22] These delightful dilemmas were gradually superseded by a more painful predicament, a recurring pattern taking shape. At Trinity, Mahaffey's double-edged praise had been a rejection, tasting of sour grapes: 'you're not quite clever enough for us here, Oscar'. At Oxford Wilde was one of the most brilliant Greek scholars of his generation: he got a double first and, furthermore, won the Newdigate Prize for poetry. But he was not offered a college fellowship.

True, the Freemasons accepted Wilde. He adored their outfits. But Wilde was not made welcome in the Oxford Union, traditional gateway to the British imperial establishment. In fact, the Oxford Union rubbed Wilde's face in the mud. In 1881 their governing committee refused to accept his first book of poems. He had presented a copy in response to a request made by the Union librarian. However, the committee accused Wilde of plagiarism and disliked his homoerotic sensuousness. This was not deemed acceptable, even when cleverly rhymed.

After Oxford, Wilde moved to London and shared accommodation in Chelsea with a university friend. This was Frank Miles, a society painter whose father was the rector of Bingham in Nottinghamshire. The family entertained Wilde at Bingham Rectory. Wilde got to know Miles's well-connected sitters like Lillie Langtry (1853–1929). They offered useful pathways into fashionable high society in the empire's capital. Wilde used his opportunities well. He became adept at playing the court jester. But the pattern of half-acceptance, half-rejection continued. He was an outsider in that insiders' world, often mocked and sometimes brusquely excluded. Frank Miles's father was upset by the scandalous reputation Wilde's poetry book was given by its critics and insisted his son move out from the rooms he shared with Wilde. The son dutifully complied. Wilde was furious at this betrayal and let it show. Other barriers went up. Wilde belonged to various London clubs like the Albemarle and the Rhymers'. But in 1888 he failed to get into the Savile Club for distinguished practitioners of the arts and sciences even when sponsored by Henry James (1843–1916). The Athenaeum Club, London's most eminent haunt, would never take him into its membership.[23]

It was not Wilde's bi-sexuality that held him back. The point is that members of the English upper class establishment sometimes found Wilde a disturbing, even subversive, presence even though they enjoyed being teased by him for a while. Consider the words Wilde gave to the Duchess of Berwick in his play, *Lady Windermere's Fan*. She was talking about Lord Darlington, a tantalizing maverick, by turns flattering, witty and inscrutable, full of paradox like Wilde himself. The duchess exclaims: 'What a charming, wicked creature! I like him so much.' Pointedly, she adds: 'I'm quite delighted he's gone!'.[24] Being amused by Darlington was exhausting. Even Darlington got tired of it. He was disappointed in love, retired from London society and travelled abroad. Perhaps Wilde the playwright imagined his own fate when depicting Darlington's rejection and exile. His own end-game was similar but much more brutal.

Wilde had three ambitions. One was to attract attention. His 1882 American lecture tour, promoted by impresario Richard D'Oyly-Carte boosted his celebrity status. Dressed in velvet jackets and satin knee britches, Wilde told a hundred and forty audiences about an English Renaissance evident in the beautiful interior décor of English houses. Carried in swaying railroad cars, Wilde swept through prairie, city and suburb. Everywhere he played the hyper-confident and charming aesthete.[25] D'Oyly-Carte's comic opera *Patience* opened in New York the same year as Wilde's American tour: hardly a coincidence. Its leading character was the mock-heroic, lily-carrying Bunthorne. Wilde's own social performance was a parody of the comic operatic stereotype, upgrading the flamboyant personal style he had cultivated during his university career.

Another ambition was to taste the fruit of every tree in the world's garden, ignoring 'no trespassing' signs. Wilde coveted the responsibility and respectability that went with being a college fellow, a professor, a schools inspector, an author, a journal editor and a husband. He did not achieve the first three but managed to taste authorship, editorship and even marital bliss, for a while at least. Wilde's third ambition was to bring about a world where every person could appreciate all the beauties of life. That meant giving everyone education, knowledge, free time and material means. To do this, resources had to be wrenched from imperialist political regimes and the privileged social establishments living under their protection.

Wilde adopted his mother's political ideals as his own. His anti-war poem *Ave Imperatrix*,[26] from his 1881 collection, lamented the dead sacrificed in senseless imperialist wars and welcomed the republican future lying ahead. At about the same time Wilde wrote two intense melodramas, *Vera; Or the Nihilists* (1880) and *The Duchess of Padua* (1883).[27] Both featured anarchists keen to assassinate despots. In each case his clear target was the morally irresponsible misuse of political authority, denying others free and fulfilling lives. In 1881 *Vera* closed before opening in London because of the anarchist threat to the Russian Czar Alexander II. In 1883 the same play lasted just one week in New York because it was not making any money. It did not help that German anarchist Johann Most (1846–1904) was touring America's northeast states preaching revolution.[28] *The Duchess of Padua* was not staged until 1891 and then under a different title, *Guido Ferranti*.

Disintegration

Meanwhile, another author, definitely not radical, argued that imperialism was collapsing through British lack of resolve. His thoughts were published in the *Quarterly Review* for October 1883. Here we catch a glimpse of what higher conservative circles in Britain were thinking. The article, entitled 'Disintegration', observed that the British Empire was held together by thousands of Britons ruling over millions of colonial subjects. But this could only be done while the English were regarded as being superior. The biggest threat to this was the British liberal conscience, represented by William Gladstone.

The Liberal government was 'deliberately humiliating' the English in India before the indigenous population by giving Indians responsible office jobs previously denied to them. This undermined property rights, contract law and the conquerors' authority over subject races. Having a 'conscience of exalted sensibility' put the British nation and the British Empire in danger of disintegrating into 'a bundle of unfriendly and distrustful elements'. Meanwhile, the Irish were uppity, resentful, dissatisfied, unreasonable and implacable. Despite being beaten into submission Ireland refused to behave like a conquered people. Instead, Ireland was bargaining its way towards Home Rule. If British politicians did not resist Irish demands, this would hasten the day when the British Empire disintegrated.

The anonymous author of 'Disintegration' was Robert Gascoyne-Cecil, Marquess of Salisbury (1830–1903).[29] In fact, Salisbury became a very effective imperialist. He was British prime minister between 1885 and 1902, apart from short breaks, and had close links to South Africa's powerbrokers. These included Cecil Rhodes (1853–1902), Cape Colony's prime minister from 1890 to 1896, and Alfred Milner (1854–1925), appointed Cape Colony's governor in 1897.[30] Rhodes's style was: if you want it, take it. Salisbury backed Rhodes's vision of an imperial estate in Africa stretching from the Cape to Cairo. Salisbury's task was to help keep rivals such as the Germans and Portuguese at bay.

Wilde was certainly in Salisbury's field of vision. Salisbury and Wilde, both bulky men, could hardly have avoided brushing past each other in June 1894 at the wedding of Salisbury's son, Lord Edward Cecil. Oscar Wilde was a guest. The bride was his friend, the free-thinking Violet Maxse. In later years this lively lady allegedly had a fling with Alfred Milner, also one of Wilde's old acquaintances. Milner was invited to Wilde's own wedding in 1884.[31]

Respectable radical

Like Rhodes in Africa, Wilde in London wished to explore the territory and undermine its indigenous rulers. How could he disrupt the self-image, intentions and behaviour of the English upper class? By the mid 1880s Wilde was treading carefully. He wanted to get his radical message across but he also needed a steady income. How was he going to make his point and at the same time make his money?

The richest pickings were in London Society so Wilde sought entry, making his living as a hunter-gatherer journalist specializing in cultural criticism. He needed to clothe himself in greater respectability. To maximize public attention in the early 1880s Wilde had cleverly exploited the image of the foppish aesthete promoted by the opera *Patience* with its comic hero Bunthorne. Wilde became Bunthorne but this effete stereotype soon became an obstacle to obtaining the security and status he desired. Wilde needed to change his public profile and become recognized as a dependable sort of chap.

As Wilde approached the age of thirty it was time for him to settle down. Perhaps his mother kept reminding him of this. She lived only a few hundred yards away from Oscar in Chelsea along with elder son Willie Wilde (1852–99), a leader writer for the *Daily Telegraph*. Jane Wilde was the planet around which her two sons circulated like moons. Jane transmitted her views and needs regularly, signing off her notes as *La Madre*. Chelsea residents could hardly miss the family likeness of mother and sons, all three tall and ample of figure. Willie used to joke that Oscar paid him to grow his big black beard so nobody would mistake him for his brother.

The three helped each other out, financially and professionally. They were all writers and regularly wrote reviews, for example, in *Pall Mall Gazette, Burlington Magazine* and so on. Oscar and Jane's pushiness compensated for

Willie's indolence, some of the time at least.[32] Jane Wilde could not come up with a suitable match for Willie but she did find a good wife for Oscar. This was Constance Lloyd (1859–98), daughter of a rich Queen's Counsel. Constance and Oscar married in 1884. Wilde was soon putting other ticks in the box of respectability: fathering Cyril (1885) and Vyvyan (1886), then editing a serious magazine, *The Woman's World*, for two years (1887–9). Wilde developed links with a network of New Women including Olive Schreiner (1855–1920), feminist author of *The Story of a South African Farm*,[33] who sent three short stories.[34]

Wilde loved his wife and children and this was reciprocated. But by 1888 Wilde was strapped for funds and starting to stray from domesticity. He turned away from editing other people's writing and focused on elaborating his own vision. He spent more time away from home, more evenings in restaurants, and more nights in hotels. By the late 1880s Wilde had been coming to terms with his own bi-sexuality for at least a decade. In 1878, he had a long talk with a Catholic priest about his unsettling penchant for attractive youths.[35] Once he got all that off his chest he returned to flirting with both men and women, just as he had done since student days.

After marriage in 1884 the pattern changed. Honeymooning in Paris Wilde picked up a copy of *A Rebours*, a tale of sexual dissolution published that year by Joris-Karl Huysmans.[36] The excitement generated by this work was hinted at in *The Picture of Dorian Gray*. Huysmans also sketched out the outlines of the story Wilde later told in his *Salome*.[37] There was another factor. Childbirth did not add allure to Constance in her husband's eyes. By 1885 Wilde was moving into a new groove, actively pursuing young men.[38] Casual sex was a passionate hobby he followed alongside editorial work and his longer-term project: to get under the skin of the imperial establishment by assiduous observation and sparkling performance on the dinner party circuit.

Meanwhile, Wilde kept half an eye on parliamentary politics, the profession he once said he would have made his own if he had stayed in Dublin.[39] During the early 1880s Parnell's Irish parliamentary party was beginning to make the weather. They looked for political allies in the United States and throughout the empire. In South Africa they made common cause with the Boers, opponents of the British. By 1885 Parnell had enough MPs to hold the parliamentary balance of power. He first backed the Conservatives who promptly started the third Anglo-Burmese war (1885–6), taking the bloody road to Mandalay. Parnell then switched to the Liberals who brought in an Irish Home Rule Bill, splitting the Liberal party. The Liberal Unionists, including Joseph Chamberlain (1836–1914), moved towards the Conservatives and gradually merged into their social circles. As Lady Bracknell put it: 'They count as Tories. They dine with us. Or come in the evening, at any rate'.[40]

Irish issues were explosive.[41] Oscar Wilde was a hot and heavy piece of shrapnel: an enthusiastic Celt, a dedicated Parnellite, and always an Irish patriot. More by coincidence than design, Wilde's wit offered a counterpoint to Parnell's whip. The crack of both, the wit and the whip, worked up to a high pitch during the late 1880s. Wilde attended several meetings of the Parnell Commission (1888–9), which examined, and eventually dismissed, the phoney charge that the Irish leader had been involved in a political assassination.[42] Wilde's radical political views were refined in the Eighty Club. This was a London-based pressure group and think tank within the Liberal Party founded in the wake of the party's election victory of 1880. Supporters of Irish Home Rule argued out their policies and tactics at its meetings. In 1887 the conservative-minded *Spectator* suggested the club's principles were those of 1798, the year of the great Irish rebellion inspired by the American and French revolutions.[43]

Wilde was an active Eighty Clubber in the late 1880s and made a speech to fellow members in 1889. It has not been preserved but a review by Wilde in the *Pall Mall Gazette* during that same year perhaps conveys its flavour. Wilde argued that 'what captivity was to the Jews, exile has been to the Irish'. It taught them how 'indomitable' the force of nationality could be.[44] Wilde argued that English hatred and prejudice in the past was being superseded by well-intentioned stupidity. Fortunately, the rise of the Irish-American had transformed the situation, enabling Ireland to extend its boundaries to the New World. Greater Britain would have to contend with Greater Ireland, in other words, the United States of America.[45] Here Wilde's undiminished allegiance to the Irish cause came to the surface. It was a sign he was keen to make a more decisive impact on the world around him.

Wilde was hankering after more satisfaction, more cash and more credit, financial, social and intellectual. As editor, he had explored the female point of view. As a father, he had taken an interest in children as an audience for imaginative fiction, especially short stories with moral and political messages buried just below the surface. His stories were about responsibility and fulfilment, exploring the conflicts and limitations experienced by both the powerful and the powerless.[46] However, by the late 1880s Wilde was searching for new perspectives and satisfactions.

Smiling saboteur

Wilde's long-term objective was to undermine the class he memorably portrayed through the figure of Lady Bracknell, the ferocious aunt in *The Importance of Being Earnest*, first performed in 1895. Lady Bracknell lived in a tidily uniform world. It was a world she and her kind felt they owned and controlled. They made its rules and enjoyed enforcing them. Wilde's fellow Oxonian Lewis Carroll (1832–98) is worth mentioning at this point because of two characters from *Through the Looking Glass*: the White Queen and the Red Queen.[47] Wilde did not make the following comparison but it seems apt. He entered London Society with the support of a would-be revolutionary White Queen who believed 'six impossible things before breakfast'.[48] That was his mother, *La Madre,* who lived just down the road from him in Chelsea, a district that was bohemian rather than fashionable. Lady Wilde hated the idea of being conventionally respectable.

On the other side was the highly conservative Red Queen: his ultimate adversary, Lady Bracknell. She represented the stuffy and snobbish sociopolitical order. She evidently lived in a high-class London square, certainly on the fashionable side. Lady Bracknell was interfering, organizing, and sure that she was right, always telling others what was good for them and what the rules were. She was monstrous but, unfortunately, not mythical. Like the Red Queen she was 'cold and calm – ... formal and strict'.[49] The White Queen had daring visions but the Red Queen was forever stamping down on social gaffes and upstart fakes. Between them stood Wilde, determined to subvert the Bracknell worldview. His basic message was that the world experienced by Lady Bracknell is straightforward, plain to see and, in her view, just as it should be. But Lady Bracknell has got it wrong, no matter how assertively she issues her commands.

In fact, Wilde insists, we live in three worlds: the world as it seems to be; the world as it really is; and the world as it might become. The existing social and political order seems to be strong and immovable. But is it more than an empty façade, a moral abomination, based on falsehoods and the wearing of masks; more pernicious than it seems and much weaker than it looks? If so, perhaps we should deny its claims and stop obeying its commands. Perhaps things could be different and better. Wilde was keen to rip off the false masks that concealed the true faces of the world's Bracknells, male and female, who set the tone and made the rules operating throughout Britain's vast international sphere of influence.

But masks properly used, in the hands of ingenious artists, could release new creative energies, liberating new possibilities. They could help us to imagine others and ourselves differently.[50] Oscar Wilde once asked Olive Schreiner why she lived in the East End.[51] She said because it was the only place in London where people did not wear masks. By implication, you could observe their true values and intentions. Wilde replied that he lived in the West End because he was only interested in masks. Wilde surely meant that in high society he could find the two kinds of people he was most interested in: immoral fraudsters, who should be exposed, and creative artists, who should be encouraged.

By 1891 Wilde was prepared to be more open and direct. This was a year of powerful artistic declarations. In 1891 he published *The Picture of Dorian Gray*,[52] a vivid gothic tale of luxuriant gardens, lavish jewellery, sexual licence, explicit violence and Egyptian cigarettes. This scandalous text was just one note in a complex chord Wilde strummed as he demanded attention. Wilde's play Salome[53] was another shocker, written in French that same year. This moonlit melodrama showed familiar Biblical characters in a sensational way totally without reverence. Wilde's script put on stage a mother without a heart, a father without his senses, a daughter without her clothes, and, finally, a prophet without a head; or, more accurately, a head without a prophet. Rehearsals began, with plans to produce the play in Paris and London. But the play was banned from the English stage and the Paris production did not go ahead until 1896. *Punch* celebrated with a cartoon showing Wilde in a French military uniform with the caption: 'A Wilde idea. Or, more injustice to Ireland!'[54]

A third horror story also took shape in 1891. This time it was Wilde who lost his heart and his head. He met and fell in love with Bosie, Lord Alfred Douglas. This was much more dangerous ground than gothic or biblical romancing. Bosie was not just gorgeous and needy. He was also greedy, selfish, vain, spiteful and stupid, as Wilde recognized much too late. Wilde's utopian and rebellious spirit, driven into hiding in the early 1880s, was resurfacing in a highly articulate, open, and sometimes reckless way. In 1891 he finally managed to stage *The Duchess of Padua*, rechristened as *Guido Ferranti*. It ran for three weeks in the Broadway Theatre, New York. Meanwhile, Wilde insisted that Matthew Arnold, author of *Culture and Anarchy*,[55] published in 1869, was wrong to treat central government as a necessary disciplining force in society. On the contrary, only noble anarchy would produce a truly worthy modern culture.[56]

Wilde was getting the public's attention but not yet their approval. At least he was now expressing his vision directly. Wilde was being judged on his own words and ideas, no longer confined to being an editor, a reviewer or a cartoon image in *Punch*. His next task was to find a way to get his message through even more effectively, to open the minds of his audience as well as their eyes and ears. He needed to get their relaxed and receptive attention. To achieve that Wilde added another note to the complex chord he was strumming, one that would enable him to cut through to the large and sympathetic audience he wanted. He accomplished this with another project he was working upon in 1891. It was a very watchable fable about London in the 1890s.

Lady Windermere's Fan opened in 1892 at the St James's Theatre in the West End. This was a play full of recognizable everyday characters. We see Wilde the cultural anthropologist at work, drawing on his practical understanding of the dynamics of family life. This was an arena Wilde no longer wished to inhabit but he had scouted out its perils and opportunities pretty fully. Reading the play one can almost hear the sigh of relief behind the audience's thunderous applause: at last, something from Wilde they could recognize, understand, sympathize with and smile at, sardonically at least. The West End was where Gilbert and Sullivan had twitted Wilde as the idiotic Bunthorne in their lampooning comic opera *Patience*. That work, produced in 1881, aimed to diminish Wilde through mocking laughter, although Wilde had used the image to his advantage as he toured the United States. A decade later, Wilde returned to the West End in triumph. Aged thirty-seven, he finally had his theatrical pulpit and a willing paying, congregation. His chosen subject was the English public that had previously mocked him. Especially its leaders in London high society, whose members occupied the most expensive theatre seats. Wilde conducted a surgical dissection of the imperial establishment over a sequence of four witty but pitiless plays.

Lady Windermere's Fan was Wilde's breakthrough back into the big time, the first since his American tour. It brought him substantial critical acclaim, social kudos and a rich flow of ready cash. Wilde's Lady Windermere is a young wife who fears, wrongly, that her husband is having an affair. She considers leaving him and goes for help to an admirer, Lord Darlington. Lady Windermere does not know it but the other woman is her own mother, Mrs Erlynne, who years before abandoned her own husband and child for another man. Mrs Erlynne's new lover abandoned her in turn, leaving her to survive alone, unprotected and unrespectable. Mrs Erlynne is using the threat of causing a scandal to get her son-in-law, Lord Windermere, to give her money and help her get back into Society. Mrs Erlynne acts behind the scene to rescue the Windermeres' marriage, and meanwhile acquires a new husband for herself and the prospect of a decent life. The Windermeres are reconciled. In other words, in the play Wilde shows that people who are socially marginalized and sneered at can behave with more care, compassion and responsibility than their supposed betters.

Three more plays followed. The playwright's message in each case was conveyed through his plots rather than his aphorisms, although those witty formulations kept audiences alert and listening. In *A Woman of No Importance*, staged in April 1893, the rich and powerful Lord Illingworth offers the dream job of being his secretary to Gerald Arbuthnot, a young man of humble circumstances. All is well until Arbuthnot's mother and Illingworth meet and realize that Gerald is their illegitimate child from a brief liaison finished long ago. Illingworth had swiftly moved on. Mrs Arbuthnot, her son and his bride-to-be form an alliance against Lord Illingworth. He retreats from the scene, hurt and defeated. This time Wilde shows that the weak may combine to become powerful when faced with injustice.

In *An Ideal Husband*, performed in January 1895, the stakes are even higher. Sir Robert Chiltern, MP, a leading figure in the House, has a shameful secret: his fortune was founded on a fraudulent business conspiracy he joined as a young man. It involved shares in the Suez Canal company. His past comes back to bite him in the shape of the scandalous and sensational Mrs Cheveley, a sophisticated charmer with an impressive European-wide network of ex-lovers in the worlds of diplomacy, politics and finance. Mrs Cheveley knows Chiltern's secret. She threatens to reveal it if he fails to give public support for another fraudulent scheme of international investment she is helping to promote. Chiltern has a world-wise friend, Lord Goring, who helps him wriggle free of this predicament. Meanwhile, Chiltern's pure and prudish wife is left ignorant of the whole business. The moral: even the most apparently noble and virtuous statesmen in Britain's imperial parliament carry the taint of corruption.

Wilde's fourth play in the sequence was *The Importance of Being Earnest*, which opened in February 1895. This sharp shooting farce was a piece of hard-hitting revenge, as deadly as any *Punch* cartoon. *The Importance of Being Earnest* pulled the rug out from beneath the upper class, and left it sprawling, cut down to size. Remember the scene in Francis Ford Coppolla's *The Godfather Part III* where a glorious performance of *Cavalleria rusticana* is made the background for a coordinated massacre of Mafia enemies. In a similar way, Wilde uses the sustained hilarity produced by *The Importance of Being Earnest* as cover for a literary assassination of his direst foes, the arrogantly rich and powerful.

In this work Wilde was able to carry out the task of anarchic destruction that his leading characters had failed to achieve in his early melodramas, *Vera* and *The Duchess of Padua*. Wilde's farce had shock value. We should not be deceived by how well we know the plot. We should also remember that *The Importance of Being Earnest* was preceded by three other plays that had already drawn up a hefty charge sheet of selfishness, foolishness and degradation against the social types now being put on stage once more. Beneath the stream of witty patter Wilde hammered home a number of plain truths: that the socially marginalized can follow higher moral standards than the high and mighty, that those low in the pecking order become strong when they combine, and that the power game corrupts its players.

In *The Importance of Being Earnest* Wilde showed much less empathy than before with his characters as they faced agonizing social pressures that drove them to put on false masks and engage in desperate acts of deceit. Instead they were lined up like cardboard ducks in a shooting gallery. There is, indeed, a laugh a minute but notice that the play is subtitled 'a trivial comedy for serious people'. Those serious people were in the audience, including many in the cheaper seats. Any hard working office clerks, board school teachers or station masters who bought tickets for *The Importance of Being Earnest* or read the play, were able to sit in judgment over the shallow posh folk that Wilde had transported from Chelsea, Mayfair and, perhaps, Bingham Rectory.[57]

Algernon and Jack, two feckless bachelors, are exposed as inveterate liars. Lady Bracknell is revealed as a selfish bully with a merciless tongue. The Anglican Church is twitted as a refuge for out-of-touch time-servers. London Society is portrayed as a perpetual drill parade of obsequious hypocrites keen to cling onto their position in the hierarchy of prestige and privilege. This was Bunthorne's revenge. However, there was one other very big casualty. Barely two months into the run of *The Importance of Being Earnest* Wilde found himself in court, and then in prison.

Hard cell

Wilde's subtle assault on English high society and the answering ripostes of conservatives had initially taken place mainly in the exclusive dining rooms of the privileged. They later moved to the more widely accessible arena of literary journals and satirical magazines such as *Punch*. During the early 1890s the action moved into the most open forum so far, the West End theatre where productions played to large audiences and were reviewed in the popular press.

After the St James's Theatre Wilde's next public forum was the Old Bailey in April 1895. He was initially drawn there out of loyalty to Bosie who was engaged in a long-running feud with his father, the Marquess of Queensberry. This was a highly dysfunctional family, containing unhappy, reckless people.

Bosie apparently believed he could get his own father thrown into jail on the grounds that the marquess had libelled Wilde. He asserted that Wilde was 'posing as a sodomite', engaging in homosexual acts that were illegal at that time. The difficulty was this libel had plausibility. Wilde thoughtlessly complied with Bosie's wishes. He issued a writ against Queensberry who was duly arrested. However, it was not difficult for Queensberry's legal team led by Edward Carson to provide evidence that Wilde had kept company with homosexual prostitutes. They also claimed on the basis of writings such as *The Portrait of Dorian Gray* that Wilde had a bad character, liable to corrupt others.[58]

Wilde had spent the previous three years mounting a highly effective campaign on the West End stage to undermine the character and reputation of the English upper class. Now his foes seized upon Wilde's chief weapon, character assassination, and used it against Wilde himself. His reputation was thoroughly besmirched in open court and on the world stage. His libel case was thrown out. Soon after that it was Wilde's turn to be arrested on a charge of gross indecency, backed up by the evidence Queensberry's team had already gathered.

Wilde did not try to escape by leaving the country. Bosie pleaded with him to stay. Just as significant, his mother was adamant he should face the music. She was determined her son should be a hero or a martyr, as she had always wished to be herself. Yeats later remembered her taking this position. According to another sympathetic source, Wilde's brother Willie expected him to stay and face the music like 'an Irish gentleman'.[59] It was a matter of family honour. Unfortunately, so it was for Bosie's father, the Marquess of Queensberry. He struck Wilde down without mercy and the popular press was finally able to feast upon him without restraint, stripping off all semblance of respectability from their victim. Wilde was painted for all to see as a man of diabolically bad character with a propensity for corrupting the young.

The details of the court proceedings are less important that the outcome, a guilty verdict. There was considerable collateral damage. Neither his mother nor his wife survived very long after the trial: Lady Wilde died in 1896, Constance in 1898 aged thirty-nine. Wilde himself was jailed for two years with hard labour. His literary voice was virtually silenced apart from the long letter that became known as *De Profundis*[60] and a poem, *The Ballad of Reading Gaol*, originally published under the name of C.33, which was Wilde's cell number at Reading.

Carson, a fellow Anglo-Irishman, had not been keen to instigate the second trial but the government told him it could not afford any suggestion of a cover up. At the time there were strong rumours that the Liberal prime minister, Lord Rosebury, had been in a homosexual relationship with his private secretary, Lord Drumlanrig, who was Lord Alfred Douglas's elder brother.

Drumlanrig was found shot dead in 1894. It was recorded as a hunting accident but suspicions about suicide or murder persisted. Queensberry, Drumlanrig's father, was distraught and thirsty for revenge. Perhaps it was convenient for the prime minister's protectors to throw Wilde off the sledge in front of the hotly pursuing Marquess. Was this a way of distracting him from pursuing the case of the prime minister and his other son?

It is very telling that no Society heavyweight stepped in to save Wilde the way Wilde had saved John Barlas three years before, or to commute his sentence, as happened to Cecil Rhodes' brother following the notorious Jameson Raid in South Africa at the end of 1895. In any case, following Wilde's sustained West End assault on the integrity of the imperial establishment over the previous three years, his disappearance from the scene was surely quite convenient in political terms.[61]

Wilde enjoyed danger, whether political, social or sexual. He did not enjoy prison. He paid a heavy price for love, loyalty and an inability to grasp likely consequences staring him in the face. His months spent on the treadmill and picking okum ruined his health and undermined his morale. Wilde bemoaned the deadening effect of prison life on intellect and imagination: 'in the sphere of thought ... motion is no more'.[62]

Wilde's punishment was harsh but his response was acceptance and self-blame. If this was a mask it fitted close enough to become Wilde's face, for a while at least. In any case, as Wilde had argued in happier days, masks can engender creativity. In fact, Wilde was as creative in responding to humiliation as he had been reckless in incurring it. *De Profundis* records this process. Wilde describes a personal journey in which he stifles the temptation to hatred, since that would disable his artistic personality, so reliant on openness, empathy and sensitivity. Instead, he accepts his own culpability and blames his appalling self-neglect. He had allowed Bosie to lead him to the slaughter 'as an ox to the shambles'. At the same time, Wilde envies the wonderful performance opportunity his trial had offered the barrister making the case against him: '*How splendid it would be if I was saying all this about myself*'.[63]

In fact, Wilde decided to enact his own retrial in the pages of *De Profundis*, acting as his own judge and prosecuting counsel. This enabled him to transform humiliation, a degradation undeservedly imposed, into a mixture of guilt and shame. He accepted that he had failed to meet his own standards. Wilde also became his own therapist. He adopted an attitude of humility. His plan was to work imaginatively and philosophically upon his experience of suffering. Never a modest man, he compared his situation to the passion of Christ. By 1897 Wilde had lost his reputation, his mother, his wife and his children. He wanted to move on to a new phase of conciliation, especially between himself and the world. He wished to reintegrate himself with the beauty of nature.

Wilde also wanted to reintegrate himself with Bosie. For all his highly cogent analysis of the damage this relationship had done to him, Wilde still hoped that his long letter would somehow reform the younger man. As he revealed in *De Profundis*, they had broken up and come back together on several occasions. Wilde still hungered for another round, to bring him some comfort. His hopes for conciliation were short-lived. Wilde soon lost Bosie, the man who once cruelly told him: '*When you are not on your pedestal you are not interesting*'.[64] Sadly, Wilde could no longer enact the public persona he had arduously constructed. His appreciative audience became a jeering mob. Wilde was soon forced to escape from England and drift around France and Italy. He spent his last years travelling under a pseudonym.[65]

Wilde's triumph was a posthumous one. As late as the 1920s it was common to disparage him, although *The Importance of Being Earnest* was singled out for special praise. W.B. Yeats, André Gide and Wilde himself all acknowledged that his conversation and living self were a very large part of his sensational impact.[66] However, his writings undermined the British imperial elite's morale and self-image, providing an antidote to Rider Haggard (1856–1925), who wrote up the Empire as noble and exciting.[67] Wilde also contradicted the conservative bent of works such as Rudyard Kipling's *Plain Tales from the Hills*, published in 1888, which humanized the Raj.[68]

Rudyard Kipling (1865–1936) normalized the exotic, bringing the breezes of Shimla into cosy British parlours. He told gossipy stories about deception, cruelty and contempt in a rather fatalistic, worldy-wise tone of voice, an approach taken much further by Saki and Maughan.[69] Kipling's objective was not to condemn the imperial project but to show his readers that colonials were no better or worse than other people. By contrast, in Wilde's plays the main source of dramatic tension is the quiet terror felt by corrupt and neglectful members of rich and influential families when they realize their grossly immoral behaviour could lead to disgrace. Kipling shows us pitiful mice; Wilde delineates merciless monsters. He exposes scandalous selfishness on the part of those with power, met by strong and intelligent resistance by those who are nominally weaker.

Wilde made London high society look first corrupt, then ridiculous. He blazed a trail for P.G. Wodehouse (1881–1975) with his own repertoire of upper class drones and nincompoops. Wilde also opened a literary door for E.F. Benson (1867–1940) who directed attention to the upper middle class versions of these selfish, small-minded types in places like East Sussex where Mapp and Lucia peered through telescopes at their neighbours. Also for George Orwell (1903–50) who depicted their demoralized and suicidal cousins in colonial Burma during the 1920s.[70] Wilde became a gay martyr as lipstick tributes in Père Lachaise Cemetery attested. The cause is noble but Wilde never sought that honour. He probably would be just as pleased to hear another judgment: that his assault on the hypocritical and arrogant British imperial establishment was pathbreaking. It prepared the way for other voices and campaigns against imperial regimes. Mahatma Gandhi (1869–1948) was in London in the late 1880s and early 1890s. He disliked Wilde's theories about art but surely benefited from the work Wilde did in undermining the Raj's self-confidence. Wilde helped plough the ground that Gandhi sowed and harvested with his campaign to shame the British out of India.

The influence of Wilde is more overt in the case of Karl Kraus (1874–1936) in Vienna, one of his greatest admirers. Jean Améry was familiar with Kraus's essays. These poured scorn on the decaying structures of the Austro-Hungarian empire, the corruption and incompetence exhibited during World War I, and the confusion reigning after 1918, compounded by the backwash of the Russian Revolution (1917). Like Wilde, Kraus saw the wicked intent of people up to no good but wearing masks to hide that fact. His masterpiece was the blistering satire *The Last Days of Mankind*,[71] an epic play echoing with contempt for the lies, self-deception, false hope and cruelty reshaping Europe, turning it into a moral wasteland.

Empire and Reich

Before moving on to Jean Améry, we need to explore briefly the relationship between the British Empire, Wilde's ultimate earthly foe, and the Third Reich, the murderous regime from whose ferocious jaws Améry amazingly slipped free. Gerwin Strobl has shown that Adolf Hitler and the Nazis constructed their own favourable image of British imperialism based on assertive overlords such as Robert Clive and Warren Hastings in India, Cecil Rhodes in Africa, and George Arthur in Tasmania. The Nazis admired their brutality and ruthlessness, and their cold calculation of the British interest. In Nazi eyes these daring characters exemplified the British disregard for moral scruples, their relentless drive for territorial expansion and their dominant masculinity. An SS researcher was delighted to discover in 1935 that the British had the harshest penal sanctions against homosexuality of all Europe's 'Nordic-Germanic' nations.[72] These sanctions had, of course, been applied to Oscar Wilde.

The Nazis enjoyed finding evidence of British tough-mindedness. They relished reading about: the genocide that virtually wiped out the Aboriginal population of Tasmania (1825–31); the devastating famines in Bengal (1769–73) and Ireland (1845–52); the Fashoda incident (1898) when the British bullied the French out of the upper Nile region; the Boer War (1899–1902) during which the British had no qualms about inflicting disease and starvation upon other white Europeans in concentration camps; and the British attack at Mers-el-Kébir on the navy of Britain's ally, the beleaguered French, to prevent French ships from being useful to the Germans (1940).[73] Hannah Arendt argued in *The Origins of Totalitarianism*[74] that Hitler's approach echoed certain aspects of British imperialism. She was thinking, for example, of the aggressive enthusiasm for violent mastery displayed by white adventurers in Africa. Also, the autocratic approach to so-called subject races espoused by many colonial administrators. At the centre of the colonial relationship she saw fear, disgust and repressive zeal.

Hannah Arendt had her own list of ghastly imperialist practices. European disregard of the rights and humanity of the African population led to gruesome massacres; for example, in Matabeleland where troops employed by the British South Africa Company used Maxim guns to slaughter Ndebele warriors on an industrial scale. Meanwhile, in South Africa itself Boer farmers forced indigenous inhabitants of the Transvaal to work in virtual slavery tending land and cattle. The Boers imposed this arrangement with a good Christian conscience. Rifles and whips reinforced their worldview, which was sanctified by their version of Dutch Calvinism. Arendt argued that the Nazis re-imported this repressive spirit into Europe.

According to Arendt, the Nazis also copied another imperialist practice, governing subjects through bureaucratic autocracy. A prominent practitioner of this approach was Evelyn Baring, ennobled as Lord Cromer (1841–1917).[75] He made himself omnipotent in the role of Consul-General in Egypt between 1883 and 1907. Cromer, a friend of Alfred Milner, was able to shrug off all external controls on his behaviour. As far as possible, Cromer ignored local and colonial law. He wanted maximum flexibility, secrecy and personal discretion. He relied on his personal judgment as an experienced and civilized Englishman. That was sufficient qualification, in his view. He did not offer his actions for public discussion. Nor did he justify them, at least not until he had retired from his Egyptian responsibilities.

Cromer was proud of this achievement, which he described in his essay entitled 'The Government of Subject Races'.[76] Cromer dismissed any idea of introducing 'free institutions in the full sense of the term' in India or Egypt 'for generations to come'. Cromer assured readers that colonial officials sent out from Britain could be relied on to take all key decisions because 'the habit of assuming responsibility, coupled with national predispositions, acting in the same direction, generates a capacity for the beneficial exercise of power'.[77] In other words, what we say goes because we are used to being in charge and we are always right. In Cromer's world, the power of government rested with the all-mighty chief on the spot. A reliable and efficient corps of officials should implement his commands to the letter. The colonial subjects should obey without question.[78]

That autocratic spirit certainly flourished in India. Some evidence comes from the writings of Bennet Christian Huntingdon Calcraft-Kennedy (1871–1935), a British High Court judge based in Bombay for over thirty years. In 1924 he published a book entitled *The Lost Dominion* under the pseudonym of Al Carthill. Arendt mentions this work only briefly. On investigation, it turns out to be a disturbing read.[79] Calcraft-Kennedy summarized the British style of colonial administration as 'bureaucracy and despotism'.[80] He wanted it to be even more despotic. Like Salisbury, Calcraft-Kennedy thought good government was hindered by misplaced liberalism. This had acquired 'an extreme left wing tinged with sympathy for the subversives'.[81] Perhaps Calcraft-Kennedy was thinking of people like George Orwell, who encountered reactionary views of the kind retailed by the judge in Burma where Orwell served as a colonial policeman. Orwell's novel *Burmese Days*[82] makes it crystal clear he found this approach totally repulsive. Perhaps Orwell read *The Lost*

Dominion. It was certainly on sale in 1924 at his favourite bookshop in Rangoon when he was posted to nearby Syriam (now Thanlyin).[83]

Calcraft-Kennedy proposed an administrative style that would, in his view, appeal to 'the real genuine inarticulate public opinion of the masses.' They would respond well, he thought, to a government that declared: 'If you agitate, you will be punished; if you preach sedition, you will be imprisoned; if you assassinate, you will be hanged; if you rise, you will be shot down'.[84] If necessary, the colonial masters could resort to a specific measure he described as the '"administrative massacre"'.[85] By this he meant the deliberate and systematic slaughter of any group of people posing an obstacle to effective government; for example, those who broke official curfews, either deliberately or accidentally.

Calcraft-Kennedy was making this argument just five years after the Amritsar massacre occurred in the Punjab. In 1919 General Reginald Dyer ordered his troops to fire upon a gathering of Punjabi families holding a public meeting in defiance of a curfew he had imposed. His attack left 379 people dead and over 1,200 wounded. This action generated immense bitterness and anger throughout India.[86] Dyer's military superiors reprimanded him but he had some support in the British press. According to Calcraft-Kennedy, liberal policies were to blame for massacres of this kind. It is, he asserts, 'the policy of the humanitarian … that … makes them necessary'.[87] However, once they took place the results were impressive: 'All disorder disappears as if by magic.' What remains? '(N)othing but corpses and ruined buildings, and smiling faces and salaaming multitudes'.[88] These words leave a very sour taste.

Orwell and Calcraft-Kennedy were on opposed wings of the imperialist enterprise that gave them both employment. Autocratic imperialism was opposed by a humanitarian and egalitarian movement that was gathering strength within the increasingly democratic British parliamentary system. All this is well known. But Arendt's argument still carries weight. Conquests carried out in Queen Victoria's name were brutal operations organized for prestige and profit. Harsh repressive techniques were indeed used on those who dared to rebel against the British Empire. However, when Adolf Hitler published *Mein Kampf* just a year after *The Lost Dominion* appeared, this work made Calcraft-Kennedy, the self-styled would-be despot, seem like a fumbling amateur.[89]

Hitler's text gave due warning that the future Führer intended to take personal control of a dictatorial Nazi state. His object was to destroy his enemies, eliminate his chosen victims, and create a new world order under Aryan rule. Undesirable elements in the population would be surgically eliminated. As a result of this approach, Jean Améry and millions of others became victims in the 1930s and 1940s.

Notes

1 Wilde is not recorded as ever visiting Burma, although Mrs Chan-Toon, an adventurous Irishwoman with an inventive imagination, suggested he did. See Mackie 2011. For reflections on Wilde, colonialism and opium, see Marez 1997.

2 Alford 1995; Yeats 1922, 53–8, 171–2.
3 Sherard 1906, 104–8; *Times Law Court Reports*, 8 Jan 1892, 5 and 16 Jan 1892, 4; Cohen 2012; Buckland 1906, 111; *Register of Admissions to Middle Temple, London, 1850–85,* 631 at http://www.middletemple.org.uk/library-archive/archive-information-contacts/digitised-records/registers-admissions (accessed 10th January 2018); https://www.geni.com/people/Colonel-Thomas-Arthur-Harkness-Davies/6000000038910661347 (accessed 10 Aug 2016); Barnes 2005.
4 Edmonds 2014; Ellmann 1984; Ellmann 1988; Fryer 2014; Holland 1997; Holland 2004; Kaylor 2006; Kiberd 1996; Kilroy 1970; Knox 1994; McKenna 2004; Melville 1999; Pearce 2000; Powell and Raby 2013; Robertson 1981,129–38; Ross 2014; Sherard 1906; Smith 2013; Smith and Helfand 1989; Toughill 2009; and Varty 1998. See also the following books on Wilde which unfortunately appeared too late to be taken properly into account here: Frankel 2017; Lee 2017; O'Sullivan 2017.
5 Wilde 2011.
6 Wilde 1891b.
7 December 28 1895, *Acton and Chiswick Gazette*; Stepniak 1883.
8 Douglas 1914 63–6; Longford 1979, 289–93; Kaylor 2006, 98.
9 Holland 2004.
10 Bartlett 2010; Connolly 2011; Foster 1990; Hoppen 2016; Lee 2010.
11 Coogan 2013; Bew 2012; Foster 2010; Davitt 2015; Marley 2007.
12 Marjoribanks and Colvin 1932–36; Belford 1996.
13 Coakley 1994, 49–75, 106–17.
14 Ellmann 1988, chap 1; De Vere White 1967; Melville 1999; http://www.oscholars.com/TO/Appendix/A_Brother_of_Any_Sort.htm (accessed 11 Aug 2016).
15 Eagleton 1999.
16 Ellmann 1984; Wilde 1887.
17 *Proceedings of the International Meridian Conference 1884.*
18 Pearson 1893.
19 Darwin 2009.
20 Allen 2008; Kipling 1937.
21 Whelehan 2012.
22 Ellmann 1988, 36–96.
23 Waller 2008, 510–22; Beerbohm 1923.
24 Wilde 1994, 375.
25 Friedman 2014; Hofer and Scharnhorst 2013; Morris 2013.
26 Wilde 1994, 375.
27 Wilde 1994, 561–673.
28 See Emma Goldmann's biographical note on Johann Most, originally published in *American Mercury*, VIII, June 1926, reproduced by the anarchist history blog at https://anarchisthistory.noblogs.org/files/2015/01/johann-most-imposed.pdf (accessed 31st August 2017).
29 Robert Cecil (Lord Salisbury), 'Disintegration' in *Quarterly Review* 156, October 1883, 559–95, 563; Roberts 1999, 39.
30 O'Brien 1979; Nimocks 1968; Rotberg 1988; Packenham 1992; Darwin 2013, 217–54.
31 Holland and Hart-Davis 2000, 64, 83, 227; Cecil and Cecil 2005.
32 Melville 1999.
33 Schreiner 1989.
34 Moyle 2012; Stanley 2016; Schreiner and Cronwright-Schreiner 1896.
35 McKenna 2004, 20–21.
36 Huysmans 2014.
37 Huysmans 2014, 28–32.
38 McKenna 2004.
39 Melville 1999, 178.

40 Wilde 1994, 332.
41 Henry 1920.
42 Davitt 1890.
43 *Spectator*, 21 May 1887, 2; www.archive.org/eightyclub00eighiala (accessed 10 Aug 2016); Various 2015; Wright 2014; Wright and Kinsella 2015.
44 Wilde 1889.
45 Seeley 1883; Bell 2011; Janis 2015; Wright 2014; Wright and Kinsella 2015.
46 Wilde 1994, 168–317; Aransáez 2014, e.g. 168–219; Tattersall 1998; Killen 2007; Zipes 2006.
47 Woolf 2010; Carroll 2003; Carroll 1887.
48 Carroll 2003, 174.
49 Carroll 2003, 296.
50 Wilde develops these arguments in his collected essays published as *Intentions* (Wilde 1891a). The essays included 'Pen, Pencil and Poison', 'The Critic as Artist', 'The Decay of Lying' and 'The Truth of Masks.' Aransáez 2014.
51 Ellmann 1988, 258.
52 Wilde 2011.
53 Wilde 1894.
54 *Punch*, 7th September 1892; http://punch.photoshelter.com/image/I0000lic65 0N7qDg (accessed 12 Aug 2016). Tydeman and Price 1996.
55 Arnold 2009.
56 Arnold 1867; Wilde 1891b.
57 Eltis 1996; McCormack 1998; Coakley 1994; Kiberd 1996.
58 Holland 2004; Edmonds 2014.
59 Melville 1999, 270.
60 Wilde 2013.
61 McKenna 2004, 472–5, 507–9.
62 Wilde 2013, 89.
63 Wilde 2013, 53, 148; italics in original.
64 Wilde 2013, 65; italics in original.
65 This name, Sebastian Melmoth, was taken from a gothic horror story written by his great uncle Charles Maturin (1782–1824). That story begins with the burning of a portrait and ends with the gruesome death of the portrait's subject, the man who gave the book its title: *Melmoth the Wanderer*. Despite the pressure he was under, Wilde still became involved in issues such as the Dreyfus affair. See Maguire 2013.
66 Beckson 1970, 241, 397.
67 Monsman 2006; Haggard 2002.
68 Kipling 2009.
69 Byrne 2008; Hastings 2009.
70 Kuchta 2010.
71 Kraus 2015; originally published in 1922.
72 Strobl 2000, 83.
73 Strobl 2000, 41–4, 62–7, 77–8, 168–9, 176–80, 212.
74 Arendt 1973.
75 Arendt 1973, 185–222.
76 Baring 1908, 1913.
77 Baring 1913, 31.
78 Milner 1891; Owen 2004; Reid 2004.
79 Arendt 1973, xvii, 128, 143, 178, 186, 216.
80 Carthill 1924a, 70.
81 Carthill 1924a, 239; See also Carthill 1924b; Patterson 2009; Wilson 2017.
82 Orwell 1989.
83 Smart and Mookerdum, 58 Barr Street, Rangoon. See Orwell 1989, 66 for evidence of his enthusiasm for this Rangoon bookshop. For a photograph of

Carthill's *The Lost Dominion* with a Smart and Mookerdum label on the title page see http://wormwoodiana.blogspot.co.uk/2015/11/smart-mookerdum-booksellers-rangoon.html (accessed 12 August 2016).
84 Carthill 1924a, 236–7.
85 Carthill 1924a, 93.
86 Narain 2013; Lloyd 2011.
87 Carthill 1924a, 99.
88 Carthill 1924a, 100.
89 Hitler 1992; originally published in 1925.

Bibliography

Alford, N. (1995). *The Rhymers' Club. Poets of the Tragic Generation*. London: Palgrave Macmillan.
Allen, C. (2008). *Kipling Sahib. India and the Making of Rudyard Kipling*. London: Abacus.
Aransáez, C. P. (2014). *The Role of the Reader in Oscar Wilde's Works*. Norderstedt, Germany: GRIN.
Arendt, H. (1973). *The Origins of Totalitarianism*. San Diego, CA: Harcourt Brace & Company; originally published in 1951.
Arnold, M. (1867). *On the Study of Celtic literature*. London: Smith, Elder and Co.
Arnold, M. (2009). *Culture and Anarchy*. Oxford: Oxford University Press; originally published in 1869.
Baring, E. (Lord Cromer). (1908). 'The Government of Subject Races'. *The Edinburgh Review*, January 1908, reprinted in Baring 1913.
Baring, E. (Lord Cromer). (1913). *Political and Literary Essays, 1908–1913*. London: Macmillan.
Baring, E. (Lord Cromer). (1913). 'The Government of Subject Races' in *Political and Literary Essays, 1908–1913*. London: Macmillan; originally published in 1908.
Barnes, J. (2005). 'Gentleman Crusader: Henry Hyde Champion in the Early Socialist Movement', *History Workshop Journal*, 60, 1, 116–138.
Bartlett, T. (2010). *Ireland. A History*. Cambridge: Cambridge University Press.
Beckson, K. (Ed.). (1970). *Oscar Wilde. The Critical Heritage*. London: Routledge.
Beerbohm, M. (1923). *A Peep into the Past*. Privately printed, 1923.
Belford, B. (1996). *Bram Stoker: A Biography of the Author of Dracula*. London: Weidenfeld and Nicolson.
Bell, D. (2011). *The Idea of Greater Britain*. Princeton, NJ: Princeton University Press.
Bew, P. (2012). *Enigma. A New Life of Charles Stewart Parnell*. Dublin: Gill & Macmillan.
Buckland, C. E. (1906). *Dictionary of Indian Biography*. London: Swan Sonnenschein.
Byrne, S. (2008). *The Unbearable Saki*. Oxford: OUP.
Carthill, Al. (1924a). *The Lost Dominion*. Edinburgh and London: William Blackwood and Sons.
Carthill, Al. (1924b). *The Legacy of Liberalism*. London: Philip Allan & Co.
Carroll, L. (1887). 'Alice on the Stage', *The Theatre*, 9, 52, 179–184; reprinted in Carroll 2003, 293–298.
Carroll, L. (2003). *Alice's Adventures in Wonderland and Through the Looking Glass*. London: Penguin; originally published 1865–1871.

Cecil, H. and Cecil, M. (2005). *Imperial Marriage: An Edwardian War and Peace*. Stroud, UK: The History Press.

Coakley, D. (1994). *Oscar Wilde. The Importance of Being Irish*. Market Harborough, UK: Tower House.

Cohen, P.K. (2012). *John Evelyn Barlas, A Critical Biography: Poetry, Anarchism and Mental Illness in Late-Victorian Britain*. High Wycombe: Rivendale Press.

Coogan, T.P. (2013). *The Famine Plot: England's Role in Ireland's Greatest Tragedy*. London: Palgrave Macmillan.

Connolly, S.J. (2011). *The Oxford Companion to Irish History*. Oxford: Oxford University Press.

Darwin, J. (2009). *The Empire Project. The Rise and Fall of the British World System 1830–1970*. Cambridge: Cambridge University Press.

Darwin, J. (2013). *Unfinished Empire. The Global Expansion of Britain*. London: Penguin.

Davitt, M. (1890). 'The Report of the Parnell Commission', *Nineteenth Century*, March, 357–383.

Davitt, M. (2015). *The Fall of Feudalism in Ireland: Or the Story of the Land League Revolution* (Classic Reprint). Charleston, SC: Forgotten Books; originally published 1904.

De Vere White, T. (1967). *The Parents of Oscar Wilde. Sir William and Lady Wilde*. London: Hodder and Stoughton.

Douglas, A.B. (1914) *Oscar Wilde and Myself*. New York: Duffield and Company.

Eagleton, T. (1999). *Scholars and Rebels in Nineteenth-Century Ireland*. Oxford: Blackwell.

Edmonds, A. (2014). *Oscar Wilde's Scandalous Summer*. Stroud: Amberley.

Ellmann, R. (1984). 'Oscar at Oxford', *New York Review of Books*, 29 March.

Ellmann, R. (1988). *Oscar Wilde*. London: Penguin.

Eltis, S. (1996). *Revising Wilde: Society and Subversion in the Plays of Oscar Wilde*. Oxford: Clarendon Press.

Foster, R. (1990). *Modern Ireland 1600–1972*. London: Penguin.

Foster, R.F. (2010). *Charles Stewart Parnell. The Man and His Family*. London: Faber and Faber.

Frankel, N. (2017). *Oscar Wilde. The Unrepentant Years*. Cambridge, MA: Harvard University Press.

Friedman, D.M. (2014). *Wilde in America. Oscar Wilde and the Invention of Modern Celebrity*. New York: W.W.Norton.

Fryer, J. (2014). *Wilde*. London: Thistle Publishing.

Haggard, H.R. (2002). *King Solomon's Mines* edited by Gerald Monsman. Peterborough, Ontario: Broadview Literary Texts.

Hastings, S. (2009). *The Secret Lives of Somerset Maugham*. London: John Murray.

Henry, R.M. (1920). *The Evolution of Sinn Fein*. New York, NY: B.W.Huebsch.

Hitler, A. (1992). *Mein Kampf*. London: Pimlico; originally published in German in 1925.

Hofer, M. and Scharnhorst, G. (2013). *Oscar Wilde in America. The Interviews*. Urban, Chicago and Springfield: University of Illinois Press.

Holland, M. (1997). *The Wilde Album*. London: Fourth Estate.

Holland, M. (2004). *Irish Peacock and Scarlet Marquess. The Real Trial of Oscar Wilde*. London and New York: Fourth Estate.

Holland, M. and Hart-Davis, R. (eds) (2000). *The Complete Letters of Oscar Wilde*. London: Fourth Estate.

Hoppen, K.T. (2016). *Governing Hibernia: British Politicians and Ireland 1800–1921*. Oxford: Oxford University Press.

Huysmans, J.K. (2014). *Against the Grain*. London: CreateSpace Independent Publishing Platform; originally published in French as *A Rebors* in 1884.

Janis, E.M. (2015). *A Greater Ireland. The Land League and Transatlantic Nationalism in Gilded Age America*. Madison, WI: University of Wisconsin Press.

Kaylor, M. (2006). *Secreted Desires. The Major Uranians. Hopkins, Pater and Wilde*. Brno, CZ: Masaryk University Press.

Kiberd, D. (1996). *Inventing Ireland. The Literature of the Modern Nation*. London: Vintage.

Killen, J. (2007). *The Fairy Tales of Oscar Wilde*. London: Routledge.

Kilroy, J. (1970). *James Clarence Mangan*. Cranbury, NJ: Bucknell University Press.

Kipling, R. (1937). *Something of Myself*. London: Macmillan.

Kipling, R. (2009). *Plain Tales from the Hills*. Oxford: Oxford University Press; originally published in 1888.

Knox, M. (1994). *Oscar Wilde. A Long and Lovely Suicide*. New Haven and London: Yale University Press.

Kraus, K. (2015). *The Last Days of Mankind*. New Haven and London: Yale University Press.

Kuchta, T. (2010). *Semi-Detached Empire. Suburbia and the Colonization of Britain, 1880 to the Present*. London: University of Virginia Press.

Lee, J.J. (2010). *Ireland 1912–1985. Politics and Society*. Cambridge: Cambridge University Press.

Lee, L. (2017). *Oscar's Ghost. The Battle for Oscar Wilde's Legacy*. Stroud: Amberley.

Longford, E. (1979). *Pilgrimage of Passion. Life of Wilfred Scawen Blunt*. London: Weidenfeld & Nicolson.

Lloyd, N. (2011). *The Amritsar Massacre: The Untold Story of One Fateful Day*. London: I.B.Tauris.

Mackie, G. (2011). 'Forging Oscar Wilde: Mrs. Chan-Toon and For Love of the King', *English Literature in Transition, 1880–1920*, 267–288.

Marez, C. (1997). 'The Other Addict: Reflections on Colonialism and Oscar Wilde's Opium Smoke Screen', *ELH*, 64, 1, Spring, 257–287.

Maguire, J.R. (2013). *Ceremonies of Bravery. Oscar Wilde, Carlos Blacker, and the Dreyfus Affair*. Oxford: Oxford University Press.

Mckenna, N. (2004). *The Secret Life of Oscar Wilde*. London: Arrow Books.

McCormack, J., Ed. (1998). *Wilde the Irishman*. London: Yale University Press.

Marley, L. (2007), *Michael Davitt: Freelance Radical and Frondeur*. Dublin: Four Courts Press Ltd.

Marjoribanks, E. and Colvin, I. (1932–6). *The Life of Lord Carson*, 3 vols. London: Victor Gollancz.

Melville, J. (1999). *Mother of Oscar. The Life of Jane Francesca Wilde*. London: Allison and Busby.

Milner, A. (1891). *England in Egypt*. London: Edward Arnold.

Monsman, G. (2006). *H. Rider Haggard on the Imperial Frontier: The Political and Literary Contexts of His African Romances*. Greensboro, NC: ELT Press.

Morris Jr., R. (2013). *Declaring His Genius. Oscar Wilde in North America*. Cambridge, Mass: The Belknap Press.

Moyle, F. (2012). *Constance. The Tragic and Scandalous Life of Mrs Oscar Wilde*. London: John Murray.

Narain, S. (2013). *The Jallianwala Bagh Massacre*. New Delhi: Lancer Publishers.
Nimocks, W. (1968). *Milner's Young Men: The "Kindergarten" in Edwardian Imperial Affairs*. London: Hodder and Stoughton.
O'Brien, T.H. (1979). *Milner. Viscount Milner of St James's and Cape Town 1854–1925*. London: Constable.
O'Sullivan, E. (2017). *The Fall of the House of Wilde*. London: Bloomsbury.
Orwell, G. (1989). *Burmese Days*. London: Penguin Books.
Owen, R. (2004). *Lord Cromer: Victorian Imperialist, Edwardian Proconsul*. Oxford: Oxford University Press.
Packenham, T. (1992). *The Scramble for Africa*. London: Abacus.
Patterson, S. (2009). *The Cult of Imperial Honor in British India*. London: Palgrave Macmillan.
Pearce, J. (2000). *The Unmasking of Oscar Wilde*. London: HarperCollins.
Pearson, C.H. (1893). *National Life and Character. A Forecast*. London: Macmillan.
Powell, K. and Raby, P. (eds) (2013). *Oscar Wilde in Context*. Cambridge: Cambridge University Press.
Proceedings of International Meridian Conference, Washington 1884.
Reid, D. (2004). 'Review of Lord Cromer: Victorian Imperialist, Edwardian Proconsul (review no. 414)', *Reviews in History*, July 2004 at http://www.history.ac.uk/reviews/review/414 (accessed 13 August 2016).
Roberts, A. (1999). *Salisbury. Victorian Titan*. London: Weidenfeld & Nicolson.
Robertson, W.G. (1981). *Time Was*. London: Quartet Books.
Ross, I. (2014). *Oscar Wilde and Ancient Greece*. Cambridge: Cambridge University Press.
Rotberg, R.I. (1988). *The Founder: Cecil Rhodes and the Pursuit of Power*. Oxford: Oxford University Press.
Seeley, J.R. (1883). *The Expansion of England*. Cambridge: Cambridge University Press.
Sherard, R. (1906). *The Real Oscar Wilde*. London: T. Werner Laurie.
Schreiner, O. (1989). *The Story of a South African Farm*. London: Virago; originally published 1883.
Schreiner, O. and Cronwright-Schreiner, S.C. (1896). *The Political Situation*. London: T. Fisher Unwin at https://archive.org/details/politicalsituat00crongoog (accessed 19th August 2016).
Smith, D. (2013). 'Forced Social Displacement: the "inside stories" of Oscar Wilde, Jean Améry, Nelson Mandela and Aung San Suu Kyi', in Nicolas Demertsiz (ed.) *Emotions in Politics*. London: Palgrave-Macmillan (2013), 60–83.
Smith, P.E. and Helfand, M.S. (1989). *Oscar Wilde's Oxford Notebooks. A Portrait in the Making*. New York and Oxford: Oxford University Press.
Stanley, L. (2016). *Imperialism, Labour and the New Woman: Olive Schreiner's Social Theory*. London: Routledge.
Stepniak, S. (1883). *Underground Russia. Revolutionary Profiles and Sketches from Life*. London: John W. Lovell.
Strobl, G. (2000). *The Germanic Isle: Nazi Perceptions of Britain*. Cambridge: Cambridge University Press.
Tattersall, C.A. (1998). 'Oscar Fingal O'Flahertie, the Wilde Colonial Boy: Social and Political Subversion in Oscar Wilde's Fairy Tales' Ph.D. thesis, University of Toronto.
Toughill, T. (2009). *The Ripper Code*. Stroud: The History Press.

Tydeman, W. and Price, S. (1996). *Wilde: Salome (Plays in Production)*. Cambridge: Cambridge University Press.
Various. (2015). *The "Eighty" Club, 1895*. Paris: Leopold Classic Library/Babelio; originally published in 1895.
Varty, A. (1998). *A Preface to Oscar Wilde*. London and New York: Longman.
Waller, P. (2008). *Writers, Readers, and Reputations: Literary Life in Britain 1870–1918*. Oxford: Oxford University Press.
Whelehan, N. (2012). *The Dynamiters: Irish Nationalism and Political Violence in the Wider World, 1867–1900*. Cambridge: Cambridge University Press.
Wilde, O. (1887). 'Mr Mahaffey's New Book', *Pall Mall Gazette*, 9 Nov. 1887.
Wilde, O. (1889). 'Mr Froude's Blue Book', *Pall Mall Gazette*, 13 April 1889.
Wilde, O. (1891a). *Intentions*. London: Methuen.
Wilde, O. (1891b). 'The Soul of Man under Socialism', *Fortnightly Review*, 49, Feb 1891, 292–319.
Wilde, O. (1894). *Salome*, London: Elkin, Mathews & John Lane.
Wilde, O. (1994). *The Complete Plays, Poems, Novels and Stories of Oscar Wilde*. London: Parragon.
Wilde, O. (2011). *The Picture of Dorian Gray. An Annotated, Uncensored Edition*, edited by Nicholas Frankel. Cambridge, MA and London: The Belknap Press; originally published in 1891.
Wilde, O. (2013). *De Profundis and Other Prison Writings*. London: Penguin.
Wilson, J. (2017). *India Conquered. India's Raj and the Chaos of Empire*. London: Simon & Schuster.
Woolf, J. (2010). *The Mystery of Lewis Carroll*. New York: St. Martin's Press.
Wright, T. (2008). *Oscar's Books*. London: Chatto and Windus.
Wright, T. (2014). 'Party political animal. Oscar Wilde, Gladstonian Liberal and Eighty Club member', *Times Literary Supplement*, 4 June 2014.
Wright, T. and Kinsella, P. (2015). 'Oscar Wilde, A Parnellite Home Ruler and Gladstonian Liberal: Wilde's Career at the Eighty Club (1887–1895)', *The Oscholars*. https://oscholars.files.wordpress.com/2013/02/wright-kinsella-on-wilde-2.docx (accessed 10 August 2016).
Yeats, W.B. (1922). *The Trembling of the Veil*. London: T. Werner Laurie.
Zipes, J. (2006). *Fairy Tales and the Art of Subversion: The Classical Genre for Children and the Process of Civilization*. New York: Routledge.

3 Jean Améry

Colossi in conflict

Jean Améry (1912–78), born in Karl Kraus's Vienna, grew up during and after the First World War. Améry, with his dome-like forehead and deep eyes, differed from Wilde, Mandela and Aung San Suu in one key respect.[1] He was not born into his society's intellectual aristocracy, royal establishment or political elite. He was a provincial tavern keeper's son.[2] By the early 1920s he was living in Bad Ischl, a picturesque spa resort in provincial Austria.

Later, Améry was a victim of the Nazis' concentration camps and rebelled against that fact. Not just the desperation of living in inhuman conditions under a perpetual death sentence but also the life sentence that followed. This brought repeated migraines, frequent panic attacks and continuing mental trauma along with the discomfort of being forever marked out as a surviving victim.[3] Améry knew he was very lucky to live through the experience but he wanted to keep control over his victimhood, not be controlled by it. He did not want his whole life and entire reputation to be reduced to his agony in the Nazi concentration camps during the early 1940s. He had other plans. He wanted to be a great novelist.

Jean Améry's birth name was Hans Mayer, which he kept from 1912 until 1955, the year of his second marriage. Then he adopted as his first name Jean, the French equivalent of Hans, and as his surname Améry, an anagram of Mayer. In this way he rejected Germany and Austria, and paid a tribute to French existentialism, the philosophical path he wished to tread. By that time Améry was living in Belgium. Nearly a quarter of a century later, aged sixty-six, he packed his suitcase, travelled to Salzburg in Austria, booked into a hotel, and committed suicide, leaving notes for his wife and the hotel manager. On his gravestone are engraved, as he instructed, his adopted name, his dates and his Auschwitz number. Améry's other plans had not worked out. He had not been acknowledged as a great novelist. But he retained control over when and how his life ended. He went out of his way to make sure his voluntary death, as he called it, was seen as a rational and deliberate act with philosophical, moral and political significance. He was choosing to make his point, and his exit, in his own way.

It was not his first decisive exit. In 1938 Améry, an active anti-Nazi, an intellectual and a Jew, chose to leave Austria rather than be persecuted there. Améry spent the rest of his life, apart from two years as the Nazis' unwilling guest, wandering across Europe's frontiers, observing, analysing and weaving his way amongst the various military, political and business forces competing to dominate the continent. Améry studied this process and concluded that the United States was a big winner and the British Empire a big loser.[4] Not in itself a controversial conclusion but Améry's key contribution is a discerning narrative report from the ground level of his personal experience of living in the midst of this intensely fought struggle between competing power-wielders. He shows us the wounds inflicted on German, French and British citizens caught up in this prolonged struggle. Above all, he shows us the wounds inflicted on himself.

Following Améry we are taken in two complementary directions. We go with him beyond Britain's national and imperial frontiers. Améry provides an external observation point from which we may watch, through his eyes, the British and others trying to adjust to the West's reshaping and the British Empire's decline. But Améry does more than that. He helps us reach inwards, encountering our feelings. Améry enables us to understand the dynamic workings of anxiety and resentment within individuals and groups who lose out in such confrontations. At the same time, he starkly depicts the ruthless urge towards domination that drives many of those who humiliate them.

We need some context. Let us return to the 1930s when Améry's European odyssey began. The British were still masters of the Indian Raj and behaved like top dogs. Internationally, they had two powerful rivals, the United States and Nazi Germany, with Japan looming in the East. The American state and Germany's rulers both foresaw an enlarged future role for themselves on the world stage. But for the moment they were waiting and watching. Hitler admired two great virtues, as he saw it, of the British Empire's rulers: their hypocrisy and their ruthlessness. In September 1938 Neville Chamberlain hoped to settle a few local difficulties with Adolf Hitler by flying over to Munich and discussing matters face to face. Hitler responded by talking Neville Chamberlain into accepting Germany's annexation of the Sudetenland within Czechoslovakia. Ironically, nearly half a century before, Joseph Chamberlain, Neville's father, had served as British colonial secretary (1895–1903). In those days the British backed up reasoned arguments with overwhelming force. They were able to obstruct Germany's territorial ambitions in southern Africa. But times had changed.

Compare Ireland and Austria, homelands of Wilde and Améry, during the late 1930s. Ireland, England's western neighbour, won its freedom in 1922. After fifteen years of home rule, the Irish government enacted a new republican constitution asserting the Irish people's 'inalienable, indefeasible, and sovereign right' to self-determination. According to the 1937 Constitution, the Irish state was 'sovereign, independent, [and] democratic'.[5] In 1938 Austria, another small Catholic country in Europe, also decided to rewrite its constitution. Like Ireland, Austria had a powerful neighbour with big ideas: Nazi Germany. The First World War shattered the Austro-Hungarian empire. The new sovereign state of Austria was about twice the size of Ireland. As Hitler began his campaign of expansion during the mid-1930s many Austrians wanted to belong to his victorious columns. After all, Hitler was Austrian-born. They wanted their compatriot to be their *führer*.

In 1938 the Austrian government, encouraged by Berlin, discarded its sovereign independence and submerged itself within the Third Reich. Austrians waving Nazi flags welcomed the German *Wehrmacht* with cheers as its soldiers crossed the border. From that point Hitler ruled Austria.[6] The Nazis intended, if they could, to refashion Europe on racial lines according to their own blueprint. When the Nazis came to power they murdered on a massive scale, disposing of whole population groups they defined as defective or poisonous. Jews were prominent on their list. Karl Kraus, who died in 1936, would have regarded *Anschluss* (annexation) as a tragedy. For Jean Améry it was, above all, an emergency.

Austrian beginnings

But we should start at the beginning. Jean Améry enjoyed his youthful freedom at Bad Ischl in Austria's Salzkammergut region. From the top of nearby Mount Katrin he could see seven sparkling lakes. Salzburg, home of the Mozart festival, was close by. Bad Ischl had been fashionable before the First World War, with strong imperial connections. Franz Joseph, the last Hapsburg emperor, used to make annual visits to his Kaiservilla in the spa town. During the 1920s remnants of Bad Ischl's old classy atmosphere lived on but the emperor had abdicated and Tom Mix cowboy films were playing in the local cinema.

Améry was a child of the mountains and of the German romantic tradition. He did not like school but loved the written word, imaginative, theoretical or preferably both. By the time he was eight he had made his way through the works of Friedrich Schiller, poet, playwright and philosopher, author of the ode 'To Joy'. Schiller, friend of Goethe, wanted to have a beautiful soul: to enjoy aesthetic delight while also recognizing his moral duty. Perhaps Améry mingled such reflections with memories of his father who died at the Italian front during the First World War in 1916 when his son was only four. The father's demise was not heroic: a strangulated hernia. But he lost his life as an Austrian patriot in military uniform.[7]

Améry's home in Bad Ischl was a guesthouse, the *Gasthaus zur Stadt Prag*, run by his mother and her sister, both widows. These lodgings were nicely situated by the confluence of two rivers, the Traun and the Ischl, near the lower slopes of the renowned Kalvarienberg (Mount Calvary). During the summer months the town was at the service of richer folk visiting from Vienna and beyond. But when winter arrived everyone relaxed and let their hair down. Améry recalls that in his early youth he sported white knee socks and *lederhosen* like the others. His mother wore the *dirndl*, traditional Alpine clothing common throughout the town. Améry recalled dionysian evenings when 'Everybody talked, trampled, spat as they liked' and danced while the accordion played. Améry was part of 'the happy crowd' singing as couples 'skipped and stomped'. Later in the early morning hours there was the occasional jingling of a 'horse-drawn sled' passing by outside. Inside 'things could get rough' as aggressive feelings kept under control during the day were released, making 'the floors tremble'.[8]

Did those late night arguments sometimes have an anti-Semitic edge? After all, Jewishness was a long-standing issue in the Austrian countryside. Jews were not welcome in some spa centres including Kitzbühel, Schladming, and almost the entire Wachau region. Nearby was Berchtesgaden, already becoming a favoured retreat for the Nazi senior leadership. But Bad Ischl and some other spa towns including Bad Aussee and Bad Gastein were different. They traditionally did not discriminate.[9] Bad Ischl was a rural haven with its relatively civilized and tolerant ambience.

In fact, Améry's mother and father had both moved away from Judaism. Améry's father, Paul, was non-observant, secular and assimilated. His birthplace, Hohenems, near Austria's Swiss border, was a mixed community where Catholics and Jews intermingled in relative amity. Améry's mother, born Valerie Golschmidt, came from a 'good' Viennese family schooled in bourgeois ways. She retained some Yiddish phrases but was resolutely Catholic and ensured that her son received a Christian upbringing. At school Améry shone in religion and loved going to church. Like Wilde, he enjoyed the atmospherics and drama.

Améry's mother moved from Vienna to Bad Ischl for several reasons: she needed a steady income after her husband's death; anti-Semitism had increased in Viennese since Mayor Karl Lueger made hatred of Jews a central plank of his administration (1897–1910); and her son was diagnosed as needing treatment for his lungs.[10] Her sister's husband ran a sanitorium a few kilometres south of Bad Ischl. So Améry's mother acquired a guesthouse in that spa town.

In Bad Ischl and throughout his life Améry pursued three interests with enthusiasm. One was women, a lifelong passion. He needed them for excitement and comfort.[11] Another interest was literature, a kingdom in which Améry wished to be granted high nobility in recognition of his achievements. Did Améry's veneration of literature reflect the interests of his dead father or, perhaps, his grandfather who was still very much alive? Both men surely came under the influence of the inspirational Moritz Federmann (1840–1916), master at the renowned Jewish school at Hohenems. At this school, educational standards were high and the spirit liberal. Jews and non-Jews worked alongside each other amongst both pupils and staff. Améry, too, belonged to that tradition of cooperation and inclusivity amongst scholars and citizens.[12]

The third of Améry's major interests was wandering. His strongest early memories evoke the alpine tracks around provincial Ischl. His walks were a way of hiding. Améry felt excluded by poverty from the bright lights of sophisticated Vienna. Burying himself in the forest gave Améry protection from his provincial embarrassment. He would escape to his secret cave high in the mountains or wander along forest footpaths listening to the echoing sound of farmers at work in their fields.[13] Améry's grandfather recommended stricter discipline. Améry decided to move on. In 1926, aged fourteen, he quit school without obtaining his *baccalaureate* and went to Vienna. His mother came too but the change of venue meant she had less chance of controlling or guiding her son. She was no Speranza. There is surely no doubt that Frau Mayer spent the next decade worrying about her son. She died in 1939, aged sixty.

Vienna, the city of Sigmund Freud and Arnold Schoenberg, was exciting and dangerous, a magnet for people left vulnerable by the Austro-Hungarian empire's collapse. For half a millennium the empire had been a congenial political shelter for many groups, including Jews.[14] Vienna's most influential cultural figure at that time was Karl Kraus. His newspaper *Die Fackel* (*The Torch*) had been attacking hypocrisy since 1899 and his regular one-man shows drew large audiences. Kraus responded with great enthusiasm to Wilde's message that artists should assert their freedom to wear whatever mask they wished, and explore alternatives to those aspects of the present they found morally and aesthetically unacceptable.

In the pages of *Die Fackel* Kraus published extracts from 'The Soul of Man under Socialism',[15] *The Picture of Dorian Gray*[16] and 'The Decay of Lying.'[17] He praised *Salome*[18] as an unparalleled masterpiece, and described Wilde as 'a genius murdered by the spirit of the philistines'.[19] Wilde wanted to undermine imperialism and release the oxygen of freedom. However, by the 1920s Kraus had a more pessimistic view of the future than Wilde a generation earlier. He thought the collapse of empires brought more conflict. Young Améry, by contrast, was optimistic about prospects for peaceful reconciliation within Austria and beyond.[20]

While political battles raged, Améry advanced his literary and philosophical education at college. He found work where he could, sometimes playing a bar piano. He became a bookshop assistant, which helped him towards other openings such as teaching at the Vienna Adult Education Centre (*Volkshochschule Wien*). Soon he was having conversations with writers like Robert Musil, Elias Canetti and Hermann Broch. Améry made himself familiar with members of the Vienna Circle led by Moritz Schlick. From Rudolf Carnap he learned that rational human beings with a disciplined critical capacity should be able to get along well with each other. Life could be sorted out with the right approach.[21]

That spirit inspired a new literary journal named *Die Brücke* (*The Bridge*). Améry inaugurated and co-edited this journal in 1934 with his lifelong friend, Ernst Mayer. The journal's title summed up their mission: to construct new social links and cultural bonds between potentially antagonistic groups. The city could learn from the countryside, the rich from the poor, and *vice versa*, and so on. This youthful optimism was surely inspired, in part, by the thrill of moving from the countryside to a culturally diverse metropolitan city. A similar surge of enthusiasm was experienced by Nelson Mandela when, a decade later, he moved from the countryside into the multiracial circles of radical intellectuals and activists in Johannesburg. Like Améry in the early 1930s, Mandela in the early 1940s drank deep of a lively urban scene. But in both inter-war Vienna and post-war Johannesburg this freedom was soon struck down by rigid race laws and police oppression.

In Vienna disagreements were pursued through rational debate in civilized salons, and also through angry clashes on hard cobbled streets. Améry learned the difference between these approaches the hard way. In February 1934 the first issue of his new peace-promoting journal appeared. Ironically, its calls for reconciliation and mutual understanding coincided with a three-day violent uprising in Vienna by the Republican Defence Corps against Engelbert Dollfuss's fascist regime. Améry was soon transporting socialist rifles across Vienna. But rifles were no match for the regime's heavy artillery on the surrounding hills. Dollfuss survived and continued to rule until July when he was assassinated during an attempted Nazi coup. The following year, the Nuremberg laws in Germany restricted the rights and freedoms of Jews. This made it very clear the future held serious threats for people like Améry. These anxieties found their way into *The Shipwrecked* (*Die Schiffbrüchigen*), a novel Améry was writing in 1935.[22]

The central character of *The Shipwrecked* is a young Jewish intellectual whose Austrian world is disintegrating, leaving him consumed by disorienting despair. His girlfriend leaves him for a rich admirer. Struggling against failure and passivity, he decides to force something meaningful and decisive to happen. He picks a quarrel with an Aryan stranger who kills him in the resulting duel.[23] But in fact Améry's love life flourished. Against his mother's wishes, he married a Jewish woman, Regine (or Gina) Berger, in December 1937. Three months later Hitler annexed Austria and made it part of the Third Reich. An old school chum in a new Nazi uniform came to see Améry at home. He worked in the Office of Genealogy and brought some advice. To save himself Améry had to divorce his Jewish wife and get his mother to swear he was illegitimate, the bastard son of a true Aryan. Instead, Améry and Gina prepared to escape.

Like his father at the front in the First World War, Améry knew hostile forces had him in their sights. But there was one big difference. This time the threat was coming from other Austrians inspired by the Austrian-born Adolf Hitler. Améry made a shocking discovery, rather like the one African-American writer James Baldwin later made in his youth. Like many other American kids, Baldwin enjoyed watching films about cowboys and Indians; but he finally realized he was one of the Indians destined to be slaughtered.[24] Likewise, Améry saw that his enemy, the Nazis, were in uniform in his own country and he was on the target list. The battle had begun. His task was to get himself enrolled in the anti-Nazi army, wherever that might be.

Fateful trains

Late in December 1938 Améry and Gina travelled to Cologne by rail.[25] They went to see a young man on *Brüsseler Strasse*. He arranged for them to go on a carefully chosen sequence of trains running over New Year that took them into Belgium. Soon they were in Antwerp and found lodgings in the port district. Améry quickly came to terms with the Flemish language and found his way around this new stamping ground.

He met friends, gave classes, visited the library, and enjoyed cheap and delicious horsemeat served by the Salvation Army. Sometimes he called in at the *Gounod* tavern to discuss politics, war, and more amorous topics with the delightful and friendly Denise. This relatively pleasant existence lasted for over a year. In September 1939 war broke out in Europe. Améry was desperate to get into military uniform to fight the Nazis. But Belgium was neutral at that time. He was stymied. Eight months later Germany invaded Belgium. Gina went into hiding, helped by her friend Maria Leitner, a key figure later.

Meanwhile, Améry was deported from Belgium as a German alien and put on a train to southern France. He jumped off the train, got arrested again, and was sent to Gurs, a transit camp in Vichy France near the Pyrenees. The camp had been set up to receive fighters returning from Spain after Franco's victory in the Civil War. Améry planned to escape from the camp, easily the best option since staying meant eventual death at German hands. When spring 1941 arrived it was time to go. His chosen companion, Jacques Sonnenschein, was an Austrian mathematician with a good scientific background.[26] They agreed to sleep during the day and travel by night, following local streams. This would take them to the River Adour, which would lead them to the port of Bayonne in German-occupied France.

It was a dangerous strategy but the only way Améry could rejoin his wife, now in Brussels. On their journey they encountered a thoroughly defeated French population but received help: a good meal, a gift of shoes and enough money to buy tickets for a crowded train. After four months on the road, and a brief spell behind bars in Bayonne, they made it to Brussels where Améry was reunited with his Gina. It was September 1941 and the people of Brussels were quietly respectful of their new German masters. Améry admired the flexibility and initiative of the Belgians who managed to get around food rationing through a highly efficient black market. They accepted the fate of the Jews with equanimity, pragmatically assuming that a group being treated so badly must deserve it in some way. Brussels in 1941 was very different from Antwerp in 1940. Améry was forced to adapt to being a 'non-person' who hid in doorways whenever police vehicles drove by. He spent a lot of time in cheap cinemas watching Nazi propaganda about the worthlessness of Jews and the advances made by German forces against the Soviet Union. Améry was determined to engage in acts of resistance, however small. One day he queued at the counter of a Flemish vegetable seller ostentatiously dealing with his customers in loud German. Améry coolly asked in Flemish for a '*Witte kool'* (white cabbage). The trader angrily indicated he was being handed an impeccably Teutonic '*Weißkohl*'.

Améry repeatedly broke the eight o'clock curfew imposed on all Jews. Sometimes he would walk briskly past one of the larger, slower policemen from the Belgian countryside, boldly looking him straight in the eye. It was a way to feel 'victorious in the midst of defeat', to say 'I am not afraid'.[27] After a while, Améry noticed graffiti about America's entry into the war, and the stalling of the *Wehrmacht*'s advance into Russia. He became bolder. As in Vienna during the 1934 uprising, Améry was keen to be part of the action. He began to work with the Belgian underground resistance.[28]

His task was to drop subversive leaflets around police and army barracks. These would be read, hopefully, by the occupying German forces and their Belgian collaborators. One night in 1943 Améry went out from his lodgings with some highly compromising subversive material under his arm. He did not return until twenty-one months later. Améry was arrested by the police on 23rd July 1943 and taken to the Gestapo headquarters on Avenue Louise. He was interrogated but gave nothing away, no names or addresses. He did not know them. He was then moved to Fort Breendonk, on the northern outskirts of Brussels. The regime was harsh. Executions occurred frequently and all prisoners were required to watch.

Améry was tortured as a suspected resistance worker. His wrists were handcuffed behind his back and then lifted up by a hook, which was attached to a chain hanging from the ceiling. Améry's body swung in mid air and this put an intolerable strain upon his shoulders as he tried to defeat the force of gravity. After a while his muscles gave way: 'there was a crackling and splintering in my shoulders that my body has not forgotten until this hour. The balls sprang from their sockets'.[29] The immense pain made him lose consciousness. While this was happening Améry was subjected to a vigorous assault using a leather horsewhip. The whole thing lasted about half an hour. He was then taken back, semi-conscious and still bound, to his cell.[30]

For the next three months Améry was kept in solitary confinement. He tried without success to commit suicide. On 2nd November Améry, by now identified as a Jew, was consigned to Auschwitz. He arrived there on 17th January 1944. He was in a new intake of 655 prisoners, 417 of whom were killed immediately. Améry was assigned to hard physical labour outdoors carrying cement sacks. After six months the camp authorities discovered he could decipher and write German script. He became a member of the clerical staff at the Buna factory manufacturing synthetic rubber run by I G Farben at Auschwitz.

Améry had to stand for several hours on the parade ground, and survive on 200 grams of bread plus two bowls of soup a day. But, crucially, he was working indoors and known to be useful because of his very high level of functional literacy. He was too fit and valuable to be disposed of quickly, and too resourceful to betray vulnerability. By January 1945, a year after Améry's first arrival, the Soviet army's advance caused the Nazis to evacuate

Auschwitz in a hurry. The surviving inmates were forced to march on foot over sixty kilometres to Gliwice. Then they travelled westwards by rail into Germany in open trucks.

Early in February they got to Dora-Mittelbau, near Nordhausen. Two months later the Nazis moved them even further West, this time to Bergen-Belsen where they arrived in 5th April. On 15th April 1945, the British army liberated Bergen-Belsen, bringing to an end Améry's period of 642 days as a prisoner in German concentration camps. He was thirty-three years old and weighed 45 kilograms (99 lbs). He made his way back to Belgium. When he got back to his apartment his wife was nowhere to be found. It was only four years later that Améry discovered Gina had died of heart failure in 1944, twelve months after his arrest.[31]

A new start

In 1945, Améry was halfway through his life. He spent the second half of his life coping with the effects of the first. He tried to move on from victimhood and establish a dignified and satisfying frame for his social identity and sense of selfhood. Améry did not want to be forever defined by his condition in Auschwitz, which had been appalling and unacceptable. However, he could not return to Austria. The pre-war atmosphere no longer existed and he could not settle permanently in the country that had so eagerly united with Nazi Germany. The most attractive option was to enter *Kultur*'s hall of fame. That was where he really wanted to be but it was difficult to arrange.

Améry faced several immediate problems: how to cope with the loss of Gina; how to earn his living; how to get proper official papers; and how to find a guiding belief. By 1948, Améry was in regular touch with Maria Leitner, Gina's friend, by then estranged from her husband. In 1955 Maria, a non-Jew originally from Vienna, became Améry's second wife. This was definitely a lucky break. Maria admired Améry's intellect and looked after him with care for the rest of his days. To earn money Améry took to journalism. His reporter's beat covered Switzerland and Belgium, especially Zurich and Brussels.[32]

Maria was the main organizer of his complex working life as a freelance feature writer. She did a lot of the background research for her husband's newspaper articles. In 1955 Hans Mayer became Jean Améry. The most pressing reasons were strictly practical. He had become entrapped in lengthy bureaucratic tangles in Belgium while trying to get his civic identity recognized. His birth name was compromised by an opportunistic but false claim he had made just after the war. He did not, in fact, have a doctorate. He was not, in fact, Dr Hans Mayer.[33]

Becoming Jean Améry was also a symbolic act of refusal and a switch of allegiance. He was rejecting the Germany and Austria that had rejected him. His new name was an expression of comradeship with the French Resistance, warriors against Nazism. Also with the man whose philosophy of existentialism became closely associated with that movement: Jean-Paul Sartre (1905–80).[34]

Existentialism was a philosophy built on the idea that human beings created the present, the future and themselves through their choices and their actions. It brought a Cartesian spirit to bear on the density of Heidegger and other Germanic writers from whom its basic ideas were drawn.

Sartre was not just a philosopher and political commentator but also a novelist, dramatist and poet who communicated effectively with the French people. The thoughts of Sartre ran through café conversations in Paris during the late 1940s just as the sayings of Karl Kraus had reverberated in Viennese cafés a quarter of a century before.

Both commentators were exciting but Sartre was more upbeat and forward-looking. Kraus had condemned the corruption of contemporary Austria, recalling its nobler past. By contrast, Sartre identified himself with the heroism of the French Resistance and pointed optimistically towards the future, along the road towards liberty. Sartre told Améry what he wanted to hear. He keenly wished to belong to the network of exciting authors that included Albert Camus (1913–60), Maurice Merleau-Ponty (1908–61) and Simone de Beauvoir (1908–86). But when Améry met Sartre, briefly, in Brussels in 1946 he found himself tongue-tied. He could only mutter a short conventional greeting. Améry began to accept that he would not find his way into these Parisian networks. He had to make his own way.

In time, Améry came to see that two false illusions had sustained him immediately after the war. For a start, he wrongly believed he was undefeated by the Nazis. In *Love's Crown of Thorns* (*Dornenkrone der Liebe*), a fictional narrative he wrote in 1945, Améry presented Fort Breendonk as a 'battlefield of death' on which he triumphed. In this story, the Gestapo tried to make Améry a helpless victim but he was too clever for them. He invented 'fairy tales' that bamboozled his interrogator, leading to 'an absolute triumph of mind over matter',[35] the reverse of his later judgment on his time at Auschwitz. By the mid 1960s Améry's reollection was that brute horror had turned him into mere suffering flesh beyond any help the mind might offer.

Améry's second post-war illusion was that the Germans would become better people. He had been optimistic in his essay 'On the Psychology of the German People,' written in 1945.[36] At that time he thought the Germans had stopped thinking for themselves or worrying about others' suffering. Instead, they worked dutifully without asking questions. He expected the Germans would soon realize the hatred they had brought upon themselves, transform their ways of thinking and behaving, and rediscover the more humane aspects of German culture. But by the 1960s Améry was forced to conclude that the Germans were not likely to improve. They had known what they were doing during the Third Reich and would do it again.[37]

For his part, Améry wanted to demonstrate he could make a difference through his books. When writing *Love's Crown of Thorns,* Améry told Ernst Mayer that 'If it turns out well, there will be meaning to my life; if it is nothing, I will know that I myself am nothing.' In other words, as Heidelberger-Leonard put it, this new text was 'a test of his right to exist'.[38] The book did not find a publisher but Améry continued to test himself in this way. He was determined to write novels that would portray the human condition and express his own powerful sense of justice.

For years Améry could not get his novels into print. He made his living as a highly readable journalist who knew a great deal about European culture and politics. He published books on jazz, teenage stars, and even Gerhart Hauptmann, a writer he did not like.[39] This was commodity production, dictated by the needs of the market, giving the public what it would buy but Améry showed his determination to get to the heart of his subjects, judge their worth and locate them within a cultural and even moral field. This spirit is clear, for example, in the distinctly commercial project, *Karrieren und Köpfe* (*Careers and Leaders*), which he published in 1955.[40] This book portrays sixty celebrities in science, literature, philosophy, music, art, sculpture, architecture, the stage, film and the cocktail circuit – and in that order, beginning with Albert Einstein and ending with Elsa Maxwell, an American gossip columnist. Améry gives priority to high culture, and the selection reflects his own high standards.

But Améry wanted to be much more than a perceptive impresario. In 1961 he finally spoke openly and directly, with his own voice, in a survey of the post-war West. This was initially published in German as *Geburt der Gegenwart* (*Birth of the Present*). Three years later it came out in English entitled *Preface to the Future. Culture in a Consumer Society*.[41] By this time Améry had trodden the European landscape for over two decades, traversing the continent from North-East Germany to South-West France, and from Vienna to Brussels. During the mid 1950s he spent some months living in London. His experiences and reflections arising from these wanderings were recorded in talks he gave on the radio, a medium Améry relished for its open and experimental character, not hemmed in by big business.[42]

Preface to the Future was a systematic analysis of the new West: not heavily theoretical but empirical, pragmatic and almost conversational in tone. This book surveyed the human and political landscape in the wake of the cataclysmic struggle that had pitted the British Empire against the Third Reich. Both these mighty powers were totally destroyed by the war, although the British Empire took a little longer to die than its enemy. Two other forces eventually settled the war in the West: the obdurate heroism of the Russian people and the wholehearted commitment of the Americans.

In Améry's view, the post-war West was shaped by the Cold War and the expansion of American mass production and mass consumption. Culture became a commodity. Products in film, music, theatre and art were promoted across national boundaries to maximize the audience. Taste became standardized and the distance between high and popular culture reduced, resulting in a general levelling up of production values.

Theodor Adorno (1903–69) and Max Horkheimer (1895–1973) had already explored the relations between capitalism and mass culture in their *Dialectic of Enlightenment* in 1944.[43] They did it from a great theoretical height, lodged in the Marxist stratosphere, and from the vantage point of the United States, where they had arrived in 1937.[44] By contrast, over fifteen years later Améry provided something very different: a distinctively European perspective, one empirically explored at ground level, applying an intellect that had been profoundly conditioned by two things. One was the many years he spent tramping the roads and tasting the air of Europe. The other was the many months he passed in conditions of daily terror and watchfulness during the mid 1940s, times that made him profoundly distrustful of theoretical abstraction, as he made clear in *At the Mind's Limit*.[45]

Améry's experience in Auschwitz brought about a significant moment of inner creative destruction: destruction because the utter inhumanity of the camps shattered his confidence in the world and the cultural lens through which he had habitually examined it; creative because Améry was forced to undergo a very painful but, as it turned out, very fruitful rebirth. He had to reconstruct his view of himself and the world. Those moments of intense fear and his desperate determination to survive shaped Améry's methodological approach to observing and interpreting the world. By paying close attention to his immediate environment Améry learned how to stay out of trouble and seize opportunities. Améry gained confidence in his capacity to conduct penetrating analyses of concrete situations, sometimes at extreme and intense moments where his life might easily be at stake. This was a vital survival technique that increased his ability to understand, describe and, if necessary, avoid or even divert the dynamics of those situations.

Améry accumulated and reflected deeply upon an immense and diverse internalized store of personal lived experiences spread over time and space. Sustained reflection on such situations generated insights about the structures and processes that brought them about. Améry looked beneath surfaces for the mechanisms that held large and small worlds together and gave them direction and meaning. As a result he garnered valuable insights on the ordering and disordering of life and society, on how the world works. He had the inner means to apply this approach, especially his combination of intense sensitivity and deep robustness, qualities that made him such an effective freelance journalist for two decades after the war.

Preface to the Future is a virtuoso performance, converting accumulated street-level reporting into systematic comparative analysis of national cases. Briefly, Améry argued that France, England, Germany and the United States were the key national populations making the greatest impact upon the West in the immediate post-war period. The steadfast defiance of the French Resistance and the independent attitude of General de Gaulle as leader of the Free French enabled France to include itself amongst the victorious Allies in 1945; defeat was turned into victory. By contrast, the costs of the war meant London had to relinquish possession of the British Empire, including the British Raj in India and Burma. The British endured food rationing and other shortages until the mid 1950s; for them, victory in the war was turned into 'the greatest defeat in British history'.[46]

By the late 1950s the Empire was rapidly being taken over by indigenous rulers. But English heads preserved 'a kind of consciousness of Empire'[47]

They were caught between a past they could not recover and a future they could barely face. They cherished their national health service based on socialist principles while simultaneously adoring the monarchy, which helped sustain a snob-ridden class system. There was an abundance of high culture but in the late 1950s the works of so-called angry young men such as John Osborne (1929–94), Kingsley Amis (1922–95) and John Braine (1922–86) were especially interesting. Their writing seemed to rise directly out of the country's sociopolitical conditions. Améry's judgments on their work were not aesthetic but sociological. In *Lucky Jim*[48] he discerned self-satisfied anti-intellectualism and a petty-bourgeois contempt for other people. *Look Back in Anger* was a tirade of destructive egocentricity fed by disappointment and irresponsibility.[49] *Room at the Top*, the most repellent of all, featured a greedy and ambitious central character, a man who behaved as if he had a right to exploit others or push them brutally aside, whatever the cost.[50]

Améry shrewdly discerned in these works an undercurrent of cruelty and violence, possibly derived from 'an older more brutal England' before the welfare state.[51] This earlier epoch was, in fact, the age of empire, when the imperial master's strength prevailed over any opposition mounted in the name of nationalism or universal human rights. The vicious undercurrent noticed by Améry expressed the postwar generation's intense resentment at the loss of their past imperialist supremacy. These young men were angry because Britain's dominant global position had been destroyed by a war they had supposedly won. They had been deprived of their inheritance. The British fed deep upon their resentment, which became part of the British national myth.

Améry's survey of the stressful emotional and moral landscape inhabited by those angry young men echoes Wilde's own dissection of the anxious mental universe of their upper-class predecessors seventy years before in his West End domestic comedies: *Lady Windermere's Fan* and so on. Many of the same dynamics reappear: egocentricity, self-satisfaction, irresponsibility and contempt, all mixed with fear lest everything be lost. Améry found two dominant themes in contemporary English culture. One was a deep isolationism. There was 'almost hostile indifference to Europe'[52] in spite of the British government's attempt to join the Common Market. The second theme was a spirit of rejection, a profound lack of interest in the rest of the world beyond Britain. The English said 'no' to how the world was changing, and only very reluctantly joined in the 'general mutual enlacement of the West'[53] under American leadership.[54]

Turning elsewhere, Améry noted that America and Germany were business-centred societies that prized innovation, efficiency and profit. German employees were even more suited to capitalist business than their American counterparts. Americans' hard work flowed from an unshakeable conviction that the dedicated corporate employee could win a future blessed with comfort and security. By contrast, Germans worked relentlessly to displace past moral failures from their minds and avoid the discomfort and insecurity brought by a 'tormented conscience'.[55] In fact, for many the Third Reich was remembered as a happy time. Meanwhile, the Cold War placed West Germany in the front line of the struggle against communism, mobilized against the same enemy as the one Hitler had opposed. Basically, Améry concluded, the people remained the same in the early 1960s as two decades earlier.

Améry's verdict on the new West was negative. Its powerful mass media promoted a materialistic life style focused on consumption, free from communist oppression. The books of the embittered ex-communist Arthur Koestler (1905–83) were as culturally influential in the United States as those of Sartre were in Europe.[56] But how should this Western freedom be used? Western civilization had no coherent message about moral values and political purposes. It reached out in many directions through its dense networks but culturally it had little depth. It was horizontally extensive but vertically shallow.

The West had no overarching sense of civilizational purpose and direction; no clearly defined and solidly grounded moral and intellectual structures; nothing to give coherence and meaning to the emotions and mentalities of particular individuals or groups. In the early 1960s, Améry noticed the vigour of China, India and Japan, nations that 'give rise to cultural impulses of the greatest intensity'. These Asian cultures might 'in the end prove to be stronger and more viable than our Western tradition'.[57]

By the time *Preface to the Future* appeared in English Améry was deeply engaged in another project, the radio broadcasts soon to be published as *At the Mind's Limits*.[58] This involved drilling down into German Nazism. For example, he noticed the delight it took in torture as a way of achieving self-realization. Améry conveyed the moral and emotional shock of becoming the victim of such deliberate cruelty. He wanted his German audience to accept responsibility for allowing those things to happen. In his radio talks and in the book that followed, Améry reflected on his time in Fort Breendonk, at Auschwitz and after his release.

Améry's key themes in *At the Mind's Limits* are in sharp contrast with *De Profundis*. Oscar Wilde presented a lengthy *mea culpa* from his prison cell. By contrast, Améry drew up an extensive charge sheet. Torture diminished and fragmented its victims while making torturers, and by extension the nation that produced them, feel great. Améry had been turned into a catastrophe Jew, marked out for misery. His home, his *heimat*, was taken away from him and destroyed, leaving him with an unfocused longing, impossible to satisfy. In his most abrasive chapter, entitled 'Resentment', Améry argued that contemporary Germans could not be easily relieved of their guilty conscience. In Améry's words, 'Only I possessed, and still possess, the moral truth of the blows that even today roar in my skull.' He felt this left him 'more entitled to judge' than others. He was adamant that 'resentments are there in order that the crime become a moral reality for the criminal, in order that he be swept into the truth of his atrocity'.[59]

Améry could neither forget nor forgive. In his view, a central issue was the estrangement between victim and perpetrator. Fellow feeling between them could only be achieved if the perpetrators were harshly punished or came to experience in some other way the sense of loneliness and abandonment they had imposed on their victims. By suffering victimhood themselves, they would become capable of empathizing with those they had victimized.

He lamented his own past inability to strike back when he and other Jews were being victimized. How could he justify being spared since he had not responded effectively to his tormenters' abuse? One acquaintance, the writer Fritz J. Raddatz, recalled that when visiting Améry in Brussels he was often met by a depressed silence and Améry's repeated assertion that he could not forgive himself.[60]

Justice and honour

At the Mind's Limit and *Preface to the Future* were major achievements.[61] With these two books behind him, Améry freed himself from daily dependence on routine journalistic production, which was, in his own words, a 'non-career, an anti-career'.[62] His next task was to free himself from an unsatisfactory self-identity. He did not want to make his living by forever playing the irreconcilable victim dwelling at length on the details of his suffering and resentment.

Améry's default inner condition was gloom. But that gloom predated Auschwitz. In an imaginary letter to Améry composed two years after his suicide, Maria wrote: 'it was all in you from an early date'. She recalled that his favourite poets as a youth were preoccupied with 'decline, melancholy, and death'. Améry spent his life wrestling with an endemic feeling of loneliness. Was it caused by losing his father when he was four years old, removing a guide and protector? By the time young Améry arrived in Vienna he was already feeling out of place and disjointed. He tried to find a meaningful cultural niche through his work on the journal *Die Brücke* in 1934 but that did not work. In *The Shipwrecked* (*Die Schiffbrüchigen*), written the following year, Améry was already imagining how to engineer an acceptable form of suicide that would express his sense of personal honour.[63] In that book, as we have seen, the chosen device was a duel.

Two relationships were especially important to Améry. One was the interplay between the self and the world. Améry thought people acquired their sense of self by struggling for recognition and freedom. The self should push back against unwelcome social pressures and take from the surrounding world only what it wants, resisting confinement.[64] That was, indeed, how Améry lived, through a series of experimental involvements, short and long: with women, with the Vienna circle, with Sartre, with anti-Nazi resistance, with journalism, with literature, and with life. These experiments were interspersed with moments of escape: wandering in the forest, hiding in mountain caves, jumping onto trains, jumping off trains, changing his name, changing his location, and changing his mind. In Auschwitz there was no escape through the fence or gate. Instead, Améry, like others, hid behind a mask of willing compliance in his duties to avoid being defined as disposable. Much later, Améry made his own escape from life, by choice.

The other relationship that interested Améry was between words and things. His message from the torture chamber was that conceptual reasoning embedded in culture and philosophy had no purchase on pain and suffering. Culture and philosophy could not alleviate, communicate or explain that experience. Améry also concluded that people's perceptions of reality were filtered and shaped by embedded habits of feeling and judgment enacted in body language and speech, of which they might be only half-aware.

So how should we manage? As far as Améry was concerned, facts, things and experiences should be directly perceived with as little mediation as possible and, once received, those perceptions should be reflected upon deeply to tease out their most important attributes. The eponymous central character in Améry's novel *Lefeu oder der Abbruch* (hereafter *Lefeu*)[65] has contempt for modern literature that deliberately plays with words in ways that distort and destroy their received meaning. The artist Lefeu paints everyday objects rather than fashionable abstract canvases. Améry assumed that facts about the world and the self would gradually clarify through careful and sustained attention. On that basis one could also make some practical comparisons and empirical generalizations.

Améry enjoyed language. But he mistrusted its influence. In Vienna as a young man he had discovered how perilous it was to construct worlds that exist only in the sphere of language. During the 1960s, he saw these old erroneous ways regaining strength in the dialectical reasoning of Sartre, and the language games of post-modernity.[66]

As he came to realize that Sartre was not his saviour, Améry redefined his mission. He asked how it was possible to live in a world where his own high ideals were impossible to achieve. He became preoccupied with two linked thoughts: individuals are almost bound to fail in their efforts to establish a satisfactory existence for themselves in society; but it is both possible and important to make a meaningful fight of it, to live nobly and with honourable intentions. There is something of Cervantes in this approach.[67] Not that Améry ever saw himself as Don Quixote. Sancho Panza, perhaps, commenting sardonically on his master's adventures.

Améry put a real-world human problem at the centre of his thinking. He began exploring what made people's lives and deaths either satisfactory or unsatisfactory, and how individuals moved between these different conditions. As part of this quest he reworked the Sartrian concept of disgust (*la nausée*) for his own purposes.[68]

Améry sought out pathways leading from feelings of disgust with the world towards various forms of either revolt or resignation.

In *On Aging*[69] (1968) and *On Suicide*,[70] Améry directly addresses his fellow humans whom he believes are all, like him, experiencing unsatisfactory lives. For example, the old have diminishing time available and have lost their command over space: 'they stay quietly in their place'. Meanwhile, their past visions fade away: 'The real has washed over what was once possible'.[71] Aging makes us vulnerable strangers in the changing world.[72] That is the down side but Améry also tries to identify forces that might allow us to have more satisfying lives and deaths. This concern flows through his own biography as a resistance fighter, his views on aging and suicide,[73] and the plots of *Lefeu* and *Charles Bovary*.[74]

In Améry's view, people can have satisfactory lives if they are able to engage in an active struggle to establish their self-identity, defend their honour and advance their beliefs. Not just in literary confrontations but also by striking back at bullies and joining in battles either on the streets or the military front line. Améry believes that death should have a noble meaning. Satisfactory deaths might include, for example, being fatally wounded in an honourable duel, falling on the field of battle for a noble cause, being executed for carrying out a crime of passion to preserve one's honour, or enacting a freely-chosen suicide in a rational and composed frame of mind.

In 1970 Améry was elected to the Berlin Academy of Arts and won the Critics Literary Prize of the League of German Writers.[75] This was mainly for his book on aging, and not quite what he wanted. Améry believed a writer such as himself should produce great novels, books worthy of being placed alongside authors such as Thomas Mann (1875–1955), Robert Musil or the early Jean-Paul Sartre. Such works showed readers how to understand themselves more completely, overcome their moral weaknesses, and behave in a better way. In that spirit, Améry complemented his explorations in *On Aging* and *On Suicide* with his two highly innovative novels, or novel-essays: *Lefeu* and *Charles Bovary*.[76]

Lefeu is about a rebellious artist contesting the advance of capitalist modernity. *Charles Bovary* is about the husband of the adulterous Emma Bovary, whom Améry rescues from the contemptuous dismissal to which his creator Gustave Flaubert (1821–80) subjects him. In both these works Améry depicts his central characters going into battle to defend their honour and strike out at mediocrity and deception in the world around them. At the same time, Lefeu and Charles Bovary show distinct signs of an inclination towards death, behaving in ways likely to lead to self-destruction. Lefeu and Bovary find themselves, like Améry himself, struggling for a life worth living while seeking out a death worth having.

Let us return to *On Aging*,[77] because here Améry argues that our sense of who we are and what we can do in the world is shaped by struggles over several years that typically end in minor but humiliating defeats. By the time we have established our identity and know what we are capable of doing our chance to shape our world has practically disappeared. We are exhausted and disheartened. In such a condition getting old is an unpleasant experience, even for those who tasted great success when young. Améry once heard the aging Sartre give a lecture. He was shocked to see how much virility and power had drained out of Sartre; also, how the young preyed on him, taking what they wanted from his presence without offering genuine respect.[78]

Améry recalls living with death at Auschwitz, under the oppressor's thumb. He strongly implies that such an experience, however horrible, was better than the trauma of growing old. After all, he writes, 'There is no nicer death in the world than being killed by an enemy'.[79] How different from the slow internal constriction of life that disease administers to the aging body. Among the aging, relish for life is replaced by fear of death. Growing old is humiliating. Faced with that challenge, will his aging readers adopt an attitude of resignation or one of revolt?

Revolt is the stance taken by the artist Lefeu in his run-down apartment in the 15th *arrondissement* of Paris. He faces two enemies. One is the corrosively intrusive capitalist market. Developers wish to demolish the homes of the small community of experimental artists to which Lefeu belongs. Most of his friends have sold out but Lefeu is a rebel. He follows his own aesthetic inclination. This leads him to paint real objects or scenes such as the dome of the Panthéon and cultivate a delight in decadence that is totally opposed in spirit to those who want to buy him out.[80] Their cynical offers to promote his work as metaphysical realism disgust him.[81] This leads us towards Lefeu's second enemy, which is the pervasive misuse of language to spin a web of self-referential semantics. This verbiage illuminates nothing beyond the vacuity of its practitioners. These sadly include his girlfriend Aline whose poetry Lefeu criticizes harshly.[82]

Lefeu reads like a prolonged session on the psychiatrist's couch. Lefeu has flashbacks and visions. One intermittent character is the so-called bird of misfortune that takes flight during the night.[83] This weird bird had appeared in the work of Améry's friend, the artist Erich Schmid.[84] Like Améry, Schmid was an Austrian from Vienna who fled the Nazis, lived in Belgium, was deported to a detention centre in southern France, escaped, and joined the resistance. Unlike Améry, Schmid was never captured or sent to an extermination camp. Instead he spent the war fighting the Nazis, took part in the liberation of Lyons, and joined the French Foreign Legion. Then he spent the rest of the war in Italy, the battleground where Améry's own father had died. That was a life Améry would, no doubt, have liked to lead but he was denied the opportunity.

Lefeu begins to recall a previous existence in which his name was Feuermann. His parents were rounded up by the Gestapo and killed in the gas chambers, although he escaped destruction. Gradually, Lefeu comes to understand that he is a survivor of the Holocaust. He dreams he is the *Feuerreiter*, the red-capped Fire Rider imagined by the poet Eduard Moricke (1804–75). He has vengeful thoughts, which centre on a plan to burn Paris to the ground. Consumed with this idea, Lefeu, whose very name means fire, paints a picture of Paris in flames. Finally, Lefeu rejects his dreams of arson and burns the painting itself, an act that coincides with his own death from a sudden seizure in front of the burning picture.[85]

At this point, the temptation to make a comparison with Wilde's *The Picture of Dorian Gray* becomes overwhelming. In Wilde's novel, as in *Lefeu*, the main protagonist dies just after destroying a picture that encapsulates his nightmares. Wilde based the main characters in his novel on different aspects of himself – the dedicated artist, the urbane man about town, and the reckless pleasure-seeker – exploring their potential if taken to extremes. In a similar way, in *Lefeu* Améry sets free various fragments drawn from the resources of his own complex personality such as Lefeu the artist, Feuermann and the *Feuerreiter*, allowing them each of them to live out their drives and come to various sticky ends.

The Picture of Dorian Gray evokes the implosion of a way of living. Dorian leaves a trail of ruin, damaging or destroying anyone who stands in his way. He gradually realizes the depth of his own depravity, the terrible harm he has done to others and himself. Likewise *Lefeu* witnesses the demolition of a form of human existence, in this case his much-valued artists' colony overthrown by the brute demands of commercialized, consumerist modernity. Lefeu begins to understand for the first time just how much he has been abused. He has been the victim of hostile, alienating forces that find his presence inconvenient and wish to destroy him.

The two novels complement each other. Wilde focuses on the powerful who abuse their position, Améry on the victims who receive such abuse. Neither Lefeu the victim nor Dorian the perpetrator can live with the self-knowledge they finally acquire. Wilde explores the self-destructive psychology of exploitation and indulgence carried out at the cost of humiliating others. Améry examines the emotional effects of suffering intense humiliation. Wilde includes some heady dream-like sequences evoking Dorian's sensuous excesses. Améry's book overrides mundane rules of space, time and physics to depict some tormenting psychological truths that Améry had learned the hard way.

Lefeu had only lukewarm reviews. He was criticized for trying to convert himself from an essayist to a writer of full-length novels. Améry found this devastating and within two years published his treatise on suicide.[86] In this book Améry argues that a decision to take one's own life may be reasonable, not a symptom of mental disturbance. He had already tried to kill himself in 1974, and previously in 1943 at Fort Breendonk. Améry draws upon this inside knowledge to identify mechanisms that lead a person in a suicidal direction.

One is a gradually strengthening inclination towards death rather than life. This shows itself in a chronic reluctance to engage with the world, a melancholic sense of resignation. This may be compounded by a second factor, a chronic feeling of disgust with the society's brute indifference to human needs and aspirations. The third factor is the experience of some great setback or failure that produces depression and disillusionment. The setback brings indignity and humiliation. Committing suicide may, in these circumstances, be a way of taking back full control of the self. In other words, it may be a declaration of independence, a way of escaping society's clutches. The decision to take one's own life, and the act itself, are both assertions of absolute sovereignty.

These feelings of affronted dignity and self-assertion are what Améry restores to Charles Bovary, the well-meaning country doctor who is the husband of Emma Bovary. Améry is correcting an error of omission, as he sees it, by the original author, Gustave Flaubert. Like *On Suicide*, this is a work of advocacy. Much of it evokes the courtroom. Améry is offended on Charles's behalf by Gustave Flaubert's contempt for petty bourgeois provincials. Flaubert neglects to explore the socio-political dynamics of the lives led by the Bovary family and their neighbours. The author of *Madame Bovary*[87] ignores the strong progressive ethos found in provincial medicine whose practitioners moved between peasant hovels and the mansions of the local aristocracy. Flaubert treats such people with a mixture of mocking irony and indifference.[88] Améry argues that Flaubert's worship of art as an ideal, his predilection for erotic fantasy, his resentment towards the world, and his bad conscience towards himself all combine to shape the author's attitude of contempt. The one character Flaubert takes seriously is Emma whose romantic excesses mirror his own inclinations. Both of them, Emma and Flaubert, identify with the aristocracy.

Améry takes the side of the betrayed bourgeois husband saddled with ruinous debts by a wife who escapes her own shame by poisoning herself. Flaubert kept Charles ignorant and gave him an ignominious death caused by the shock of finding his wife's love letters. Améry remakes Charles as a man who knew what was going on, challenged his wife, killed both her lovers, and refused to ask for a reprieve from the death sentence. In *Charles Bovary*, Améry manages to combine a strong dose of outraged bourgeois morality with a keen sense of aristocratic honour.[89] He condemns Flaubert for his ungenerous treatment of Charles Bovary and dismisses Sartre's sympathetic analysis of Flaubert in his book *The Family Idiot* (Sarte 1971–2). With great gusto, Améry wipes the floor with two great novelists: Flaubert, whom he evidently dislikes, and Sartre, his own god that failed. At the same time, Améry puts in a good word for victims everywhere. They are not, he insists, either stupid or ignorant, whatever their oppressors might think. The book is a decisive settling of accounts.

In *Charles Bovary* Améry is a trenchant and articulate opponent of those who oppressively deny others their rights. He frames the struggle against these enemies in the manner of a medieval knight or a Wild West gunfighter. In other words, he does not rely heavily on the democratic or liberal state as an agency enforcing justice but on strong individuals asserting themselves against their enemies. As already seen, Améry expects people to constitute their self-identity in the process of asserting their claims for recognition. He manages to combine his strong bourgeois ethic defending universalistic human rights with a knightly code that gives respect to those who can deploy bodily force to fight for their honour and self-identity.

Charles Bovary was not a critical success. Shortly after the reviews appeared Améry made his last attempt at suicide, last because it was successful.[90] Améry's reputation has been steadily climbing ever since. Améry's suicide was a premeditated act, signalled long beforehand. It was an act of defiance: on the one hand, a chosen death by someone who had cheated that unwelcome fate in Auschwitz; on the other hand, the lighting of a funeral pyre intended to blaze fiercely. Perhaps Améry hoped that his death would draw attention not only to the wronged victim but also to the noble rebel that dwelt within the victim, one who knew the odds were stacked against him but fought on for righteousness and honour.

Notes

1. Heidelberger-Leonard 2010, an indispensable guide; *Örtlichkeiten* (Améry 1980b, henceforth *OK*); and *Unmeisterliche Wanderjahre* (Améry 1985a, henceforth *UW*). I have used the Spanish translations, respectively *Lugares en el tiempo* (henceforth *Lugares*), which is a translation of *Örtlichkeiten*, and *Años de andanzas nada magistrales* (henceforth *Años*), which is a translation of *Unmeisterliche Wanderjahre*. Cross references to the German texts are given.
2. See also Brudholm 2008; Bukey 2001; Doll 2006a; Gehl 1963; Howland 2015; Levi 1987; Levi 1988; Leask 2013; Lorenz and Weinberger 1994; Zolkos 2011. See also Smith 2013.
3. *Años*, 138; *UW* 100.
4. Améry 1964; Darwin 2009, 514–655; Brendon 2008.
5. http://www.taoiseach.gov.ie/eng/Historical_Information/The_Constitution/February_2015_-_Constitution_of_Ireland_.pdf (accessed 12th August 2016).
6. Hochmann 2016; Bukey 2001; Gehl 1963.
7. Heidelberger-Leonard 2010, 4, 10.
8. Quoted in Beckerman 1994, 79; *Lugares*, 20; *OK* 12.
9. 'Anti-Semitism and tourism in Austria: Jews in Austria's 19th century spa towns' at http://www.tourmycountry.com/austria/anti-semitism-austria.htm and http://www.tourmycountry.com/austria/anti-semitism-austria2.htm (both accessed 14th August 2016).
10. Améry was pronounced cured some months later.
11. Heidelberger-Leonard 2010, 6, 12–13.
12. http://www.jm-hohenems.at/en/jewish-quarter/jewish-school and http://www.hohenemsgenealogie.at/en/genealogy/getperson.php?personID=I0431&tree=Hohenems (both accessed 15th August 2016)
13. *Lugares*, 31–57; *OK*, 24–48.
14. Judson 2016; Lieven 2002, 158–98.
15. Wilde 1891b.
16. Wilde 2011.
17. From *Intentions* (Wilde 1891a).
18. Wilde 1894.
19. Tims 1989, 188–92.
20. Kraus 2015; Tims 1989; Tims 2005; Broch 1986; Canetti 1982, 65–74; Canetti 1982, 55–263; Janik and Toulmin 1973; Musil 2017; Olsen 1986; Schorske 1981; Zweig 2009.
21. Doll 2006b; Janik and Toulmin 1973, 202–39.
22. *Lugares*, 21–34; *OK*, 13–27. In 2010 *The Shipwrecked* (*Die Schiffbrüchigen*) was published in a French translation as *Les Naufragés*. See Améry 2010.
23. Heidelberger-Leonard 2010, 29–40; also Weiler 2006.
24. Baldwin 1965.
25. *Lugares*, 37–81; OK, 28–69.
26. Heidelberger-Leonard 2010, 53, 70.
27. *Lugares*, 77–8. *OK*, 65–66.
28. On Belgian Resistance see, for example, Bodson 1994; De Ridder Files 1991.
29. Améry 1980a, 32.

30 Heidelberger-Leonard 2010, 54–60; Améry 1980a, 21–40.
31 Heidelberger-Leonard 2010, 50, 61–72.
32 *Lugares*, 71–81, 85–95.
33 Heidelberger-Leonard 2010, 89, 93.
34 Baert 2015; Flynn 2014; Sartre 1958; Sartre 1974; Sartre 2000; *Años*, 115–39; *UW*, 79–101; *Lugares*, 107–28; *OK*, 91–111.
35 Quoted in Heidelberger-Leonard 2010, 59.
36 Heidelberger-Leonard 2010, 78–84.
37 *Lugares*, 131–52; *OK*, 112–32; *Años*, 143–68; *UW*, 102–24.
38 Heidelberger-Leonard 2010, 40.
39 Améry 1960; Améry 1961; Améry 1963.
40 Améry 1955.
41 Améry 1964.
42 Améry 2003: *Lefeu o la demolición*,192; *Lefeu oder der Abbruch*, 176.
43 Adorno and Horkheimer 1970.
44 See also Adorno 1973. For another analysis of Améry's approach see Grøn and Brudholm 2011.
45 Améry 1980a.
46 Améry 1964, 220.
47 Améry 1964, 214.
48 Amis 2000; originally published in 1954.
49 Osborne 2015; play originally produced in 1956.
50 Braine 2013; originally published in 1957.
51 Améry 1964, 233.
52 Améry 1964, 236.
53 Améry 1964, 239.
54 *Lugares*, 96–105; *OK*, 81–90.
55 Améry 1964, 189.
56 Koestler 1994; Scammell 2011.
57 Améry 1964, 301.
58 Améry 1980a.
59 Améry 1980a, 70.
60 Raddatz 2012; Sebald 2003, 149–71. See also Dickens 2003.
61 Améry 1980a; Améry 1964.
62 Quoted in Heidelberger-Leonard 2010, 103.
63 Heidelberger-Leonard 2010, 241–2.
64 Améry 1999, 118–19.
65 Améry 2003.
66 *Años*, 113–95; *UW*, 79–147. See also Améry 1971; Améry 1982; Améry 1985b.
67 Cervantes 2003.
68 Sartre 2000.
69 Améry 1994; originally published in 1968
70 Améry 1999; originally published in 1976.
71 Améry 1994, 12, 19.
72 Améry 1994, chapters 2, 3 and 4.
73 Améry 1994, 27–52 (chapter entitled 'Stranger to oneself'); Améry 1999, 93–122 (chapter entitled 'Belonging to oneself').
74 *Charles Bovary, Landarzt. Porträt eines einfachen Mannes* is the original German title, which translates as *Charles Bovary. Country Doctor. Portrait of a Simple Man*. Reference is also made to the French text entitled *Charles Bovary, médecin de campagne* (Améry 1991). Referred to in the main text as *Charles Bovary*. References in the notes from the German translation will be to *Bovary Lanzart*, and from the French translation to *Bovary médecin*. See, for example, *Bovary médecin*, 171; *Bovary Lanzart*, 160.

75 Heidelberger-Leonard 2010, 179. See also 187–8.
76 Améry later planned a novella to be entitled *Rendez-vous in Oudenarde* but this did not come to fruition. Heidelberger-Leonard 2010, 230–4.
77 Améry 1994.
78 Améry 1994, 69–73.
79 Améry 1994, 116.
80 *Lefeu o la demolición*, 53–5; *Lefeu oder der Abbruch*, 55–6.
81 *Lefeu o la demolición*, 43; Lajarrige 2006.
82 *Lefeu o la demolición*, 73–104; *Lefeu oder der Abbruch*, 61–88.
83 *Lefeu o la demolición*, 88; *Lefeu oder der Abbruch*, 74.
84 It also, perhaps, appears briefly in Améry's discourse on suicide where he argued that to understand the mental state of someone contemplating this act we needed 'to stare with the eye of a nocturnal bird' (Améry 1999, 30). Zisselsberger 2011; http://www.erichschmid.com/en/biography (accessed 29th March 2017).
85 *Lefeu o la demolición*, 194–8; *Lefeu oder der Abbruch*, 165–8.
86 Heidelberger-Leonard 2010, 208–12.
87 Flaubert 2008. Sartre produced a lengthy biographical study of Flaubert entitled *The Family Idiot* (Sartre 1981-93; originally 1971–2).
88 *Bovary médecin*, 63–89; *Bovary Lanzart*, 58–83.
89 *Bovary médecin*, 119–73; *Bovary Lanzart*, 110–62.
90 http://anathanwest.wordpress.com/translations/jean-amery-suicide-notes (accessed 14th August 2016)

Bibliography

Adorno, T. (1973). *The Jargon of Authenticity*. London: Routledge; originally published in 1964 in German.

Adorno, T. and Horkheimer, M. (1970). *The Dialectic of Enlightenment*. London: Verso; originally published in 1944 in German.

Améry, J. (1955). *Karrieren und Köpfe* (*Careers and Leaders. Portraits of Famous Contemporaries*). Zürich: Thomas Verlag.

Améry, J. (1960). *Teenager-Stars. Idole unserer Zeit* (*Teenage Stars. Idols of Our Time*). Zürich: Thomas Verlag.

Améry, J. (1961). *Im Banne des Jazz. Bildnisse Grosser Jazz-Muziker* (*Under the Spell of Jazz. Portraits of Great Jazz Musicians*). Zürich: Albert Müller Verlag.

Améry, J. (1963). *Gerhart Hauptmann. Der Ewige Deutsche* (*Gerhardt Hauptmann. The Eternal German*). Mühlacker: Steiglitz-Verlag.

Améry, J. (1964). *Preface to the Future. Culture in a Consumer Society*. New York, NY: Frederick Ungar; originally published in 1961 as *Die Geburt der Gegenwart* (*The Birth of the Present*). Zurich: Walter.

Améry, J. (1971). *Widersprüche* (*Contradictions*). Stuttgart: Klett-Cotta.

Améry, J. (1980a). *At the Mind's Limits. Contemplations by a Survivor on Auschwitz and its Realities*. Bloomington, IN: Indiana University Press; originally published in 1966 in German as *Jenseits von Schuld und Sühne* (*Beyond Crime and Punishment*). München: Szczesny.

Améry, J. (1980b). *Örtlichkeiten* (*Localities*). Stuttgart: Klett-Cotta; also published in Spanish in 2010 as *Lugares en el tiempo*. Valencia: Editorial Pre-Textos.

Améry, J. (1982). *Weiterleben-aber wie? Essays 1968–1978*. (*To Live On But How? Essays 1968–1978*) Stuttgart: Klett-Cotta.

Améry, J. (1985a). *Unmeisterliche Wanderjahre (Unmasterly Journeyman Years)*. Stuttgart: Klett-Cotta; also published in Spanish in 2006 as *Años de andanzas nada magistrales*. Valencia: Editorial Pre-Textos.

Améry, J. (1985b). *Der integrale Humanismus. Zwischen Philosophie und Literatur Aufsätze und Kritiken einers 1966–1978 (Integral Humanism. Between Philosophy and Literature. Essays and Reviews 1966–1978)*. Stuttgart: Klett-Cotta.

Améry, J. (1991). *Charles Bovary. Médicin de Campagne. Portrait d'un Homme Simple (Charles Bovary. Country Doctor. Portrait of a Simple Man)*. Paris: Actes Sud; originally published in 1978 in German as *Charles Bovary, Landarzt. Porträt eines einfachen Mannes*. Stuttgart: Klett-Cotta.

Améry, J. (1994). *On Aging. Revolt and Resignation*. Bloomington and Indianapolis: Indiana University Press; originally published in 1968 in German as *Über das Altern. Revolte und Resignation*. Stuttgart: Klett-Cotta.

Améry, J. (1999). *On Suicide. A Discourse on Voluntary Death*. Bloomington and Indianapolis: Indiana University Press; originally published in 1976 in German as *Hand an Sich legen. Diskurs über den Freitod*. Stuttgart: Klett-Cotta.

Améry, J. (2003). *Lefeu o la demolición (Lefeu or Demolition)*. Valencia: Editorial Pre-Textos; originally published in 1974 in German as *Lefeu oder der Abbruch*. (1974). Stuttgart: Klett-Cotta.

Améry, J. (2010). *Les Naufragés*. Paris: Actes Sud (*The Shipwrecked*); originally published in 2007 in German as *Die Schiffbrüchigen*. Stuttgart: Klett-Cotta.

Amis, K. (2000). *Lucky Jim*. London: Penguin; originally published in 1954.

Baert, P. (2015), *The Existentialist Moment. The Rise of Sartre as a Public Intellectual*. Cambridge: Polity.

Baldwin, J. (1965). 'The American Dream and the American Negro', *New York Times*. 7th March 1965.

Beckerman, R. (1994). 'Jean Améry and Austria' in Lorenz and Weinberger 1994, 73–86.

Bodson, H. (1994). *Agent for the Resistance. A Belgian Saboteur in World War II*. College Station: Texas T&M University Press.

Braine, J. (2013). *Room at the Top*. Richmond VA: Valancourt Books; originally published in 1957.

Brendon, P. (2008). *The Decline and Fall of the British Empire 1781–1997*. London: Vintage.

Broch, H. (1986). *The Sleepwalkers*. London: Quartet Books; originally published in German in 1931.

Brudholm, T. (2008). *Resentment's Virtue. Jean Améry and the Refusal to Forgive*. Philadelphia, PA: Temple University Press.

Bukey, E.B. (2001). *Hitler's Austria: Popular Sentiment in the Nazi Era, 1938–1945*. Chapel Hill, NC: University of North Carolina Press.

Canetti, E. (1982). *The Torch in My Ear*. London: Granta.

Cervantes, M. (2003). *Don Quixote*. London: Secker & Warburg; originally published in 1605 and 1615 (2 vols).

Darwin, J. (2009). *The Empire Project. The Rise and Fall of the British World System 1830–1970*. Cambridge: Cambridge University Press.

De Ridder Files, Y. (1991). *The Quest for Freedom. A Story of Belgian Resistance in World War II*. Santa Barbara, CA: The Narrative Press.

Dickens, C. (2003). *A Christmas Carol and Other Christmas Writings*. London: Penguin Classics, 27–118; originally published in 1843.

Doll, J. (ed.). (2006a). *Jean Améry (1912–1978) De l'expérience des camps à l'écriture engagée (Jean Améry (1912–1978) From Experience of the Camps to Engaged Writing)*. Paris: L'Harmattan.
Doll, J. (2006b). 'Réminiscences de Vienne la Rouge? A propos de *Livres de la jeunesse de notre siècle* de Jean Améry' in Doll 2006a, 179–192.
Flaubert, G. (2008) *Madame Bovary*. Oxford: Oxford University Press; first published in French in 1857.
Flynn, T.R. (2014). *Sartre: A Philosophical Biography*. Cambridge: Cambridge University Press.
Gehl, J. (1963). *Austria, Germany, and the Anschluss, 1931–1938*. Evesham, UK: Greenwood Press.
Grøn, A. and Brudholm, T. (2011), '"Nachdenken"' in Zolkos (2011), 193–215.
Heidelberger-Leonard, I. (2010). *The Philosopher of Auschwitz. Jean Améry and Living with the Holocaust*. London and New York: I.B.Taurus.
Hochman, E.R. (2016). *Imagining a Greater Germany: Republican Nationalism and the Idea of Anschluss*. Ithaca, NY: Cornell University Press.
Howland, J. (2015). 'Intellectuals at Auschwitz: Jean Améry and Primo Levi on the Mind and its Limits', *Holocaust Genocide Studies* (Winter) 29, 3, 353–373.
Kraus, K. (2015). *The Last Days of Mankind*. New Haven and London: Yale University Press.
Janik, A. and Toulmin, S. (1973). *Wittgenstein's Vienna*. Chicago, IL: Elephant Paper backs.
Judson, P.M. (2016). *The Hapsburg Empire. A New History*. Harvard, MA: Harvard University Press.
Koestler, A. (1994). *Darkness at Noon*. London: Vintage; originally published in 1940.
Lajarrige, J. (2006). '"Rue sans espoir, sans vouloir, sans temps". Lefeu oder der Abbruch (1974): essai de roman', in Doll 2016a, 159–177.
Leask, P. (2013) 'Losing Trust in the World: Humiliation and its Consequences.' *Psychodynamic Practice*, 19, 2, 129–142.
Levi, P. (1987). *If This is a Man and The Truce*. London: Abacus.
Levi, P. (1988). *The Drowned and the Saved*. London: Abacus.
Lieven, D. (2002). *Empire. The Russian Empire and its Rivals from the Sixteenth Century to the Present*. London: Pimlico.
Lorenz, D.C.G. and Weinberger, G.Eds. (1994). *Insiders and Outsiders. Jewish and Gentile Culture in Germany and Austria*. Detroit, MI: Wayne State University Press.
Musil, R. (2017). *The Man Without Qualities*. London: Pan Macmillan; originally published in 1943.
Olsen, D.J. (1986). *The City as a Work of Art: London, Paris, Vienna*. New Haven, CT: Yale University Press.
Osborne, J. (2015). *Look Back in Anger*. London: Faber and Faber.
Raddatz, F.J. (2012). 'Wer gefoltert wurde, bleibt gefoltert', *Die Welt*, 31 October 2012.
Sartre, J.P. (1958). *Being and Nothingness. An Essay on Phenomenological Ontology*. London: Methuen.
Sartre, J.P. (1974). *Between Existentialism and Marxism*. London: NLB.
Sartre, J.P. (1981–93) *The Family Idiot. Gustave Flaubert 1821–57*, Chicago: Chicago University Press; originally published in French in 1971–2.
Sartre, J.P. (2000). *Nausea*. London: Penguin; originally published in French in 1938.
Scammell, M. (2011). *Koestler: The Indispensable Intellectual*. London: Faber and Faber.

Schorske, C.E. (1981). *Fin-de-Siécle Vienna. Politics and Culture.* New York, NY: Vintage Books.

Sebald, W.G. (2003). *On the Natural History of Destruction.* London: Penguin Books.

Smith, D. (2013). 'Forced Social Displacement: the "inside stories" of Oscar Wilde, Jean Améry, Nelson Mandela and Aung San Suu Kyi', in Nicolas Demertsiz (ed.) *Emotions in Politics.* London: Palgrave-Macmillan (2013), 60–83.

Tims, E. (1989) *Karl Kraus. Apocalyptic Satirist. Culture and Catastrophe in Hapsburg Vienna.* New Haven and London: Yale University Press.

Tims, E. (2005) *Karl Kraus. Apocalyptic Satirist. The Post-War Crisis and the Rise of the Swastika.* New Haven and London: Yale University Press.

Weiler, S. (2006). 'Les débuts littéraires de Jean Améry/Hans Mayer: *Die Schiffbrüchigen* (1935)' in Doll 2006a, 137–157.

Wilde, O. (1891a). *Intentions.* London: Methuen.

Wilde, O. (1891b). 'The Soul of Man under Socialism', *Fortnightly Review,* 49, Feb 1891, 292–319.

Wilde, O. (1894).*Salome.* London: Elkin Mathews & John Lane.

Wilde, O. (2011). *The Picture of Dorian Gray. An Annotated, Uncensored Edition,* edited by Nicholas Frankel. Cambridge, MA and London: The Belknap Press; originally published in 1891.

Zisselsberger, M. (2011). 'Aufbrechen/Abbrechen. Towards an Aesthetics of Resistance in Jean Améry's Novel-Essay *Lefeu oder Der Abbruch*' in Zolkos 2011, 151–192.

Zolkos, M. (ed.) (2011). *On Jean Améry. Philosophy of Catastrophe.* Lanham, MD: Lexington Books.

Zweig, S. (2009). *The World of Yesterday.* London: Pushkin Press.

4 Nelson Mandela

Nazism and apartheid

The stories of Nelson Mandela and Jean Améry are interwoven through the interconnections between *apartheid* and Nazism. *Apartheid* was a system of racial segregation, discrimination and exploitation in politics, government, housing, education, social services and employment. It systematically humiliated the majority of the nation's population, treating Black South Africans as intrinsically inferior. South Africa under *apartheid* was not genocidal and did not seek world domination. By the late 1980s *apartheid* was less harsh than in the late 1940s.[1] But racism was hardwired into its law and governance.

When South Africa's National Party (NP) imposed *apartheid* in 1948, it was continuing a sequence of cultural exchange between Africa and Europe. As Hannah Arendt and Gerwin Strobl argue, European colonialism in Africa and elsewhere gave encouragement to fascism in Europe.[2] This dubious gift was returned to Africa with the birth of *apartheid* as a programme between the two world wars. Afrikaner Nationalists, supposedly guided by God, wanted no earthly *führer*. However, during the 1930s the Nazi example stirred a sense of fellow feeling in many of *apartheid*'s founders.

J.B.M. (Barry) Hertzog (1866–1942) once compared his people's anguish after the end of the Boer War in 1902 to German misery after 1918: in both cases the vanquished endured 'humiliation and belittlement and insult'.[3] B.J. (John) Vorster (1915–83), South Africa's prime minister for over a decade (1966–78), openly sympathized with Hitler, Mussolini and Salazar in his younger days. During the early 1940s Vorster became a general in the paramilitary wing of the *Ossewabrandwag* (OB), which translates as *Ox-wagon Sentinel*. The OB came into existence in 1938, centenary year of the so-called Great Trek made by the Boers (or Dutch farmers) in 1838. The OB was anti-British, anti-Semitic and pro-Nazi; supposedly a cultural organization but involved in militant street politics and violent sabotage.

By 1942 Vorster was in a South African jail and Nazi victory in World War II seemed unlikely. The National Party led by D.F. (Daniel) Malan distanced itself from Hitler. The German defeat at Stalingrad in February 1943 settled matters. Hitler could no longer win. However, there were strong echoes from

Hitler's Berlin in the thought and behaviour of the National Party's leading members. Their mission was to unite and elevate South Africa's white *herrenvolk* or master race, the Afrikaners. They would bring Christian civilization to Africa. This meant putting indigenous Africans in their proper lowly place. These ideas united successive South African leaders: Daniel Malan (1948–54), J.G. (Hans) Strijdom (1954–8), H.F. (Hendrik) Verwoerd (1958–66), John Vorster (1966–78), and P.W. (Pieter) Botha (1978–89). The gospel of white supremacy was mother's milk to Mandela's fellow Nobel prize winner, F.W. (Frederik) De Klerk (1989–94), nephew of the notoriously hard-line Strijdom. Consider also Oswald Pirow (1890–1959). In 1940 he announced the creation of a 'New Order' in South Africa and campaigned for a Hitler-style dictatorship. Sixteen years later Pirow initially led the prosecution team that put Nelson Mandela and his political colleagues in the dock during the treason trial (1956–61).

Burying Madiba

The downfall of *apartheid* will always be associated with the name of Nelson Mandela.[4] Madiba was his clan name, inherited from his father. Following South Africa's first democratic election in 1994 Mandela became national president, aged 76. He was 95 years old when his life support system was switched off on 5th December 2013. The commemorative observances, long planned, took several days, and culminated in the interment near Madiba's home village. The burial took place at Qunu, deep in rural Transkei. Everything in this long sequence of events was carefully orchestrated, with some exceptions; for example, part of the crowd jeered President Jacob Zuma during the televised memorial ceremony at Johannesburg's Soccer City Stadium. Several mourners nodded off during Zuma's lengthy address at the Waterkloof Air Force Base in Pretoria a few days later.[5] In this speech the president spoke about the African National Congress (ANC)'s proud history and its mission to create a new inclusive, multi-racial South Africa.

Mandela's iconic status is the ANC's most precious asset. Over eighty heads of state and government attended the memorial service in Johannesburg on 10th December 2013, more than went to Rome when Pope John Paul II died in 2005.[6] Mandela's sanctity flickered around the South African government and the ANC, at least when seen from abroad. But this blessed condition was a diminishing asset, fading most quickly within South Africa itself.

Local South African newspapers covering the funeral's aftermath were soon reporting that an ANC regional official faced charges of fraud over the misuse of public funds earmarked for that solemn occasion. This scandal was part of a deeper malaise. The ANC in government had failed to meet the expectations of thousands of ordinary citizens still living in near-squalor. South Africa's unemployment rate in 1994 was reportedly over 20 per cent. By 2013 it had risen to nearly 25 per cent, the ninth highest in the world. These official figures almost certainly underestimated the true situation.[7]

The funeral scandal centred on Buffalo City in the Eastern Cape, a metropolitan municipality that included the township of Ginsberg, birthplace of Steve Biko (1946–77), charismatic leader of the Black Consciousness movement.[8] Biko rose to prominence during the Soweto uprising in 1976 and was assassinated the following year. The ANC appropriated Biko as a martyr of its struggle to overcome poverty and oppression but in government the ANC left the communities that Biko had represented stranded in deprivation.

In May 2015 a Ginsberg resident protested in the press about local criminal gangs. Three months later, Ginsberg's citizens were on the streets. Their message to the ANC was: give us better roads, decent services and more jobs or we will set the township ablaze. The crowd used burning tyres to close the main access road to Ginsberg. Twenty police vehicles arrived. The police threw stun grenades and made arrests. When this was reported in *The Sowetan* newspaper readers texted that it was stupid for Ginsberg folk to burn down their own township and that a much better target would be Nkandla.[9] That was the magnificent homestead built for President Zuma's private use in KwaZulu-Natal. Large amounts of public money were spent on this property, paying for its cattle kraal, chicken run, swimming pool, amphitheatre and visitors' centre, all classified as security features.

By April 2016 the president was being threatened with over seven hundred criminal charges, many for corruption.[10] After that date the situation became even worse. He was forced to resign in February 2018 several months before the official end of his term in 2019. Zuma was the ANC's intelligence chief during the struggle against *apartheid*. He became national president in 2009 against the wishes of Theba Mbeki, Mandela's immediate successor. Mandela and Mbeki were both from the Xhosa people. President Zuma is a Zulu. After 2009 his political networks in and around Durban had privileged access to the spoils of power.[11]

The condition of Ginsberg in 2015 demonstrated that South Africa remained a very violent and unequal society. It was rapidly urbanizing. At the start of the millennium just over half the nation's population lived in cities. By 2015 this had climbed to over two-thirds.[12] The cities ranged from giants such as Johannesburg and Pretoria down to much smaller places like Klerksdorp. This little mining town is the birthplace of Archbishop Desmond Tutu, who was prominent in the United Democratic Front, which mobilized protests against *apartheid* during the 1980s.

South Africa's cities have complex patterns of socio-cultural sedimentation. Historically, two rich seams have run through this complexity, two powerful systems of belief: Christianity and Communism. They have entered into various combinations: with each other, with tribal, ethnic and regional forms of solidarity, with consumerist dreams, and with neo-fascist nightmares. Neither of those belief systems can be assigned exclusively to either the high or the low moral ground. They each straddle both. Christians in the Dutch Reformed Church in South Africa practised racial segregation and blessed *apartheid*. Other Christians, including Bishops Trevor Huddleston and Desmond Tutu, campaigned against those things. Western governments, especially the United

States, demonized Communism throughout the Cold War with the help of writers such as Arthur Koestler. Meanwhile, the South African Communist Party (SACP) played a vital role alongside the ANC in resisting the oppression imposed by the white majority regime.

No one was 'simply' a Communist or a Christian. Both traditions, and others, shaped Mandela, for example. Both beliefs nurtured valuable assets: tough and flexible networks; the capacity to endure suffering; and a solid core of collective self-belief that sometimes verged on self-righteousness. These were the springs and buffers that drove forward two powerful movements. One was Afrikaner nationalism, a powerful force amongst descendants of the original Dutch settlers who bitterly resisted British imperial rule and later imposed *apartheid*. The other movement was the African revolt against *apartheid*, led by the ANC. Both movements drew upon both communal traditions. For many devoutly Christian Afrikaners, the *apartheid* regime operated as a kind of welfare state for the privileged minority, providing governmental guarantees of a decent livelihood to a large proportion of the white community. Meanwhile, for many resolutely communist ANC insurgents, Christian worship was a means of regularly resetting their moral compass.

The radical lawyer Joel Carlson has a telling account of Christianity's influence in southern Africa. In 1967 he was acting for a group of Namibian prisoners. They were freedom fighters; or terrorists, depending on your perspective. They had been treated very brutally by the South African police. The prisoners asked Carlson to make arrangements for a religious minister to hold a Christian service for them. Eventually he found a religious teacher, a so-called *dominie*, who could do this. He arranged for the *dominie* to visit the place of imprisonment and the prisoners 'greeted him with deep feeling'. He spoke to the men in their native Ovambo language then began conducting prayers in Afrikaans.

Outside stood the police with their Sten guns. Hearing Afrikaans being spoken they 'clustered in curiosity'. As the *dominie*'s voice rose 'the police recognized the prayers. One by one, they removed their hats and standing at ease, their guns in front of them, their hats on the buts of their guns, they bowed their heads'.[13] When the prisoners sang a hymn the police were 'visibly moved'. There was no blissful ending to this story. Carlson managed through immense effort to avoid a death penalty for his clients but twenty of them were imprisoned for the rest of their natural lives and nine for terms of twenty years.[14]

Historically, South Africa's internal struggles were influenced by two international factors. One was the strong pull of South Africa's gold and diamond mines, opened up during the late nineteenth century. They drew in thousands of *uitlanders* (foreigners), mainly British, to the Transvaal and the Orange Free State. The Boers originally established those two states. These people were Afrikaners, Dutch farmers who migrated north from the Cape Colony at the country's southern tip half a century before. The other international factor was the global contest between fascism, communism and capitalist democracy, culminating in the collapse of the Soviet Union at the end of the Cold War.[15]

South African politics was a never-ending battle for the upper hand. Historically, there were many lines of conflict, for example: between British and Afrikaner; between Jan Christian Smuts (1870–1950) and Barry Hertzog, two Boer politicians with diametrically opposed approaches to their British would-be rulers; and between John Vorster and Daniel Malan, Afrikaner leaders who respectively embraced and kept their distance from Nazism. Amongst the insurgent forces there were also many conflicts, for example: between Xhosa and Zulu; between Indian, African and European networks; between Nelson Mandela and Govan Mbeki (1910–2001), rivals within the ANC;[16] and between the ANC with its ideological focus of universal human rights and the Pan Africanist Congress (PAC) with its Black nationalist emphasis.

Those engaged in these conflicts had a sophisticated understanding of what was at stake and were well aware how the struggle stood at any point in time. Few white South Africans suffered cruelty or dismissive neglect comparable to that routinely experienced by the indigenous black population. But the Afrikaner guards who kept ANC activists locked up certainly knew from their own families' experience what it was like to feel marginalized and trampled upon.

In the early 1960s an Afrikaner warder in Port Elizabeth's *Rooi Hell* (Red Hell) jail told Govan Mbeki, one of the ANC prisoners: 'Remember, ... thirty years ago we Afrikaners were in a similar position to yours.'[17] If we want to understand Mandela and his fight for the rights of Black South Africans, we should begin by trying to understand the Afrikaners and their own struggle against adversity. That means going back, very briefly, to the Great Trek, and glancing at the sly and quick-footed manoeuvres of Cecil Rhodes, Alfred Milner, Barry Hertzog and Jan Christian Smuts.[18]

The Afrikaner story and Smuts

Modern South Africa has always been a violent society, and often a repressive one. White Europeans, especially British and Dutch, expelled, exterminated or enslaved its indigenous occupants. The Xhosa people in the Eastern Cape resisted the European intruders for several decades. They fought eight wars against them between the 1770s and the 1870s. Meanwhile, the two settler nations found it difficult to live together on equal terms. The British and Dutch tussled for control within the original settlement around Cape Town.

The British got the upper hand in the early nineteenth century. They gave citizenship rights in the Cape Colony to educated and propertied members of the 'coloured' population. This group was the result of unions between local white settlers and imported black slaves. The Dutch settlers did not accept this situation easily. During the 1830s many Boers headed north out of the Cape Colony towards the Orange River. Others moved still further north beyond the river Vaal. These migrations later became known as the Great Trek. The Boers trekking northwards were soon in confrontation with Zulus heading towards the region later known as KwaZulu-Natal whose main city became Durban. Blood was shed on both sides.

After many battles the Boers established the Orange Free State and the Transvaal Republic, which the British recognized as independent republics in the early 1850s. At that point the Boers seemed to have everything they most wanted. They were their own masters, in charge of their own destiny. They could farm with a subservient labour force, defend themselves, and use their own language, law and religion. They were free of British pressure to grant political and civil rights to their virtually enslaved farm workers.

But the lure of massive mineral wealth disrupted these hard-won arrangements. Between the 1860s and the 1880s abundant diamond and gold deposits were discovered along the Witwatersrand, a long ridge, deep and wide, abundantly loaded with rich ore. Kimberley and Johannesburg became dynamic centres of investment. These Afrikaner cities generated vast amounts of new wealth and soon became major centres of production and trade. They drew in many non-Afrikaner immigrants, mainly English-speaking.

Kimberley and Johannesburg threatened to eclipse Cape Town, the centre of British colonial rule, hundreds of miles to the South. But there was a downside. The dream of an Afrikaner rural idyll was gone. The biggest losers in this situation were local African peasant farmers, traditionally outside the money economy. The mines needed a ready supply of cheap labour. A poll tax was imposed on the farmers in 1905. They rebelled and were put down. Many then reluctantly became wage labourers, mainly in the mines, to get cash to pay the tax.

British dominance in South Africa was under threat. The imperial establishment in London went to war with the Boers (1880–1) who routed the British army at Majuba Hill (1881). But that was not the end of the matter. British business magnate Cecil Rhodes (1853–1902) adopted another approach. He built up a powerful position in the South African diamond market. This vicar's son made his colonial debut as a failed cotton farmer but in the 1870s and 1880s he bought up a very high proportion of the mining operations around Kimberley with the backing of the Rothschilds. He also muscled into the markets for oil and fruit in a big way, diversifying his interests and recycling his profits.

Rhodes's default strategy was to maximize returns by combining market dominance with political influence and brute force. Politics, war and business were intertwined.

During the early 1890s the British South Africa Company, controlled by Rhodes and backed by its own militia, founded the colony of Rhodesia, just north of South Africa. In 1890 Rhodes became prime minister of the Cape Colony to the south. To expand and integrate his business empire he needed to get effective political control of the Boer republics that lay between the

Cape Colony and Rhodesia. This led to the illegal and disastrous Jameson raid in 1895, led by Dr Leander Starr Jameson, an ally of Rhodes, prominent in the British South Africa Company, and the inspiration for Kipling's poem *If*.[19]

Jameson hoped to trigger a rebellion by British immigrants, and capture Johannesburg. But there was no rebellion and the raiders could not carry out their plan. Rhodes had to resign from political office. His brother Frank, who took part in the raid, was sentenced to death, although this was later commuted. Joseph Chamberlain (1836–1914), the British Colonial Secretary, somehow managed to keep his name out of the scandal. In 1897 to retrieve the situation the British sent out Alfred Milner (1854–1925), Oscar Wilde's friend and contemporary at Oxford. Milner became Governor of the Cape Colony. In effect, his mission was to protect the British stake in South Africa by building an unchallengeable British political and military presence. In that spirit the British government came back to the battlefield. During the second Boer war (1899–1902) the British military burned down thousands of Boer farms and consigned large numbers of Boer women and children to the deadly conditions prevailing in disease-ridden concentration camps, a British invention.[20]

William P. Schreiner, prime minister of the Cape Colony, opposed the war and was forced to resign in 1900. Principled opposition ran in the family. The prime minister's, sister, Olive Schreiner (1855–1920), another of Oscar Wilde's friends, returned from London to South Africa in 1889. She expressed intense sympathy not only for oppressed Black Africans but also for Boer communities suffering at the hands of the British.[21] At the peace treaty negotiations in 1902 the British gave the misleading impression that the two Boer states would be separate self-governing colonies belonging to a South African federation within the British Empire. But Boer self-government was quickly taken off the agenda, as was federalism. By 1910 the two Boer territories had been reduced to provinces within the Union of South Africa, which became a unitary self-governing dominion within the Empire, owing loyalty to the British crown. After 1931 South Africa enjoyed increased independence from London but British influence remained paramount. This was not the outcome most Afrikaners wanted, especially in the heartland Orange Free State where Barry Hertzog, a stern Boer loyalist, was the dominant political presence.

Ironically, a key political actor helping to deliver these results for the British was another Afrikaner leader, Jan Christian Smuts. In his heyday Jan Christian Smuts was as big a name as Franklin Delano Roosevelt or Mahatma Gandhi. It will be worth comparing Smuts's involvement in the resurgence of the Afrikaner people between the wars with Mandela's contribution to the post-war struggles of the African National Congress. Smuts had big plans for himself and everybody else. He trusted in his own strategic vision of a united South Africa in a united British Empire within a united world. But he had one very large blind spot. In spite of his well-advertised commitment to human rights, global peace and mutual understanding Smuts refused to put full citizenship rights for the African majority population on his political agenda. In that respect he remained true to the Afrikaner culture of his time.

Smuts was based in the Transvaal, where Afrikaner and British interests were more evenly balanced than in the Orange Free State. During the Boer War of 1899–1902 Smuts fought for the Afrikaner cause. When the Boers lost the war Smuts went into politics, joining *Het Volk* (the People's Party) formed in 1905. It was led by various former generals from the Transvaal, including Louis Botha who became prime minister of the Transvaal in 1907, and South Africa's national leader three years later. Smuts supported the British campaign to turn South Africa into a unitary state dominated by a fusion of 'civilized' elements from amongst the British and the Afrikaners. He delivered a large contingent of South African troops to fight on the British side in 1914. When Manie Maritz organized a rebellion of Boer hard-liners Smuts defeated the rebellion, then promptly annexed the neighbouring German colony of South-West Africa, a task completed in 1915.

Smuts joined Lloyd George's Imperial War Cabinet, helped shape the League of Nations after the war, and became a prominent advocate for turning the British Empire, including South Africa, into a commonwealth of nations headed up by the British crown. Smuts even sold this idea to Irish leader Michael Collins (1890–1922) who concluded a treaty with the British government making Ireland a Free State on that basis in 1922.[22] Collins could not sell that treaty to all his followers. One of them assassinated him as Ireland fell into civil war. Meanwhile, Smuts sailed on. He became South African prime minister twice: 1919–24 and 1939–48. When war broke out once more in 1939 he again brought South Africa in on the British side despite the reluctance of leading Afrikaner nationalists. True to form, Smuts had a role in Churchill's war cabinet and played a part in drafting the United Nations Charter.

The career of Smuts became directly relevant to Nelson Mandela in 1940 when he was studying at the University of Fort Hare in the Eastern Cape. Smuts visited the university and gave a talk to the students explaining the need for human rights and international harmony. Mandela was very impressed. At that time Mandela was a cheerleader for the British war effort, more enthusiastic than fellow students in the anti-colonial ANC, which he did not join till 1944. Smuts was a highly cultured and very dynamic leader promoting lofty ideals; somewhat aloof, a man with a confident and imposing manner. Is it possible that this manner influenced Mandela's own subsequent leadership style?[23]

Smuts did not have it all his own way. In 1915 dissident Afrikaner politicians founded the National Party, vowing to protect white civilization, specifically its earthly symbol, the Afrikaner worker's wage packet. The party wanted to diminish British influence and keep South Africa's majority Black population in a very lowly place. The National Party's core constituency was Afrikaners bulldozed out of their traditional existence as independent farmers. Displaced and destitute Afrikaner poor whites thronged the city streets. They had been forced to the margins of a new world of cut-throat politics dominated by international business in which British interests were highly influential.

The National Party began a fight back, using politics, networking, organization and the law. The 1913 Natives Land Act had legally confined African farmers to specified reserves in the countryside. In 1923 the Natives Urban Areas Act gave municipalities greater power to impose racial segregation in the cities. In the background was the *Broederbond*, a secret society founded soon after World War I to promote Afrikaner domination in all spheres. It demanded separate development for non-white races under white guardianship, to use the language of the day. Other groups organized boycotts of Indian and Jewish shops, especially in small country towns, replacing them with Afrikaner businesses. New insurance and banking corporations were set up to support Afrikaners moving into mining, manufacturing and commerce. Legislation was introduced favouring Afrikaner enterprises and employees, imposing large pay differentials between black and white workers. The price of maize was kept high to help Afrikaner farmers.

Leaders such as Hertzog were determined to force non-whites to live in distinct group areas, and deny them the right to vote in elections for white politicians. These measures were introduced in 1936. Meanwhile, efforts were made to raise the educational level of Afrikaner children so they could take jobs in the civil service and police, on the railways and in business. In 1948 Daniel Malan and the National Party won the general election and gained political power in Pretoria armed with their blueprint for *apartheid*. Pass laws and labour bureaux were used to regiment African workers very strictly. Black Africans were harassed in the cities and faced a high risk of arrest. Many were offered work on white farmers' land as an alternative to being taken to court. On the farms they became virtual slaves and prisoners, constantly beaten and denied the chance to travel freely.[24]

In the cities Black, Indian and coloured people were forcibly relocated in new residential areas specifically designated for each category. Meanwhile, Afrikaner politicians were creating a large sector of state enterprise, generating jobs, incomes and votes for white employees only. In all areas of life the white minority lived a superior, segregated existence. They had the best houses, schools and medical facilities. These were the benefits the South African white population reaped when the Afrikaners made their vigorous comeback after decades of defeat and retreat. The Afrikaners felt it was their right, their just reward.[25]

The ANC story and Mandela

The African National Congress (ANC) was founded in 1912. The word 'Congress' reflects the powerful influence on the ANC's founders exercised by the radical lawyer Mohandas Gandhi (1869–1948). He had set up the Natal Indian Congress in 1894 after arriving in South Africa the year before.

Gandhi spent two decades campaigning for the rights of the downtrodden. He was based in Durban and his main political opponent was Smuts, then a minister in the Transvaal government. Gandhi and Smuts were well matched: both graduated in law in Britain during the early 1890s; both were brilliant political strategists. Both were equally *slim*, meaning wily, to use an adjective commonly applied to Smuts by his Afrikaner compatriots. Smuts began by jailing Gandhi but ended up reluctantly respecting him. When Gandhi left for India in 1914 Smuts was glad to see the back of him.[26]

In South Africa Gandhi gave special support to indentured Indian labourers in conditions of near-slavery. He developed *satyagraha* (truth-force), a mixture of peaceful demonstrations and symbolic non-violent infringements of unjust laws. Gandhi publically burnt his registration card in 1908.[27] In 1952, Mandela burnt his own passbook, defiantly protesting Gandhi-style against *apartheid* in a blaze of newspaper publicity. He had joined the ANC eight years before. Elieke Boehmer likens Mandela to Gandhi in respect of their 'supremely Victorian quality of self-mastery and operation within the rule of law which they derived from the British colonial education they shared'.[28] Mandela joined the ANC when he realized his life goal of becoming a top barrister was being denied to him on racial ground.[29] By 1951 he was president of the ANC's National Youth League.

What kind of man had Mandela become by the 1950s? As an infant he lived in his mother's *kraal* in Mveso near Qunu in the Transkei (Eastern Cape). This region stretched from the east coast to the Drakensberg mountains in the West, near Lesotho. In the village of Mveso Mandela imbibed Methodist principles brought to Africa by European missionaries. His mother was Nonqaphi Nosekeni (?–1980), one of her husband's four wives. She was a devout woman who established the Methodist church in her village.[30] Mandela comes from the Xhosa people. Two of its leading branches are the Thembu and Pondo tribes. Mandela's father, Gadla Henry Mandela (1880–1930), was a chief born to a younger son of the Thembu royal family.

In the mid 1920s Gadla Henry dared to challenge an English colonial magistrate in a local dispute. In return, the magistrate sacked him from his administrative duties and fined him heavily. Mandela's father was ruined and died not long afterwards.[31] Young Mandela's uncle was the Thembu Regent, guardian of the current king, also still a youth. The Regent adopted Mandela and took him into the royal household at the Great Place, just outside the Transkei's capital, Umtata. Nelson Mandela was trained as a royal counsellor, spending his early years herding goats and sheep, learning respect for tribal customs and beliefs, and attending council meetings to gain experience. Eventually he underwent ritual circumcision along with the rest of his age cohort. Mandela had an excellent secondary education, and subsequently went to the University of Fort Hare in the Eastern Cape, where he encountered Smuts. At this time Mandela had his eye on a career as an interpreter in the courts run by the minister of native affairs. He took courses in history, English, social anthropology, Roman law and native law.[32]

After a year Mandela was expelled from Fort Hare. He had resigned from the student representative council along with others, protesting against the poor quality of the food. Mandela refused to resume his council post when the university told him to do so. When Mandela got back to the Great Place in 1941 he learned that the Regent was arranging a bride for him and had similar plans for his own son, Justice. In response, Mandela and Justice absconded from the Great Place and made their way to Johannesburg. Justice soon went back home. Mandela did not.

This episode was an early example of Mandela's willingness to break out, where possible, from any situation where his control and autonomy were seriously threatened. In the big city Mandela, good looking and confident, came into contact with highly sophisticated Africans and white Europeans from many backgrounds. They included radical cosmopolitan intellectuals such as Joe Slovo (1926–95) and Ruth First (1949–82), both committed communists. Mandela established a law practice in partnership with Oliver Tambo (1917–93). They mainly served poor African clients from the city, often without fee. By the mid-1940s, Mandela was part of the ANC's 'Xhosa Nostra,' along with Tambo and Walter Sisulu (1912–2003), both from the Transkei.

Mandela's mother was surely pleased when in 1944 her son Nelson married a deeply religious woman. Evelyn Mase was a nurse, and a cousin of Walter Sisulu. The marriage lasted thirteen years. Between 1943 and 1949 Mandela was enrolled at Witwatersrand Law School studying for an LLB degree. After repeating the final year twice he was denied his degree.[33] By that time the couple had two children and they went on to have two more. However, they drifted apart as Mandela moved increasingly into political work while Evelyn became a strongly committed Jehovah's Witness. The couple divorced in 1957.

In 1958 Mandela married a social worker, Winnie Madikizela, now better known as Winnie Mandela. It was, so to speak, a royal marriage. Winnie's father was Columbus Madikizela, counsellor to the king of East Pondoland in the Transkei. He held a position in the royal hierarchy roughly similar to Nelson Mandela's late father. Mandela's first marriage with Evelyn drew him further into the Christian circles his mother inhabited. His second marriage with Winnie reinforced his traditional tribal identity. The couple's joint network meant Mandela was on close terms with leading authority figures throughout the Transkei's traditional elite. He remained an active participant within this power structure throughout his life.[34]

Mandela led a dual existence. He was a highly respected and resourceful practitioner in law courts and tribunals, often protecting poor black African men and women against government officials or employers. On one occasion Mandela defended a domestic servant who faced the charge of purloining clothes when doing the laundry. In court Mandela walked over to the evidence on display. He lifted up a pair of knickers on the tip of his pencil, turned, and asked the white employer, standing in the witness box, 'Madam, are these yours?' The lady was far too embarrassed to reply. The magistrate dismissed the case.

Mandela's gained great respect among professional colleagues, including Afrikaner lawyers drawn into legal actions directed against Mandela himself because of his other life as a leading ANC activist.[35] Mandela was prominent in the defiance campaign and the movement for the ANC's Freedom Charter. He spoke at mass protests against forced resettlement of African families from residential areas such as Sophiatown. He took part in demonstrations against the Sharpeville massacre (1960) when police shot live ammunition into a huge crowd demanding an end to the pass laws. Like many others, he was soon placed under banning orders to prevent him from attending political meetings and gatherings.

In 1955 he and other ANC leaders went on trial for treason, but they were finally acquitted in 1961. In 1962 Mandela was back on trial again and came into court wearing a Thembu tribal costume smuggled into his cell.[36] He then went underground for some months to build up the expertise and organization required to prepare for violent resistance against the regime. At this time Mandela was delving into Marxist literature and revolutionary writings. He added these influences to the mix he had already imbibed: Christian principles, Gandhian techniques and tribal tradition. The ANC and the South African Communist Party (SACP) worked very closely together. Mandela was in the room when the SACP decided to create the organization known as *Umkhonto we Sizwe*, otherwise Spear of the Nation or, more simply, MK. He later played a leading part in persuading the ANC to make that policy its own. Mandela became a symbol of the struggle against *apartheid*, and was labelled 'the Black Pimpernel' by the press.[37]

At the Rivonia trial in 1964, when Mandela made his celebrated speech from the dock, the ANC leadership avoided death but faced considerable disorganization and demoralization. Some ANC leaders were driven beyond the country's borders, others into its jails, notably on Robben Island. Oliver Tambo led the ANC in exile from his house in North London at Haringey. Throughout the 1970s and 1980s, ANC fighters struck at police, military and industrial facilities and personnel in South Africa while the South African military attacked ANC bases in neighbouring Swaziland, Lesotho, Botswana and Mozambique. The United States and Britain treated the ANC as a terrorist organization. Meanwhile, the USSR and its ally Cuba gave it support. Boycotts were organized against companies investing in South Africa, and South African sports teams playing abroad. The United Democratic Front founded in 1983 with strong trade union backing kept many townships in a restless condition.

Throughout the 1980s the 'free Nelson Mandela' campaign grew in volume. By that time Govan Mbeki's son Thabo, a graduate of Sussex University, was coordinating the ANC's communications with foreign governments and the international press. He left South Africa in 1962 and spent nearly three decades abroad. By the late 1970s he was Oliver Tambo's political secretary, high up in the SACP, and served on the ANC's Revolutionary Council alongside Chris Hani. In 1986 Thabo Mbeki survived an assassination attempt organized by the South African regime. The following year he was engaged in secret peace talks with the same regime in Britain and Switzerland.[38]

Meanwhile on Robben Island Thabo's father, Govan Mbeki, along with Nelson Mandela and other ANC leaders, were housed in individual cells. The nastiness from Afrikaner warders ranged from mocking disrespect to utter cruelty. The rank and file, crowded into shared cells, became frequent victims of brutality from prison staff. Everyone came together during work periods, often breaking stones in the prison quarry, a regular assignment.[39] Mandela kept up an intense regime of physical exercise in his cell. He had some solitary confinement, and got beaten on occasion, but does not report being tortured. He had moments of particular distress: a son from his first marriage died; and for over a year Winnie was in jail where she suffered serious physical abuse.[40]

Conditions gradually improved. From the early 1970s news from the outside world arrived more frequently. The prisoners heard about the MK's exploits, and student protests in the townships. After the Soweto shootings in 1976 a new wave of prisoners arrived, some imbued with the philosophy of the Black Consciousness movement. By the mid-1970s, the political prisoners on Robben Island had a lighter work regime and more free time for association. They also had their own internal organization. Govan Mbeki developed an education programme, including historical aspects of the struggle against *apartheid*. There was scope for sport, music and the production of plays.

A key institution was the High Organ where matters of policy and discipline were thrashed out and disputes settled. Mandela became the High Organ's chair and spokesperson for the ANC prisoners. His main rival was Govan Mbeki, like Mandela a tall and commanding figure, also the son of a chief. Mbeki was more deeply committed than Mandela to a Marxist perspective. Govan Mbeki's frequent dissent during these years gave Mandela valuable experience of negotiating conflict in situations where it was difficult to walk away. So did dealing with conflict between prisoners and Afrikaner warders.

These situations gave Mandela training for handling other difficult confrontations still to come: between the ANC and other insurgent organizations, especially Pan-Africanists and adherents of Black Consciousness; and, eventually, between the ANC and the government. Prison had three other advantages for Mandela. It kept him alive, less likely to be the object of assassination attempts. It meant he was not implicated in the increasingly vicious and violent war waged outside the prison walls between the ANC and the *apartheid* regime. Finally, it allowed a certain magic and mystery to accumulate around his name.[41]

Unlike the most committed members of the South African Communist Party within the ANC, Mandela did not treat his support for the party as an allegiance that crowded out other commitments. Compare Govan Mbeki who once declared that Thabo was 'no longer my son. He is my comrade!' When father and son were reunited in Lusaka after nearly three decades of separation, they exchanged a formal handshake before Thabo went off to his next political meeting.[42] By then Thabo Mbeki, Jacob Zuma and others were evidently jockeying for position, fighting for primacy within the SACP and ANC, rather like siblings fighting over an inheritance. Mandela's own political capital and emotional involvements were both heavily invested in his kinship relations as well as an extensive friendship network which went far beyond ANC and SACP circles. In fact, family business and politics were closely intertwined because Mandela's kinship links included a wide network of interlocking high-status dynasties that wielded traditional authority in the Transkei.

Nelson Mandela's nephew, Kaiser Matanzima, threw his lot in with the central government's policy of separate development. In 1976 Transkei was designated as South Africa's first supposedly independent Bantustan. When Matanzima was made the Transkei's president under this new dispensation he decided to challenge the primacy of the Great Place, Mandela's early home. In 1980 he finally forced the Thembu king to abandon the Transkei and go into exile. But Matanzima soon met his own downfall. In 1986 he was, in his turn finally forced out of office, accused of corruption. For his part, Mandela opposed Matanzima's political stance for decades but still treated him as a family member. In the Transkei politics and ideology frequently cut across family ties. Likewise, family ties might help to ease the severity of conflicts.[43]

Kinship connections brought both assets and liabilities. Mandela's second and longest-lasting marriage, to Winnie Madikizela-Mandela, united both political and familial concerns since she was not just an ANC activist but also a well-born daughter within the traditional authority structure of Pondoland. Winnie was eighteen years younger than her husband. When they married he was forty, she was twenty-two. During their many years of separation she became her own woman, taking her own decisions. As is well known, she was a political force in her own right, operating in gang-ridden townships where violence and criminality were common currency. Her press coverage often brought her into dreadful disrepute but her husband remained loyal. They finally separated two years after his release, and divorced in 1996. The marriage had lasted thirty-eight years.[44]

Mandela's kinship links sustained his sense of identity and stimulated his sense of honour and duty. For over a quarter of a century his family life was conducted through occasional letters, strictly rationed visits, and the workings of his imagination. Some letters between Nelson Mandela, Winnie Mandela and others have been published, for example from 1969–70 when the security police detained Winnie under extremely unpleasant conditions for nearly five hundred days.[45] In these letters Mandela made frequent requests for detailed information about a long list of relatives, especially his wife and children but also uncles, aunts, cousins and in-laws. He wanted to know about births, marriages and deaths, health and illness, successes to be praised and failures to be salved with commiseration. His letters are full of traditional images and tales, intermingled with Christian sentiments. He shifts between a rather paternalistic style and bursts of raw affection and longing. The letters between Nelson and Winnie are full of pride and strength on both sides. These attributes surely derived from the sense of responsibility and autonomy cultivated in the high status families to which they belonged. It gave both of them an air of impunity, which others often found strangely bewitching, deeply exasperating, or both.

After apartheid

Apartheid was not overthrown. It softened, and then it crumbled. Colin Bundy points out that some of *apartheid*'s worst excesses were alleviated long before 1994. After the Sharpeville massacre in 1960 many whites left the country taking their skills with them. Between 1970 and 1987 the number of Africans in middle-class occupations grew from about 220,000 to about 600,000; a rate of increase of over 6 per cent annually. Meanwhile, the value of pensions also rose for the majority. In 1966 African pensions were on average worth only 13 per cent of those paid to whites but by 1980 that proportion had increased to 30 per cent, and to 100 per cent by 1993.

During the three and a half decades to 1996, the African population, better educated and more discontented than before, grew from about two-thirds of the national total to about three-quarters. Their discontent was expressed not just through ANC sabotage but also by trade union strikes and campaigns run by the United Democratic Front. The National Party split in 1982. Political crisis was followed by economic crisis in the late 1980s. International business began to withdraw capital and political support from the government. After 1989 the support given to the ANC from the Soviet Union and Cuba declined and then stopped altogether.[46]

Mandela came out of Robben Island in 1982 and moved to Pollsmoor prison on the mainland. A few months later, he began negotiating with the regime without consulting his ANC colleagues. Mandela slipped free of the regulating bonds of Robben Island's High Organ just as, four decades before, he had escaped from the grasp of the Great Place to avoid being forced into marriage. In both cases, in 1982 as in 1941, Mandela was able to do two things. Make a major change in his personal circumstances and then negotiate himself into a good working relationship not only with the new associates he acquired but also his old colleagues and supposed masters. The negotiations that began in 1982 ended with the jailed ANC leadership freed in 1990 and the *apartheid* regime dismantled during the early 1990s. In 1994 a coalition government of national unity was elected and Mandela became the national president.

Mandela soon made another escape. He found the duties required of South Africa's national president too burdensome and restrictive. After several months in office he slipped free of its most irksome constraints, and left his colleague Thabo Mbeki, South Africa's executive deputy president, to take them up on his behalf. When new elections came round in 1999 the African National Congress was securely established as the governing party of South Africa and Nelson Mandela was a global hero.

We need to remind ourselves how huge a triumph this was. As late as 1987 British prime minister, Margaret Thatcher, declared that the ANC was a 'typical terrorist organization' and she would have 'nothing to do with any organisation that practises violence'. But nine years later, President Mandela and Lady Thatcher had a twenty-minute chat at Buckingham Palace during his state visit to the United Kingdom.[47] Even so, Mandela remained on the US terror watch until 2008, when he reached the age of ninety.[48]

Mandela's contribution during the 1990s was crucial. Who else could have achieved the transition from *apartheid* with so little overt confrontation and disruption? It became possible because Mandela was sufficiently trusted by people in three key political locations: amongst the ANC leadership, in the African townships, and within the Afrikaner establishment. Three events illustrate this. In 1991 Mandela made a speech at Katlehong, just east of Johannesburg. It was a centre of intense conflict between Xhosa supporters of the ANC, and their rivals in the Inkatha Freedom Party, supported by many Zulu migrant workers. The audience demanded "'Give us weapons. No peace'". Mandela told them: 'If you are going to kill innocent people, you don't belong to the ANC. Your task is reconciliation.' When the audience protested, he added: 'Listen to me. Listen to me. I am your leader. I am going to give you leadership. Do you want me to remain your leader? Yes? Well, as long as I am your leader, I will tell you, always, when you are wrong'.[49] He won applause.

Two years later, Chris Hani (1942–93), leader of the ANC armed struggle, was assassinated. Crowd attacks on white communities seemed likely. Mandela went on television. He pointed out that an Afrikaner lady, a senior citizen, had been alert enough to take the number of the vehicle driven by Hani's suspected assassin. This act of inter-racial solidarity helped the police capture the suspect. Mandela's authority was invaluable in maintaining calm at this critical point.[50] Equally striking, in 1995 Mandela attended the Rugby Union World Cup as national president. This event was being held in South Africa for the first time. It was impressive to see Mandela, wearing a South African rugby shirt and a broad smile, present the trophy to the Afrikaner captain of the winning team. It was a highly symbolic occasion.[51]

It is tempting to recall young Jean Améry in traditional Alpine gear, with white knee socks and *lederhosen*. This was the Austrian equivalent, perhaps, of the South African white farmer with his shorts and long socks, supplemented by a rugby shirt or other regalia on match days. When Améry was freed from incarceration he was not inclined to get back into *lederhosen*. Instead he lived outside Austria or Germany, became an adherent of French existentialism, and changed his name.

What is the difference between Améry in 1945 and Mandela in 1995? To oversimplify: as an anti-Nazi, Améry was on the winning side; the Nazi regime was blasted to smithereens by Allied firepower; the creation of Israel soon gave Jews a state; and American military might ensured that parliamentary democracy prevailed in Western Europe. In other words, Améry had many places outside Austria and Germany where he could live in relative freedom without having to negotiate a *modus vivendi* with those who had oppressed him. By contrast, neither *apartheid* nor the ANC were defeated. Survivors on the warring sides had to find ways of living together. That was why Mandela put on his rugby shirt with such impeccable and irresistible charm. That was also the background to the Truth and Reconciliation Commission (1996–8), strongly promoted by Desmond Tutu (born 1931), who became its chair after he retired as Archbishop of Cape Town in 1996.

The Commission's rationale was that telling the truth from all sides about past violations and suffering would help those involved to understand their divisions. It would let perpetrators come to terms with what they have done and give victims back their dignity.[52] The Commission would be restorative since it: '(1) invites victims to tell their story in an open and receptive environment, (2) reveals a comprehensive truth of what transpired, and (3) promotes reconciliation between perpetrators and victims'.[53]

Thomas Brudholm shows that Desmond Tutu was unwilling to treat resentment by victims as 'a legitimate moral sentiment on any level',[54] since, in his view, it was closely related to a destructive desire for revenge. Victims should forgive those who had damaged them when they confessed their involvement and sought amnesty. If victims could not feel forgiveness they needed help to overcome their anger.[55]

But Améry, the Auschwitz survivor, argued that expressing resentment was essential. It kept the guilty ones aware of their responsibility. Neither hurt nor responsibility (or blame) could be wiped away. Resentment could only be alleviated when perpetrators and victims both sincerely recognized that something morally outrageous had occurred during their past encounters. Victims and perpetrators could only become truly reconciled with each other by accepting that neither could be reconciled with a past that troubled them both.[56]

Mahmood Mamdani deepens the Nazi/*apartheid* comparison still further.[57] He contrasts the Nuremberg trials (1945–6) at the end of World War II with both South Africa's Convention for a Democratic South Africa (CODESA), which met between 1990 and 1994, and with the Truth and Reconciliation Commission (1996–8). The Nuremberg trials were victims' justice administered by the victors. The court tried prominent individuals from the losing side on criminal charges. By contrast, CODESA in South Africa was settling accounts at the end of a prolonged conflict with no clear victors or losers. The issues to be decided concerned major interest groups, not specific individuals. The objective was not criminal justice but political reform.

CODESA was about survivors' justice. The idea was to enable people who all carried bruises as well as guilt to live together. Many people on both sides had narratives of suffering to impart as well as faults they wanted to forget.

CODESA's final deal was the outcome of a trial of strength fought out over the negotiating table, in the media and on the streets. In the end a complex compromise was reached involving: amnesty, power sharing and majority rule; dismantling the juridical and political apparatus of *apartheid*; maintaining much of the existing bureaucratic structure of government; giving monitoring powers to the Constitutional Court; and enacting a Bill of Rights that protected private property.

Two political factors protected the interests of the existing white hierarchy. The prestigious ANC exiles, charismatic returnees seeking top government positions, acquired greater influence with central government than the coalition of forces in the United Democratic Federation (UDF). Ironically, while the returnees got lucrative positions the hardened resisters who had stayed in South Africa, unable or unwilling to escape, were denied many of the root and branch reforms, expensive to implement, they had been demanding for years during their long fight for social justice in the townships. Meanwhile, in rural areas longstanding informal understandings between white settlers and the established traditional African leadership kept the balance of power weighted against workers keen to see more radical change.

This was the political context in which the Truth and Reconciliation Commission came into existence. Its focus was very narrow. The Commission respected legislation made under *apartheid*, including enactments giving law enforcement agents immunity from prosecution. This took several atrocities off the Commission's agenda. It did not consider abuses imposed upon whole groups such as those suffering forced removals from their homes. It confined its attentions to individual victims subject to acts with political motivations that infringed the law as it stood at the time. The Commission did not take account of Africans forcibly kept on farms as a virtual slave labour force, or victims of torture held in detention without trial.

Most attention was given to events since 1990 involving the violent black-on-black struggle within the ranks of those opposing the *apartheid* regime. White South Africans heard continual television reports from the Commission about ugly violence between Black South Africans in the townships. They could easily conclude that the proceedings had nothing to do with them. Mamdani regrets that the Commission ignored the chance to educate the comfortable white minority that had benefited so much from the oppression of Black South Africans. This sounds very similar to Améry's complaint about the self-satisfied ignorance he encountered amongst the German population after the war.

The ANC did not get the outright military victory and free political hand it wanted. But only the ANC had sufficient clout in the townships to deliver the relatively stable political environment business needed in the wake of *apartheid*'s failure. The ANC, in alliance with Congress of South African Trade Unions (COSATU) and the South African Communist Party (SACP), took on the task of improving the social rights of the deprived majority. At the same time this triple alliance was under intense pressure from global investors to keep government small and taxes low. The conflict of objectives is obvious: substantial social rights (education, health, welfare, social care and so on) versus business-friendly low taxes. Which would come first? Who would benefit most?

Big business acquiesced when in 2003 the ANC introduced Black Economic Empowerment (BEE) intended to favour Black African entrepreneurs. This legislation enormously benefited the new power elite that controlled the triple alliance: ANC, COSATU and SACP. These cadres and their networks were able to establish new businesses, gain lucrative contracts and build vast fortunes. Durban, the major centre of Indian business in South Africa, rose to even greater wealth and prominence. Jacob Zuma's close relationship with the Gupta family became notorious.[58] In 2006 5,580 new dollar millionaires were produced in a single year.[59] By then over a quarter of a million Africans were classified as 'upper class', compared to less than twenty thousand in 1993. Trading organizations set up through the ANC such as the Chancellor House Trust became involved, sometimes controversially, in a wide range of businesses, including mining.[60]

Big business had a very powerful position in South Africa in collaboration with the triple alliance. Whenever this composite establishment was seriously challenged a harsh response was likely. The stun grenades used by the police at Ginsberg in May 2015 were at the lower end of the scale. At the top end of the scale was an event that occurred three months later during a highly contentious unofficial strike over low wages and poor working conditions at a platinum mine near Marikana west of Pretoria. After several shooting incidents involving police and mutually opposed trade union groups, South African security forces conducted a major attack with assault rifles that ended with the death of thirty-four strikers and injury to seventy-eight others. The Marikana massacre was reputedly the most lethal police action since Sharpeville in 1960. Both massacres were carried out in defence of business and political regimes that many inhabitants of the townships regarded as repressive and exploitative. In 1960 the police were acting on behalf of the white minority government. In 2012 they were representing a state governed by the ANC.

Basic services such as piped water, electricity and sanitation improved but half the population, especially in the African townships, remained impoverished, mainly because of the very high unemployment rate. Meanwhile corruption and factionalism reigned in the rainbow nation's townships. Measured against the standards set by Mandela this seems an almighty fall. How can it be explained?

R.W. Johnson insightfully argues that one important source of the ANC's cronyism and greed as a governing party is its leaders' enormous sense of disappointment after the initial celebrations of the early 1990s. As the new ANC government shaped its economic and social policies it found that powerful global corporations set strict limits on what the new regime could do. Profits, stability and, by implication, the prevailing inequality, had to be maintained. The ANC's success had failed to deliver the socialist utopia its leaders had long expected to achieve by their hard struggle. Overwhelming forces were destroying their dreams. They needed some kind of material compensation to salve their wounds, protect their honour, and signal their greatness. The roots of cronyism and corruption lie there. The ANC politicians who took over power following *apartheid*'s downfall exhibited 'a badly wounded black persona, full of complexes and grievances'. They were plagued with 'ghosts of inferiority' The ANC's struggle to cope with its painful disillusionment had been 'working itself out in grandiloquent style since then'.[61]

R.W. Johnson argues that this situation had a major historical precedent when the Great Trek failed to deliver the isolated and independent rural idyll the Boer pioneers dreamed of achieving. This was an earlier case of a hoped-for utopia denied, snatched away when the British brutally muscled their way into the gold and diamond mining industries and forced Transvaal and the Orange Free State into their Union of South Africa. Later, British soldiers ruthlessly terrorized Afrikaner communities during the Boer War of 1899–1902. *Apartheid* was a response to the Boers' massive disillusionment. It was a way of putting right history's failure to follow the proper script, a means of ensuring that Afrikaners could be guaranteed the lion's share of the fruits produced by the land God had supposedly meant them to have. To put it another way, instead of digging their reward out of the soil on their rural homesteads, they decided to dig it out of the lives and bodies of Black Africans consigned to virtual servitude.[62]

Let us take this historical comparison one step further by comparing the careers of Jan Christian Smuts and Nelson Mandela. Neither man was able to prevent the traumas experienced by their political colleagues. However, both were able to create individual pathways for themselves that got them where they wanted to be when the odds seemed to be against them. As a royal counsellor Mandela could easily have won a kingly position for himself within a Bantustan if he had cooperated with the *apartheid* regime. However, Mandela aspired to a distinguished position at the top of South African national life. The Afrikaner rulers of the country wished to exclude Africans from such heights of influence, reserving them for whites. Likewise, the British rulers of South Africa in the late nineteenth century were determined to subordinate the Afrikaners, excluding them as a political interest from the levers of power within national government. Their plan, so it seemed, was to bottle them up in their provincial redoubts of the Orange Free State and the Transvaal. Not Bantustans exactly but certainly confining, politically speaking.

For his part, Mandela was determined to break out of his socio-political confinement, perhaps not realizing quite how long it would take. Smuts, who belonged to Transvaal's political and military elite, also wanted much more. As we have seen, Smuts was a daring and brilliant general fighting on the Afrikaner side in the Boer war. With equal daring, after the war he moved very close to the British interest and broke into their ranks not just in South

Africa but also within the wider Empire. Smuts, ambitious and looking for an upward route, was prepared to embrace a radical change of direction: making himself acceptable and well known to the British imperial masters, buying into, and sometimes shaping, their strategies, and seizing leadership roles when opportunities arose. Smuts accepted the political costs that accompanied these actions, including the mistrust of many Afrikaners.

Mandela, also ambitious, also looking for an upward route, was likewise prepared to make radical changes of direction. He distanced himself from the religious activities of his first wife. He discarded his initial intention to make a professional career in conformity with the requirements of a racially segregated society. He reinforced his traditional African identity through his second marriage to Winnie Madikizela, well placed in the Pondo status hierarchy. He got very close to the ANC, bought into, and partly shaped, their strategies, and seized leadership roles when opportunities arose.

It would be wrong to think these shifts by Mandela were part of some coldly calculated strategy. Better to recognize that through such moves Mandela acquired an increasingly complex mixture of convictions and commitments. He sometimes rebalanced his loyalties and attachments but he never abandoned any of them. His adherence was, it seems, in each case patently strong and sincere: to Christian moral standards, to revolutionary ideals, to his political colleagues, to traditional African hierarchies and values, to British 'reasonableness', to the rule of law, to human rights, to the South African nation, and to his various families. Three constants were his refusal to be put down or humiliated, his skill at maintaining his bond with the townships, and his determination to occupy the highest leadership position possible.

Mandela made another daring move by negotiating with the *apartheid* regime on his own initiative, accepting the risks this carried in terms of his ANC colleagues' trust. Like Smuts, Mandela became a very confident performer on both the national and world stage, and was prepared to make new alliances at every step of his way. Like Smuts he was a big winner and, like him, he died a hero and a world statesman.

Statues in a square

One way of summing up Mandela's achievements and putting them in context may be found in the midst of the collection of statues in London's Parliament Square. Eleven figures stand there and four of them have played a part in South Africa's history. That includes Winston Churchill. He went out to South Africa in 1899 as a journalist to report on the Boer War and was feted as a war hero for his gallant exploits that he reported in various books and articles. Later, Churchill played a part in settling the Transvaal constitution in 1907. However, three other people represented in this community of statues have much deeper and longer-lasting South African connections.

One of them is Jan Christian Smuts who brought the British and Afrikaner establishments into closer cooperation, although he did not envisage ever allowing Africans or Indians into the upper ranks of society and government. Another is Mohandas Gandhi, the Mahatma or 'Great Soul', who spent two decades cultivating bravery and ambition amongst the downtrodden Indian population in Natal. His followers taught the early leaders of the ANC the virtues of universal human fellowship and generosity, and the positive value of poverty. For Gandhi a cardinal principle was that getting politically powerful was not about personal enrichment. The third is Nelson Mandela whose charisma, courage and direct human appeal enthused the impoverished majority but also reassured the rich minority. He told the poor they deserved more and told the rich they would not be brutally dispossessed. The abolition of both poverty and violence were his most pressing priorities. None of these three visions has come to pass.

However, advances have been made on two fronts: creating pragmatic bonds of cooperation between different national elites; and making some measurable headway against poverty. Successful and well connected Africans, Indians and Afrikaners now jointly hold wealth and power in South Africa, along with the agents of international business, including Americans, Europeans and Asians, especially South Koreans.

In 2012 Martin Plaut and Paul Holden argued that 'South Africa remains what it has been since 1948: a one-party state, with democratic trimmings'.[63] However, as Plaut and Holden also showed, by 2012 the ANC was gradually losing its unchallenged grip on power. The Democratic Alliance in the Western Cape was a vocal rival. Meanwhile, the government tried to tighten controls over its critics but it faced opposition from the judiciary, most of the media, civil society, and the trade unions.[64] By 2016 Martin Plaut was writing that in South Africa 'the era of one-party rule is over'.[65]

In December 2017 Jacob Zuma ceased to be president of the ANC. His successor was Cyril Ramaphosa, born 1952, who became President of South Africa when Zuma was forced to leave office in February 2018. Ramaphosa founded South Africa's National Union of Mineworkers in 1982 and later became one of the richest men in the country. Ramaphosa is well networked internationally. What improvements will Ramaphosa make in the lives of ordinary citizens?

At least half of the South African population still lives in conditions of endemic poverty and violence even though *apartheid* has been abolished for over two decades. Some Black South Africans born in poverty have clearly benefited, especially those who, like President Ramaphosa, were able to exploit the opportunities provided by the Black Economic Employment programme. Most have not been able to do so. In the words of Colin Bundy, 'Wealth in South Africa has been partly deracialised. Poverty remains strongly racialised'.[66]

Notes

1. To see the political distance travelled between the 1940s and the 1980s, compare the biography of Malan by Lindie Koorts (Koorts 2014) with the autobiography of De Klerk (De Klerk 1999).
2. Arendt 1973; Strobl 2000.
3. Quoted in Welsh 2015, 194.
4. Barnard 2014; Boehmer 2008; Bundy 2015; Carlin 2008; Carlin 2013; Gibbs 2014; Lodge 2006; Mandela 2002; Mandela 2003a; Mandela 2003b; Meredith 1997; Sampson 2000; Smith 2010.
5. 'Boos, jeers humiliate South Africa's Zuma at Mandela memorial', 10th December 2015, *Reuters*, at http://uk.reuters.com/article/uk-mandela-zuma-idUKBRE9B90H G20131210 (accessed 16th August 2016); 'Some snooze during Zuma speech', 14th December 2013, *IOL* at http://www.iol.co.za/news/south-africa/gauteng/some-snooze-during-zuma-speech-1622506 (accessed 16th August 2016).
6. Smith 2006, 76.
7. Leibbrandt et al. 2014.
8. 'Mayor, deputy hand themselves in over Mandela scandal', 23rd June 2014, *DispatchLIVE* at http://www.dispatchlive.co.za/news/breaking-mayor-deputy-hand-themselves-in-over-mandela-scandal/ (accessed on 12th August 2016); also 'Mandela funeral-scandal accused re-elected in the ANC', 15th November 2015, *News 24* at http://www.news24.com/SouthAfrica/News/mandela-funeral-scandal-accused-re-elected-in-the-anc-20151115 (accessed on 12th August 2016).
9. 'Criminals are tarnishing Ginsberg's proud name', 13th May 2015, *Dispatch Live*, http://www.dispatchlive.co.za/opinion/criminals-are-tarnishing-ginsbergs-proud-name/ (accessed 16th August 2016). 'Ginsberg residents threaten to burn the township', 11th August 2015, *Sowetan Live*, http://www.sowetanlive.co.za/news/2015/08/11/ginsberg-residents-threaten-to-burn-the-township (accessed 16th August 2016).
10. 'Jacob Zuma "should" face 783 criminal charges, declares South African court', 29th April 2016, *The Telegraph* at http://www.telegraph.co.uk/news/2016/04/29/south-african-court-clears-way-for-jacob-zuma-to-face-783-crimin/ (accessed 14th August 2016).
11. Booysen 2016.
12. 'South Africa "two-thirds urbanized"', 24th January 2013, *South Africa.info*, at http://www.southafrica.info/news/urbanisation-240113.htm#.Vtg3tFIukfE%23ixzz41qSoFxWA (accessed 14th August 2016). See also Adedeji, Teriba and Bugembe 1991; Leibbrandt et al. 2014; Welsh 2009.
13. Carlson 1977, 107.
14. Carlson 1977, 81–122.
15. Pakenham 1992; Meredith 2008; Filatova and Davidson 2013.
16. Bundy 2012; Mbeki 1991; Mbeki 1992; Gevisser 2009.
17. Quoted by Paul Trewhela in his obituary of Gowan Mbeki, 30th August 2001, *The Independent*, at http://www.independent.co.uk/news/obituaries/govan-mbeki-9263420.html (accessed 10th August 2016).
18. Hancock 1962; Hancock 1968; Steyn 2015.
19. Kipling 1937, 191.
20. Darwin 2011, 217–54; Giliomee 2012; Marsh 1994; Meredith 2008; Ross 2008; Thompson and Berat 2014; Welsh 2000; Welsh 2009; O'Brien 1979; Nimocks 1968; Pakenham 1992; Pogrund 2000; Rotberg 1988; Smith 2013.
21. Stanley 2016; also *the Olive Schreiner Letters Project* at http://www.oliveschreinerletters.ed.ac.uk (accessed 19th August 2016); Schreiner and Cronwright-Schreiner 1896 at https://archive.org/details/politicalsituat00crongoog (accessed 19th August 2016).

22 Steyn 2015, 107.
23 Mandela 2002, 70–2.
24 Carlson 1977, 3–13. See also Beinart and Bundy 1987; Mbeki 1964; Mbeki 1992; Van der Merwe 2009; Van Rensburg 1962.
25 Mbeki 1991, 16–63; Mbeki 1992.
26 Baxter 2017; Fischer 2015.
27 Hancock 1962, 321–47; Steyn 2015, 61–4; Guha 2013; Gandhi 2012, 103–314.
28 Boehmer 2008, 103.
29 Mandela 2002, 53.
30 'Nelson Mandela's mother honoured with church restoration. Church founded by Noqaphi Nosekeni in family's home village in 1960s rescued by local community after lying in ruins', 15th November 2011, *The Guardian* at http://www.theguardian.com/world/2011/nov/15/nelson-mandela-mother-church-restoration (accessed 19th August 2016).
31 Smith 2010, 14–26; Mandela 2002, 4–9.
32 Sitze 2014, 136–9.
33 Sitze 2014, 140–4; Murray 2016.
34 Gibbs 2014, e.g. 51–3, 67–8; Mbeki 1964.
35 Mandela 2002, 217, 232–3.
36 Mandela 2002, 469.
37 Mandela 2002, 381–482. On the Rivonia trial see Brown 2012; Joffe 2004.
38 Gevisser 2009; Maharaj 2008.
39 Buntman 2003; Coetzee 2000; Dlamini 1984; Coetzee, Gilfillan and Hulec 2004; Kathadra 2011.
40 Madikizela-Mandela 2013.
41 http://www.aamarchives.org/campaigns/free-mandela.html (accessed 19th August 2016).
42 Gumede 2007, 37–9; quotation on page 37.
43 Mandela 2002, 262–4, 333–4; Gibbs 2014, 29–30, 124–5.
44 Gilbey 1994; Bridgland 1997.
45 Madikizela-Mandela 2013.
46 Bundy 2014; Filatova and Davidson 2013; Maharaj 2008.
47 'Margaret Thatcher branded ANC 'terrorist' while urging Nelson Mandela's release', 9th December 2013, *Independent* at http://www.independent.co.uk/news/uk/politics/margaret-thatcher-branded-anc-terrorist-while-urging-nelson-mandelas-release-8994191.html; 'Mandela Ends Triumphant Visit to Britain', 13th July 1996, *New York Times* at http://www.nytimes.com/1996/07/13/world/mandela-ends-triumphant-visit-to-britain.html (both accessed 11th April 2017)
48 'Mandela taken off terror watch list', 1st July 2008, *BBC News,* at http://news.bbc.co.uk/1/hi/world/americas/7484517.stm; 'Nelson Mandela's long history of support for Palestine', January 30th 2014, *Middle East Monitor,* at https://www.middleeastmonitor.com/20140130-nelson-mandelas-long-history-of-support-for-palestine/ (both accessed 11th April 2017).
49 Lodge 2006, 179–80.
50 Lodge 2006, 180–1.
51 Carlin 2008.
52 http://www.sahistory.org.za/archive/trc-final-report-volume-1 (accessed 19th March 2017).
53 Aldana 2006, 108.
54 Brudholm 2008, 47.
55 Brudholm 2008, 35–61.
56 Brudholm 2008, 72–8, 85–102, 113–16, 124–5, 131; Grøn and Brudholm 2011; Asmal 1997; Sitze 2013.
57 Mamdani 2015.

58 For some recent development see, for example, 'British PR firm Bell Pottinger apologizes for South Africa campaign', *The Guardian*, 10th July 2017 at https://www.theguardian.com/uk-news/2017/jul/10/bell-pottinger-pr-firm-apologizes-south-africa-campaign; 'Deal that undid Bell Pottinger: inside story of the South Africa scandal', *The Guardian*, 5th September 2017 at https://www.theguardian.com/media/2017/sep/05/bell-pottingersouth-africa-pr-firm both (accessed 2nd October 2017).
59 Bundy 2014, 49; Russell 2009; 'South Africa: The power of the family business', 8th March 2016, *Financial Times* at https://www.ft.com/content/abd6e034-e519-11e5-a09b-1f8b0d268c39 (accessed 10th August 2017); Madonsela 2016; Swilling 2017.
60 'Chancellor House: R26m for nine years of lies by ANC partner', 29th September 2015, *Mail&Guardian* at https://mg.co.za/article/2015-09-29-chancellor-house-r266-million-for-9-years-of-lies-by-anc-partner (accessed 10th August 2017).
61 Johnson 2015b, 240.
62 R.W. Johnson (Johnson 2015a) came from South Africa to Magdalen College, Oxford, Wilde's old college, as a Rhodes scholar in 1964. He later became a Fellow, teaching Politics at Oxford for many years, and returned to South Africa in later life.
63 Plaut and Holden 2012, 347.
64 'Secrecy bill creeps closer', 5th October 2015, *City Press*, at http://city-press.news24.com/News/Secrecy-bill-creeps-closer-20150510 (accessed 27th March 2017); and 'The practical impact of the cyber bill on you', 1st March, 2017, Michalson blog, at https://www.michalsons.com/blog/the-practical-impact-of-the-cyber-bill-on-you/25300 (accessed 27th March 2017).
65 Martin Plaut, 'Welcome to South Africa's new political landscape. The era of one-party rule is over.' 23rd August 2016, *New Statesman* at http://www.newstatesman.com/world/2017/03/world-must-wake-dangers-orphanages.
66 Bundy 2014, 49.

Bibliography

Adedeji, A., Teriba, O., and Bugembe, P. (1991). *The Challenge of African Economic Recovery and Development*. London: Frank Cass.

Adonis, C.K. (2015). 'Generational Forgiveness and Historical Injustices: Perspectives of Descendants of Victims of Apartheid-era Gross Human Rights Violations in South Africa', *Journal of Psychology in Africa*, 25, 1, 6–14.

Aldana, R. (2006). 'A Victim-Centered Reflection on Truth Commissions and Prosecutions as a Response to Mass Atrocities', *Journal of Human Rights*, 5, 1, 107–126.

Arendt, H. (1973). *The Origins of Totalitarianism*. San Diego, CA: Harcourt Brace & Company; originally published in 1951.

Asmal, K. (1997). *Reconciliation Through Truth: A Reckoning of Apartheid's Criminal Governance*. Rochester NY: James Currey.

Baxter, P. (2017). *Gandhi, Smuts and Race in the British Empire. Of Passive and Violent Resistance*. Barnsley: Pen and Sword Books.

Barnard, R. (2014) (ed.) *The Cambridge Companion to Nelson Mandela*. Cambridge: Cambridge University Press.

Beinart, W. and Bundy, C. (1987). *Hidden Struggles in Rural South Africa*. London: James Currey.

Boehmer, E. (2008). *Nelson Mandela. A Very Short Introduction*. Oxford: Oxford University Press.

Booysen, S. (2016). *Dominance and Decline: The ANC in the Time of Zuma.* Johannesburg: Wits University Press.

Bridgland, F. (1997). *Katiza's Journey: Beneath the Surface of South Africa's Shame.* London: Sidgwick & Jackson.

Brown, S.B. (2012). *Saving Nelson Mandela. The Rivonia Trial and the Fate of South Africa.* Oxford: Oxford University Press.

Brudholm, T. (2008). *Resentment's Virtue. Jean Améry and the Refusal to Forgive.* Philadelphia, PA: Temple University Press.

Bundy, C. (2012). *Govan Mbeki.* Athens, OH: Ohio University Press.

Bundy, C. (2014). *Short-Changed? South Africa Since Apartheid.* Athens, OH: Ohio University Press.

Bundy, C. (2015). *Nelson Mandela.* Stroud: The History Press.

Buntman, F. L. (2003). *Robben Island and Prisoner Resistance to Apartheid.* Cambridge: Cambridge University Press.

Carlin, J. (2008). *Playing the Enemy. Nelson Mandela and the Game that Made a Nation.* London: Atlantic Books.

Carlin, J. (2013). *Knowing Mandela.* London: Atlantic Books.

Carlson, J. (1977). *No Neutral Ground.* London: Quartet Books.

Coetzee, J.K. (2000). *Plain Tales from Robben Island.* Pretoria: Van Schaik Publishers.

Coetzee, J.K., Gilfillan, L. and Hulec, O. (2004). *Fallen Walls. Prisoners of Conscience in South Africa and Czechoslovakia.* New Brunswick, NJ: Transaction Publishers.

Darwin, J. (2011). *The Empire Project. The Rise and Fall of the British World System 1830–1970.* Cambridge: Cambridge University Press.

De Klerk, F.W. (1999). *The Last Trek – A New Beginning.* London: Pan Books.

Dlamini, M. (1984). *Hell Hole. Robben Island,* Nottingham: Spokesman.

Filatova, I. and Davidson, A. (2013). *The Hidden Thread. Russia and South Africa in the Soviet Era.* Johannesburg: Jonathan Ball Publishers.

Fischer, L. (2015). *The Life of Mahatma Gandhi.* London: Vintage.

Gandhi, M.K. (2012). *An Autobiography: Or The Story of My Experiments With Truth.* London: Penguin.

Gevisser, M. (2009). *Thabo Mbeki.* Johannesburg: Jonathan Ball.

Gibbs, T. (2014). *Mandela's Kinsmen. Nationalist Elites and Apartheid's First Bantustan.* London: James Currey.

Gilbey, E. (1994). *The Lady. The Life and Times of Winnie Mandela.* London: Vintage Books.

Giliomee, H. (2012). *The Afrikaners: Biography of a People.* London: Hurst.

Grøn, A. and Brudholm, T. (2011), '"Nachdenken"' in M. Zolkos (ed.) *On Jean Améry. Philosophy of Catastrophe.* Lanham, MD: Lexington Books. (2011), 193–215.

Guha, R. (2013). *Gandhi Before India.* London: Allen Lane.

Gumede, W.M. (2007). *Thabo Mbeki and the Battle for the Soul of the ANC.* London: Zed Books.

Hancock, W.K. (1962). *Smuts. The Sanguine Years 1870–1919.* Cambridge: Cambridge University Press.

Hancock, W.K. (1968). *Smuts. The Fields of Force 1919–1950.* Cambridge: Cambridge University Press.

Joffe, J. (2014). *The State vs. Nelson Mandela. The Trial that Changed South Africa.* London: Oneworld Publications.

Johnson, R.W. (2015a). *Look Back in Laughter*. Newbury: Threshold Press.
Johnson, R.W. (2015b). *How Long Will South Africa Survive?* London: C. Hurst & Company.
Kathrada, A. (2011). *No Bread for Mandela*. Lexington Ky: The University Press of Kentucky.
Kipling, R. (1937). *Something of Myself*. London: Macmillan.
Koorts, L. (2014). *DF Malan and the Rise of Afrikaner Nationalism*. Cape Town: Tafelberg Publishers Ltd.
Leibbrandt, M., Woolard, I., McEwen, H. and Koep, C. (2014). 'Employment and Inequality Outcomes in South Africa'. Cape Town: *Southern Africa Labour and Development Research Unit (SALDRU)*. At http://www.oecd.org/employment/emp/45282868.pdf (accessed 16th August 2016).
Lodge, T. (2006). *Mandela. A Critical Life*. Oxford: Oxford University Press.
Madikizela-Mandela, W. (2013). *491 Days. Prisoner Number 1323/69*. Athens, OH: Ohio University Press.
Madonsela, T. (2016). *State of Capture. A Report of the Public Protector*. Pretoria: South Africa.
Maharaj, M. (2008). *The ANC and South Africa's Negotiated Transition to Democracy and Peace*. Berlin: Berghof Foundation at www.berghof-foundation.org/fileadmin/redaktion/.../Transitions.../transitions_anc.pdf (accessed 19th August 2016).
Mamdani, M. (2015). 'Beyond Nuremberg: The Historical Significance of the Post-apartheid Transition in South Africa', *Politics and Society*, 43, 1, 66–88.
Mandela, N. (2002). *Long Walk to Freedom. The Autobiography of Nelson Mandela. Volume One. 1918–1962*. London: Abacus.
Mandela, N. (2003a). *Long Walk to Freedom. The Autobiography of Nelson Mandela. Volume Two. 1962–1994*. London: Abacus.
Mandela, M. (2003b) *Nelson Mandela in his Own Words. From Freedom to the Future*. Edited by K. Asmal, D. Chidester and W. JamesLondon: Abacus.
Marsh, P.T. (1994). *Joseph Chamberlain: Entrepreneur in Politics*. New Haven CT: Yale University Press.
Mbeki, G. (1964). *South Africa: The Peasants' Revolt*. London: Penguin Books.
Mbeki, G. (1991). *Learning from Robben Island. The Prison Writings of Govan Mbeki*. London: James Currey.
Mbeki, G. (1992). *The Struggle for Liberation in South Africa: A Short History*. Cape Town: David Philip.
Meredith, M. (1997). *Mandela. A Biography*. London: Simon and Schuster.
Meredith, M. (2008). *Diamonds, Gold and War: The Making of South Africa*. London: Simon and Schuster.
Murray, B. (2016). 'Nelson Mandela and Wits University', *The Journal of African History*, 57, 2, 271–292.
Nimocks, W. (1968). *Milner's Young Men: The "Kindergarten" in Edwardian Imperial Affairs*. London: Hodder and Stoughton.
O'Brien, T.H. (1979). *Milner. Viscount Milner of St James's and Cape Town 1854–1925*. London: Constable.
Pakenham, T. (1992). *The Scramble for Africa*. London: Abacus.
Plaut, M. and Holden, P. (2012). *Who Rules South Africa?* London: Biteback Publishing.
Pogrund, B. (2000). *War of Words. Memoir of a South African Journalist*. New York, NY: Seven Stories Press.

Ross, R. (2008) *A Concise History of South Africa (Cambridge Concise Histories)*. Cambridge: Cambridge University Press.

Rotberg, R.I. (1988). *The Founder: Cecil Rhodes and the Pursuit of Power*. Oxford: Oxford University Press.

Russell, A. (2009). *After Mandela. The Battle for the Soul of South Africa*. London: Hutchinson.

Sampson, A. (2000). *Mandela. The Authorised Biography*. London: HarperCollins.

Schreiner, O. (1989). *The Story of a South African Farm*. London: Virago; originally published 1883.

Schreiner, O. and Cronwright-Schreiner, S.C. (1896). *The Political Situation*. London: T. Fisher Unwin at https://archive.org/details/politicalsituat00crongoog (accessed 19th August 2016).

Sitze, A. (2013). *The Impossible Machine: A Genealogy of South Africa's Truth and Reconciliation Commission*. Ann Arbor: University of Michigan Press, 2013.

Sitze, A. (2014). 'Mandela and the Law' in R. Barnard (ed.) *The Cambridge Companion to Nelson Mandela*. Cambridge: Cambridge University Press (2014), 131–160.

Smith, D. (2006). *Globalization. The Hidden Agenda*. Cambridge: Polity.

Smith, D. (2013). 'Forced Social Displacement: the "inside stories" of Oscar Wilde, Jean Améry, Nelson Mandela and Aung San Suu Kyi' in Nicolas Demertsiz (ed.) *Emotions in Politics*. London: Palgrave-Macmillan (2013), 60–83.

Smith, D.J. (2010). *Young Mandela*. London: Weidenfeld and Nicolson.

Stanley, L. (2016). *Imperialism, Labour and the New Woman: Olive Schreiner's Social Theory*. London: Routledge.

Steyn, R. (2015). *Jan Smuts. Unafraid of Greatness*. Jeppestown: Jonathan Ball.

Strobl, G. (2000). *The Germanic Isle: Nazi Perceptions of Britain*. Cambridge: Cambridge University Press.

Swilling, M. (2017). *Betrayal of the Promise. How South Africa is Being Stolen*. Johannesburg: Public Affairs Research Institute.

Thompson, L. and Berat, L. (2014). *A History of South Africa*. New Haven and London: Yale University Press.

Van der Merwe, J.P. (2009). 'An Anthropological Perspective on Afrikaner Narratives and Myths', *Identity, Culture and Politics: An Afro-Asian Dialogue*, 10, 1, 30–50.

Van Rensburg, P. (1962). *Guilty Land*. London: Penguin Books.

Welsh, D. (2009). *The Rise and Fall of Apartheid*. Johannesburg: Jonathan Ball.

Welsh, D. (2015). 'Apartheid and the Herrenvolk Idea' in C.R. Browning, S. Heschel, M.R. Marrus and M. Shain (eds) *Holocaust Scholarship. Personal Trajectories and Professional Interpretations*. London: Palgrave Macmillan, 187–214.

Welsh, F. (2000). *A History of South Africa*. London: HarperCollins.

5 Aung San Suu Kyi

Beauty and the Beast

Nelson Mandela the South African freedom fighter was first demonized then sanctified by international opinion. The reputation of Aung San Suu Kyi of Burma (Myanmar) went the other way from sanctification to demonization. In 1991 she was given a Nobel Peace Prize, the same honour Mandela got two years later. But in 2016 200,000 people signed a petition demanding her Nobel prize be 'returned or confiscated'.[1] The petition said Suu Kyi had no respect for Muslims and criticized her failure to speak out and condemn human rights violations against the Rohingya.[2] Aung San Suu Kyi even got a public letter in September 2017 from her old South African friend, Bishop Desmond Tutu, recording his deep regret.[3] Her old Oxford college, St Hugh's, removed her portrait from display. Oxford city council voted to deprive her of the freedom of the city previously awarded to her. The City of London debated taking similar action.[4]

Hans-Bernd Zöllner draws a brilliant comparison. He says the West saw Suu Kyi's struggle against the Burmese military regime as being like the Beauty and the Beast. In this story, the Beast imprisons Beauty but her charm and civilizing influence transform him into a noble and handsome prince.[5] But by 2016 Beauty had neither civilized nor pacified the Beast. As a result, she did not seem beautiful any more. In other words, Suu Kyi allowed her supporters, especially in the West, to conjure up a vision of her as the Burmese personification of Western-style democracy, suffering for ideals of freedom that she had, presumably, imbibed during her long sojourn in Oxford and New York. Then she shattered that vision by failing to meet their expectations.

It was deeply disappointing that Aung San Suu Kyi did not condemn the Burmese military's murderous attack on the Rohingya community in 2017. Had she spoken out she would surely have been subjected to bitter counter-attacks from the *Tatmadaw*, as the Burmese military is known, and her words alone would probably not have prevented the atrocities. However, Suu Kyi might have made a significant immediate impact on the situation if she had gone further and announced her resignation from the Burmese government. Such an act would have removed the cover she has been providing, as a kind of human shield, for General Min Aung Hlaing, head of the *Tatmadaw*. If Suu Kyi had resigned this would have exposed the *Tatmadaw* to much greater international criticism. It might even have forced Burma's immediate neighbours in New Delhi and Beijing to make their views known. Their silence was also deafening.

If Suu Kyi had resigned it would also, of course, have deprived her of the influence that she had within the Burmese government, which enabled her to press forward, however slowly, with her party's programme of promoting democracy and social rights within Burma. For whatever reason, Aung San Suu Kyi preferred to remain in government and conform, in public at least, to the official line laid down by the military and monastic hierarchy, which is that the Buddhist people of Burma were under threat and must defend themselves. The damage to her prestige and moral standing internationally, was enormous. However, diplomats and governmental leaders have surely prioritized the question: what effect has the Rohingya issue had on Suu Kyi's practical ability to exercise influence on the Burmese state's internal and external policies and actions? This, almost certainly, is also the main concern both of Suu Kyi herself and the *Tatmadaw*.

Can we make sense of her actions? It is evidently difficult to get close to Suu Kyi. Since early adulthood she has been a very self-disciplined person who keeps her cards very close to her chest. She is used to being virtually alone and under siege. Entering government drew her into the counsels of an equally secretive and self-protective body, Burma's senior generals. All these factors make it a daunting task to penetrate and unravel the inner workings of Suu Kyi or the political establishment that she officially entered in 2016.

In spite of all this ambient mystery, Suu Kyi made one thing crystal clear early on in her political life. This is that her core mission, her life's work, her long-term objective, was to do her utmost to enact the mission that inspired her father, Aung San, founder of the *Tatmadaw* and independent Burma's first prime minister. This mission was to make Burma a country where all the ethnic groups within its borders could join together in peace and prosperity as emancipated Burmese citizens. That summary avoids the many ambiguities and difficulties involved in defining and fulfilling her father's vision, which did not, it seems, include particular guidance on the Rohingya people. Nevertheless Aung San's vision is the star that Suu Kyi follows. It was initially transmitted to her, when young, by his widow, her mother, Khin Kyi. Suu Kyi was early on imbued with a deep sense of having a personal responsibility to get her hands back on the levers of power in Burma that were violently wrested from her father and use that power to turn his vision into reality.

Suu Kyi has, it seems, been living a political life dedicated to fulfilling the wishes of her parents who were both ardent devotees of Burmese democracy. In this respect, Suu Kyi has been driven throughout her life by a degree of filial devotion that is, perhaps, even greater than Wilde's enormous respect for his mother, a living presence throughout most of his years of struggle and success, and a major inspiration for his anarchistic and utopian tendencies. This distinguishes Suu Kyi and Wilde from both Mandela and Améry. The latter pair shrugged off parental control and guidance while still young: Mandela in early adulthood after his first marriage broke up, and Améry in mid adolescence when he quit school without completing his *baccalaureate*.

But to investigate the case of Suu Kyi in greater depth we need to place recent events in a larger context. That means exploring through several decades the interlocking fates of the dynasty of rebels to which Suu Kyi belongs and the complex geo-political entity that has been successively known as: the Kingdom of Burma (till 1885), the Burmese division of the British Empire's Indian Raj (till 1948), the Union of Burma (till 1989), and Myanmar (since 1989) – although, as we have seen, Suu Kyi has made it clear that Burma and Myanmar are equally valid names for her country.

The best way into this geo-historical picture is some political geography. Burma is like a diamond-shaped kite. The Irrawaddy flows down the diamond's middle from north to south then empties its waters into the Bay of Bengal. Burmese territory unfolds further south beyond the Irrawaddy delta, along a narrow strip, the kite's long wavy string, occupying the western side of the peninsula that Burma shares with neighbouring Thailand.

Burma's broad central valley is flanked to the north, east and west by a wide fringe of perilous mountains and deep forests. These borderlands stretch towards Burma's frontiers with Thailand and Laos to the east, China to the northeast, and Bangladesh to the west with India beyond. Mines and dams have torn gashes in this landscape but it has only recently been tamed at the edges and along narrow internal strips of tarmac, steel and concrete.

Since the 1850s Burma had been ruled from three national capitals in turn. The first was Mandalay on the banks of the Irrawaddy at the centre of the Burmese diamond. The Burmese king made Mandalay his seat of power in 1859. He transferred his royal palace there from nearby Amarapura. This palace was the kingdom's spiritual centre, an expression of national and cosmic harmony. Nowadays it is a major centre of Chinese business influence and notorious for drug trafficking.[6]

The southern port of Rangoon, now known as Yangon, on the Irrawaddy delta, was Britain's colonial capital, the seat of government and commercial power. After 1942 it was briefly occupied by the Japanese, followed by the unstable civil government of newly independent Burma, which lasted until 1962 when an autocratic military regime took over. It ran the country for almost the next half century. From 1988 Yangon was also home to the National Democratic League, the opposition political party led by Suu Kyi, a body whose activists included disaffected officers, radicalized students and highly politicized Buddhist monks.

In 2005 the military regime inaugurated a new national capital further north at Naypyidaw, halfway between Mandalay and Yangon. Naypyidaw means abode of kings. Modern Burma's most regal figures are its senior generals, based in that city. One of its most prominent buildings is the Uppatasanti pagoda, an almost exact replica of Yangon's Shwedagon pagoda. Uppatasanti means protection against calamity. The city is designed and located with that thought in mind.[7] It is a defensible space where the regime can display its might, far away from the southern coastline, shielded on three sides by mountains and forest. One visitor described the city as 'Legoland meets Xanadu'.[8]

Arrogance and fear are built into Naypyidaw's architecture. Close by the Uppatasanti pagoda, three statues loom at the edge of a huge drill square located at the headquarters of the *Tatmadaw*, Burma's armed forces. These statues are thirty-three feet high and stand side by side, like a team of warriors. Each statue represents a great Burmese dynast: Anawrahta (1044–77), Bayinnaung (1551–81) and Alaungpaya (1752–60), founder kings of successive Burmese empires. Think Hercules, Thor and Superman. This space is reserved for the uniformed heirs to the martial glory of those champions. Ordinary people are not permitted to look upon the statues directly.

Crucially, it was Suu Kyi's own father, Aung San, modern Burma's founder, who created the *Tatmadaw* and led it until his violent death in 1947. During World War II, Aung San fought and bargained with both the Japanese and the British to win democratic freedom and national independence for Burma. His vision was a strong democracy protected by a noble and honourable army. He hoped that during the initial phase of independence a strong progressive political party would emerge as a dominant force. Its tasks would include not only maintaining order but also providing education and health. It would 'let people know that they have their rights as well as obligations as members of the state.' That would include ethnic and cultural minorities who must 'have their political, economic and social rights definitely defined and accorded'. He explicitly resisted exclusivist and domineering tendencies leading towards fascism: 'Race, religion, and language are ... by themselves not primary factors which go into the making of a nation.' Rather, it is 'the historic necessity of having to lead a common life that is the pivotal principle of nationality and nationalism'.[9]

However, during the 1950s, with Aung San dead, control of the *Tatmadaw* fell into the hands of Ne Win (1911–2002), his main rival. In 1962, the *Tatmadaw* took over Burma in a military coup and kept complete control until 2010.[10] Aung San wanted the military chiefs to serve a unified democratic nation and represent its interests. By contrast, Ne Win wanted the nation to serve the military's interests. The *Tatmadaw*'s senior officers are loyal to themselves in their self-chosen role as the nation incarnate. But where have Suu Kyi's loyalties been? In fact, she has been deeply loyal to each of her two families, in turn.[11]

For many years, Suu Kyi displayed the loyalty of a wife and mother. Her main priority at that time was her husband, whom she married in 1972, and her two sons. Later in life, Suu Kyi followed her duty as a loyal daughter. Suu Kyi acknowledged this in 1989 when she remarked: 'I'm sure this is what she [her mother] would have wanted.' She added: 'I'm doing this for my father. I'm quite happy that they see me as my father's daughter. My only concern is that I prove worthy of him.'[12] By 'they' Suu Kyi meant her followers on the streets and her opponents in the regime. The country's rulers took Suu Kyi seriously because of her capacity to exploit politically her close link to the *Tatmadaw*'s founder.

During the 1988 uprising President Ne Win promised new elections. This triggered Suu Kyi's intervention at the Shwedagon pagoda, calling for 'a strong and prosperous Union of Burma' with 'unity and friendship among national racial groups'.[13] Suu Kyi was speaking with two voices. One was her father's, the *Tatmadaw*'s best self, saying the national army should be a good servant of the people. Her other voice spoke on behalf of all Burmese, bearing witness to their suffering from repression and corruption. In her speech Suu Kyi simultaneously enacted the unhappiness of the victim and the bad conscience of the oppressor. One of her main objectives, it seems, has been to overcome that unhappiness, cleanse that bad conscience, and bring the two sides of the nation, and the two sides of herself, together.

But there were also two Burmas, mutually estranged and internally divided.[14] The tourists' Burma stretches along the Irrawaddy Valley with its dry northern plains and damp southern delta, home to the country's most fertile paddy fields. The delta and plains are where most people live. They are mainly Burman, the dominant ethnic group, and adhere to Buddhism. This Burma is focused on the three cities of Yangon, Mandalay and Naypyidaw. The other Burma lurks in the surrounding borderlands where thirty to forty per cent of the population lives, mainly belonging to highly independent minorities such as the Shan, Kachin, Karen and Chin peoples. This is the Burma of the resistance fighter, the drug smuggler, the ruby trader, and, above all, scattered communities scraping a living mainly through shifting cultivation without benefit of roads or electricity. They survive in a climate of chronic uncertainty interspersed with threats of violence and forced displacement.

The people of the borderlands are mainly Buddhist although several are Christians, Muslims or followers of more localized cults. These mountains and forests are not for wandering, Améry-style. For decades they have nurtured dozens of armed units, variously fighting, smuggling and looting in the absence of stable and coherent governance coordinated within an encompassing Burmese state. Large parts of the borderlands are difficult to traverse, win over or control. They contain much of the country's wealth such as zinc, tungsten, lead, precious stones, jade, gold, copper, antimony, tin, coal, natural gas, timber and hydropower potential. Burma's so-called 'golden triangle' is in the far northeast near the borders with Laos, Thailand and China. It is notorious for its highly lucrative opium production and drug trafficking.[15]

Burma's geo-political topography results from centuries of fighting between competing tribes and kingdoms, complicated by successive invasions. A long line of would-be conquerors preceded the British who needed three wars to get a solid foothold. In the first war (1824–6) the British secured Assam, Manipur and Arakan (now Rakhine) to the west and Tenasserim in the southeast. In a second war (1850–2) they won control of Burma's southern delta region including Yangon. This war opened up opportunities seized by merchants such as the father of Oscar Wilde's friend John Barlas. The third war (1885–6) completed Britain's military takeover by reaching northward into the central plain, capturing Mandalay and the surrounding heartland of Upper Burma. Burma's monarchy was abolished but the mountains and forests remained only half-won. The peoples of the Burmese borderlands resisted being tidied up for others' convenience.[16]

The British invaders found maintaining order by force expensive and difficult.[17] Aung San, Burma's first postwar leader, tried a more inclusive and open approach. He signed an agreement with a number of the borderland nationalities in 1947. This happened at Panglong in Burma's Shan state, a northeastern territory bordering Yunnan in China. The Panglong agreement was intended to be the basis for a lasting settlement within the newly created Union of Burma. The 1947 Constitution bound together the Burman majority and the so-called 'frontier areas' although the Shan and Karen states were promised the right to secede from the Union after ten years if they chose.[18] Suu Kyi's ambition after 2016 was to bring the Panglong agenda to fruition. She wanted to fulfil her father's vision of a united, strong and democratic Burma.

Resisting the Raj

When the Burmese monarchy fell in 1885, local strong men resisted British attempts to centralize control and objected when the British recruited warriors from the mountains and forests to staff the country's police force and military units.[19] The occupying forces treated these rebels as *dacoits*, or bandits, and called their leaders 'the Bos', 'Bo' meaning chief. As one British commander later wrote, 'It was essential to catch the "Bos," or captains of the guerilla bands, who gave life and spirit to the whole movement. Short compact men, nearly always well mounted, with a modern jockey seat, they were the first as a rule to run away. The mounted infantry man, British or Indian, a stone or two heavier, and weighted with rifle, ammunition, and accoutrements, on an underbred twelve-hand pony, had no chance of riding down a "Bo".'[20]

Min Yaung, great-uncle of Suu Kyi's father, Aung San, was a very active 'Bo' in the mid 1880s. Charles Crosthwaite, the British Chief Commissioner for Burma, wrote that 'Min Yaung ... was well provided with ponies, and even elephants.' He operated on the southern fringes of the old Burmese kingdom's zone of control, in a district that 'gave more trouble than any other in Upper Burma'.[21] Bo Min Yaung was finally executed in May 1887 but his name lived on in the region and in the family.

Colonizing Burma was a profit-seeking proposition pursued with arrogant insensitivity. Mandalay's cosmologically significant royal palace became Fort Dufferin.[22] The ex-Queen's Lily Throne Room became the British Upper Burma Club where off-duty officers could smoke, drink and take their leisure.[23] The conquerors destroyed the traditional link between Burmese royalty and the Burmese *Sangha*, the Buddhist monastic order.[24] But Buddhism remained deeply ingrained. Monks lived amongst the people, relying on food and other support given by local villagers or townsfolk. These donations earned merit for those who gave. In return, monks provided moral guidance and basic education for the poor. Buddhist boys in all walks of life spent time as novice monks during their early adolescence, a rite of passage as important as circumcision among the Xhosa.[25]

All this was below the notice of the British who saw Burma as a strictly functional conservatory bolted on to a more magnificent edifice, the Indian Raj, within which Burma was incorporated, losing its sovereign identity. Generating profit was the game. Not a straightforward task. The new rulers encouraged villagers from the plains of Upper Burma to migrate south into the delta region and become commercial rice cultivators. But things soon went wrong. Incoming Indian traders from Tamil Nadu and Kerala became very unpopular with the Burmese. This was because some of them offered substantial credit to Burmese rice cultivators but when harvests failed swiftly foreclosed their loans. Indian moneylenders soon became major absentee landlords in the region round Yangon.[26] Many Burmese felt under threat from alien invaders, not just British and Indian but also Chinese. The Young Men's Buddhist Association, established in 1906, was a focal point for discontent.

Burmese demoralization was matched by British disillusionment if George Orwell's *Burmese Days* is a reliable guide.[27] It probably is. Publishers were reluctant to take on this brilliantly subversive work for fear of being accused of libel.[28] Orwell's story is set in the 1920s. It turns on the anguish of an unmarried British teak dealer, John Flory, stationed far to the north of Mandalay. Flory hates the petty pretensions of colonial circles. Orwell, a one-time policeman in Burma, uses this tale to expose the smugness of provincial English society, transposed to Upper Burma.[29]

In *Burmese Days* the brittle snobbishness of club gossip over evening drinks on the verandah stands out starkly against lush monsoon darkness. The mix of light and shadow sharpens the scene, like a backlit X-ray. We see an aunt and her niece at different stages in the process of becoming low-powered versions of Lady Bracknell: snooty, rude and calculating but without her wit or imagination. They weave their way amongst a bevy of snobbish males whose lives revolve around maintaining caste, good form, and a plentiful supply of ice at the bar. Orwell's masterpiece is Lieutenant Verrall, younger son of a peer, whose face was 'specially constructed for ignoring unwelcome strangers'.[30] Verrall kept himself in clothes and horses by not paying bills till sued. He dismissed the 'nasty, poodle-faking, horseless riffraff' of provincial Burma, despised all Indians, apart from a few good polo players, and disliked the Army 'except the cavalry'.[31] Verrall is a colonial echo of Wilde's comic construct, the idle and deceitful cad Algernon Moncrieff, but lacks his intelligence and humour.[32]

Who shall rule?

Minor riots in the 1920s were generally nipped in the bud but during 1930 there was sustained violence against Indians and Chinese in several cities. In December, a major rebellion broke out and Burmese gangs attacked military police stations in several towns. Thousands of people died before the rebellion was quelled and its leader, Saya San, an ex-Buddhist monk, executed.[33] By this time Burmese nationalist feeling against the British was better organized. Student activists in Rangoon University joined together in the anti-colonial *Dobama Asiayone* (We Burmans Association). These radicals called themselves *thakins*, hi-jacking a Burmese term denoting imperial master, a deliberately provocative act of self-emancipation.[34]

The most influential young *thakin* in 1941 was Suu Kyi's father, highly driven and intensely pragmatic, characteristics inherited by his daughter. Aung San was ready to fight for a socially just political order and wanted to lead an armed uprising against the British. He tried to contact the Chinese Red Army but instead fell into the hands of the *Minami Kihan*, a Japanese joint Army-Navy outfit. It was recruiting Burmese fighters to help smooth the way for invading Japanese forces. The Japanese were keen to close down the supply route running north through Burma into China where they were fighting both Chiang Kai-shek and Mao Zedong.[35] They promised the Burmese independence. Aung San agreed to accept military training along with other young Burmese ex-students, later known as the Thirty Comrades. The charismatic Colonel Suzuki Keiji organized this training on Hainan Island off the coast of southern China.

Aung's San closest colleagues ranged along a spectrum between socialism and communism. The Japanese also recruited Shu Maung from a slightly earlier student generation. He took the name Ne Win, which means Radiant Sun, as his *nom de guerre*. Aung San became the unchallenged leader of the Thirty Comrades. Ne Win emerged as second-in-command. He belonged to a more conservative network, though its members described themselves as socialist. Ne Win failed his university examinations and moved into politics. In later years he cultivated a taste for horse racing, glamorous women, golf and political power.[36]

The Japanese military had a code of rigorous authoritarianism tempered by a strong *esprit de corps*.[37] The Thirty Comrades were impressed by their Japanese trainers' discipline, ruthlessness and self-belief. They learned Japanese songs and watched films about *samurai* adventures. The Japanese officers regarded themselves as superior beings, the spirit in which the Burmese military later exercised political power under the leadership of Ne Win. The postwar Burmese military felt they embodied the nation in its finest form. As Mary Callahan points out, they tended to regard all civilians as potential enemies.[38]

The Japanese attack on the American naval base at Pearl Harbor (Hawaii) in December 1941 was followed by the invasion of Malaya and the capture of the British stronghold of Singapore in February 1942. Burma was next on the list. As the Japanese advanced across the border, Aung San and his comrades recruited about five thousand men to the new Burma Independence Army (BIA). By March 1942 the Japanese forces had taken Yangon. A puppet Burmese government was appointed. Aung San accepted the position of Burma's war minister from the occupying power, and the Order of the Rising Sun from Emperor Hirohito. Aung San was a man of action in all spheres. He found time to marry Khin Kyi, Suu Kyi's mother, the nurse he met, fell in love with, and proposed to while at Yangon's General Hospital in 1942 recovering from war wounds. Radical elite politics were in the family. Khin Kyi's sister, Khin Gyi, married the leader of Burma's Communist Party, Than Tun.

In July 1942 the BIA was reconstituted as the Burma Defence Army (BDA). By September a BDA military academy had been set up in Mingaladon, a satellite town of Yangon. It recruited students from BDA units on the recommendation of officers. All training was in Japanese, using Japanese manuals. Top graduates were sent for further training in Tokyo. During 1943 a preparatory school, modelled on Japanese lines, was set up for future officers, selected at the ages of fourteen to sixteen by competitive examination. Over thirty years later Joyce Lebra noted that Burma's governing council, military commanders and diplomatic corps were mainly 'graduates of the Mingaladon Military Academy during the Japanese occupation'.[39] She added that 'Japanese training had an effect which cannot be overemphasized: the militarization and politicization of the élite of post-war Burma'.[40] In 1981, Ne Win gave awards at his presidential palace to six surviving veterans of *Minami Kikan*. He reportedly met up with his old Japanese comrades as late as the mid-1990s.[41]

Aung San and his close colleagues had a more detached approach to the Japanese. When British forces reinvaded Burma in 1944, they struck. At an agreed signal, Aung San's co-conspirators seized and killed the Japanese officers attached to the Burmese military units.[42] Aung San then threw in his lot with Field Marshal Slim who absorbed the insurgent Burmese forces into the British Army. Aung San was initially brought to see Slim by Tom Carew of the British clandestine Force 136. Slim's first response, Carew later recalled, was to 'put him in the slammer'. Slim cabled to Louis Mountbatten, Supreme Allied Commander for the South East Asia Command, asking for guidance. Mountbatten wanted Aung San on the team. Slim later acknowledged the Burmese leader was a 'genuine patriot and realist'.[43]

When the British withdrew from Burma, Aung San became head of the post-war Burmese administration. Mountbatten pushed the appointment through against the wishes of Britain's previous colonial overlords in Burma.[44] The Burmese battalions in the British forces became the basis of Burma's own national army. In January 1947 Aung San negotiated national independence with the new Labour government. Six months after securing independence Aung San was assassinated in Yangon during a meeting. A rival Burmese politician was executed for plotting the assassination but there were suspicions the British military and colonial service may have been involved.[45]

Aung San's martyrdom sealed his high reputation. His name and image were soon visible throughout Yangon, and far beyond, in street names, place names, portraits, plaques and statues. But independent Burma soon fell apart. For most of the next fifteen years Burma's prime minister was U Nu (1907–95), Aung San's old student friend: playwright, novelist and devout Buddhist, but not a strong leader.[46] U Nu tried to maintain a fractious 'anti-fascist' political alliance in government and hold together the new Union of Burma. But the politicians fell out and before long the Union became a battlefield. During the next fifteen years of civil war in Burma, politics was largely a matter of networks based on personal loyalties and shifting alliances, just as in the days of the 'Bos'. As a prominent Burmese exiled in the West later put it, 'Personalities are at the heart of Myanmar politics'.[47]

There were four problems: too little trust; too many armed groups; porous national borders; and not enough pragmatic ruthlessness. Aung San was missed. By the late 1940s three civil wars were underway: between two different brands of communists; between communists and socialists; and between the government and insurgents demanding an independent Karen state in eastern Burma. A fourth conflict began during the early 1950s when defeated Chinese nationalist forces intruded into Burma's mountains and forests. The *Kuomintang* (KMT) tried to muscle in on the regional drugs trade. Both the *Tatmadaw* and the CIA intervened.

None of this was good for agricultural production and trade in the lower Irrawaddy valley. Rice was Burma's main export. Whenever that sector faltered, the results were felt throughout society. U Nu was unable to develop Burma's economy or stabilize its parliamentary system. In 1962 Ne Win seized political power, jailed U Nu and set up a revolutionary council to govern Burma.[48] By that time Aung San Suu Kyi and her mother were in India, watching developments from overseas.

Under Ne Win's command the *Tatmadow* grew from about two thousand soldiers in 1949 to over one hundred thousand troops by 1962.[49] He made his old wartime comrades from the British-led Burma Rifles (the 'Berufs') into an elite inner corps. By the end of the 1950s the national army was virtually autonomous, a state within a state. The *Tatmadaw* set up its own businesses supplying soldiers with goods and services, profit-making opportunities, and retirement jobs. In one respect it functioned rather like the Afrikaner *Broederbond*. It looked after its own people.

Just as in South Africa, so in Burma, the dominant establishment wanted a big idea to justify its systematic pursuit of selfish gain. In South Africa the big idea was *apartheid*, supposedly ordained by God. In Burma it was socialism, although the task of fighting rebellious factions around the borderlands took precedence over elaborating this ideology. A socialist constitution was finally introduced in 1974[50] and for the next fourteen years military government in Burma was managed through the Burma Socialist Programme Party (BSPP), the military's political front. The BSPP made ambitious promises about promoting national economic self-reliance while creating harmony and prosperity through wholesale nationalization. But in practice the BSPP's main function was to provide governmental posts into which military officers could be shunted. This enabled Ne Win to readjust the balance between competing factions within the army at convenient intervals.[51]

The BSPP impoverished the nation. Misery and resentment finally brought the population out onto the streets in 1988. The popular rebellion was put down bloodily. The BSPP was discarded, undermining Ne Win's personal position. Ne Win resigned, Suu Kyi began her political campaign, won a general election in 1990, saw the result nullified by the regime, and was put under house arrest.

By 1992 the regime had found a new boss, Than Shwe, and reinforced its rule. It played up the *Tatmadaw*'s security mission, fixed food prices by government decree, maintained spies and informers in pagodas, offices and cafes, and employed strict censorship and relentless propaganda. The Department of Military Intelligence (MI) developed a sophisticated and comprehensive approach to gathering information about the population and tracking its movements.

Naypyidaw's three giant royal statues and enormous pagoda expressed the legitimizing strategy that replaced the regime's failed mock-socialism. The generals wanted to restore the politico-cosmological coherence achieved in the old Burmese kingdom. This combined the charisma of superhuman kingship, which the military by implication represented in earthly form, with the divine blessings of Buddhism. The regime's leaders were concerned with their spiritual condition. Just as the Afrikaner masters of *apartheid* included several devout Christians, so the men in charge of the *Tatmadaw* were in many cases sincere Buddhists.[52] They cared about building up the stock of merit they had allowed to diminish while in office.[53] When Thein Sein, the ex-general who became president in 2011, finally retired, he entered a monastery. He was ordained as a monk on 1st April 2016 and planned to pursue his new vocation in a 'small peaceful town'.[54]

The military was a powerful, mysterious presence at the heart of society and state, a kind of Masonic order. The *Tatmadaw* was a half-hidden inner nation. Its aspiration was to be all seeing but not all seen. A one-way mirror exposed the national population to the gaze of this secret state. By contrast, the regime's own day-by-day activities remained well out of sight of the population at large which was not permitted to share the to and fro of debate within government. Not least, Ne Win valued his own busy and varied private life too much to want to be a star, always in the public eye. He was a company man, not the object of a personality cult.[55]

Instead, Aung San, the martyred hero, provided a convenient figurehead. Rather than building up his own name, Ne Win legitimized military rule by sanctifying the image and memory of Aung San. This meant that when Suu Kyi arrived on the scene in 1988, her father's memory and image had hovered over Burmese politics and culture for over forty years. This crucial fact gave Aung San's dissident daughter enormous leverage. Her most potent weapon was her father's iconic status. Ironically, this had been assiduously fashioned and buffed up since 1962 by Suu Kyi's future political opponents, the *Tatmadaw*.

Apprenticeship

Before Suu Kyi arrived on the stage of Burmese politics she acquired an education, a husband, a young family, and a very interesting life. She received her secondary schooling in India, and followed a degree course in Oxford, writing every day to her future husband, Michael Aris, an English academic who became an expert on Himalyan and Tibetan studies. Suu Kyi lived abroad for twenty-eight years in all, bringing up two sons, travelling the world, and writing books, all interspersed with short trips back to Burma. All that time her father's memory hovered in the background. School friends in New Delhi recalled her often saying: 'I will never be allowed to forget whose daughter I am.' Her mother, Khin Kyi, kept the white scarf that had been stained with her husband's blood when he was assassinated.[56] It was a kind of holy relic.

In 1967 her mother resigned her ambassadorial post and returned to Burma to live privately. During her career, Ne Win had made efforts to undermine her. He then presented the retiring diplomat with an outsize tax bill, contrary to precedent. Ne Win also turned his attention to the daughter. He invited Suu Kyi to come and see him. Suu Kyi said she was too busy studying for her finals at Oxford. However, Ne Win was on her case, trying to make her either submit to the military regime or challenge it. Faced with this choice, Suu Kyi had sufficient skill and luck to delay till 1988 the point when she made her challenge. She reassured the regime she would not attack it from overseas.[57]

During her years abroad Suu Kyi became familiar with the culture and politics of India, Nepal, Bhutan, Tibet, Japan, Burma, Britain and the United States. She participated in the highly educated diplomatic circles of the West. Apart from Oxford, Suu Kyi studied and researched at the School of Oriental and Asian Studies in London, and at the Indian Institute for Advanced Studies at Shimla. She also wrote a scholarly comparison between Indian and Burmese intellectual life under colonialism,[58] a biography of her father,[59] and a book that appeared in 1985 entitled *Let's Visit Burma*.[60]

The most significant paragraph from all these texts was arguably in the book comparing India with Burma. Suu Kyi wrote about the need for a meaningful long-term vision to guide political action since 'A series of pragmatic moves unconnected by continuity of vision cannot be expected to sustain a long-term movement.' In the event she was able to combine a clear and durable vision for Burma's future with her father's mixture of pragmatism, daring and ruthlessness, especially with herself. As has been seen, she broadcast her vision widely during her political debut in 1988 at the age of forty-three when Ne Win's old order was gradually collapsing and a new one had not yet been established.

At that time the military regime was on the back foot. It did not know how to make the country a viable participant in the more open, globalized economy emerging as the Cold War faded. If 1962 had been Ne Win's year of opportunity, 1988 offered Suu Kyi, in turn, her own chance to influence Burmese politics. Her approach echoed two of her father's heroes. Like Eamonn De Valera (1882–1975), who participated in the 1916 Dublin uprising, Suu Kyi was prepared to take calculated and highly publicized personal risks. Like him she also knew the value of highly committed followers who would put their bodies on the frontline for the cause. Like Mahatma Gandhi, Suu Kyi played an artful double game. She insisted she was against violence but led her followers, by word or deed, into situations where violence was quite likely, and frequently broke out.

Suu Kyi thought like an artful military commander. Two of Suu Kyi's most trusted senior colleagues were Kyi Maung, one time senior army officer under Ne Win, and Tin Oo, ex-commander in chief of the armed forces.[61] They were both advocates for democracy, like their lost leader, Aung San. This military presence advertised the NLD's ingrained toughness. It also, perhaps, implied that NLD leaders knew the *Tatmadaw* from the inside and would be able to restore that organization to its former path of virtue. For herself, Suu Kyi wanted to be seen not just as a soldierly spirit, but also as a wise counsellor, and a good Buddhist. These strands of her persona developed gradually during her long journey to high office triggered by her intuitive responses to successive challenges.

Her soldierly approach distinguished Suu Kyi from U Nu, the last civilian Burmese leader. Suu Kyi refused to cooperate with him in 1988, perhaps because that would compromise her own strong but latent narrative that Aung San's daughter had returned to claim her father's stolen inheritance.[62] Her stance upset the prominent student leader Ko Ko Gyi, who helped found the 88 Generation student group in 2005.[63] This incipient fracture between Suu Kyi and the more radically democratic student leadership reappeared later. However, in 1988 the political tide was lifting up Suu Kyi, the charismatic saviour from overseas, a woman full of promise.

Early in 1989 Suu Kyi toured Burma, wearing appropriate local dress in each region, always protected by NLD workers and local supporters. She found her way into the northern territories of the Shan and the Kachin, travelled along the Irrawaddy Valley, and repeatedly scouted the towns and villages of the southern delta. The diary kept by Suu Kyi's colleague Ma Thanegi during 1989 records Suu Kyi's early months as a Burmese politician, showing, for example, how she dealt with spies from Military Intelligence (MI).[64] They were keeping an eye on her as she travelled the country, campaigning for the National League for Democracy (NLD). One day the NLD campaigners lost their way in a strange town. Suu Kyi told her bodyguard to ask two nearby MI agents to guide them. 'They did so willingly and seemed so proud when [Suu Kyi] thanked them sweetly'. Later 'she giggled and said they looked like two crooks from a movie'.[65]

Not long afterwards Suu Kyi's group stayed overnight in a Shan monastery. Predictably, it only had a men's toilet so Ma Thanegi and Suu Kyi found a public lavatory consisting of cubicles poised high above water, each with a large rectangular hole. Suu Kyi was 'terrified, said she was thin enough to slip right through'.[66] Meanwhile, she missed her sons, and sometimes wept. She displaced those feelings with laughter and exasperation, asking whatever possessed her to get involved in Burma when she 'could have stayed peacefully in Oxford!'.[67] These aspects of Suu Kyi's personality remained hidden from those she did not trust. It seems likely that early in life she acquired a strong outer shell of disciplined reserve, saying nothing when silence worked best. Later, marriage to a kind and loyal English husband evidently provided emotional release, and left her with, perhaps, more freedom and control than in a more traditional Burmese relationship.

A significant incident occurred in 1989 at Danubyu, a township in the southwest on the banks of the Irrawaddy. That was where General Maha Bandula found himself under siege by the British in early April 1825, during the first Anglo-Burmese war. According to legend, Bandula walked around the stockade walls in full uniform carrying a golden umbrella to raise morale and show Burma's fighting spirit. Unsurprisingly, he was hit and killed. The battle of Danubyu was a disaster for the Burmese kingdom. However, Bandula's courage made him the best-known general in modern Burmese military history.[68]

One hundred and sixty-four years later, again in early April, Suu Kyi and her band of NLD supporters were walking towards the local NLD headquarters in the same township of Danubyu. A line of soldiers confronted them. The captain told them to stop or he would order his men to shoot. Everybody came to a halt but Suu Kyi walked on in the middle of the road. The captain was on the point of ordering his men to fire at her. At the very last moment a superior officer intervened. Disaster was averted. Suu Kyi's deliberate risk-taking was publicized widely throughout the country and abroad. It gave her the moral right to tell her followers not to let fear inhibit them when protesting against the regime.[69]

The NLD won hands down in the 1990 election but the *Tatmadaw* dismissed the result, jailed many activists, and put Suu Kyi under house arrest in her home in the centre of Yangon. She stayed there till 1995. It was the first of three prison terms. The regime tried to humiliate its famous prisoner whom they labelled a 'whore,' a 'Western fashion girl', and a 'political stunt princess'.[70] Her mail deliveries were monitored and newspaper reports criticized her for being able to enjoy exercise videos and good quality lipstick while Burmese struggled to eat. After that Suu Kyi rejected all deliveries. She refused to ask for anything the regime might deny her or accept anything the regime might want to give her. In 1999, she rejected, with her husband's agreement, the regime's offer to let her leave Burma to visit Michael Aris, who was dying of cancer.[71]

Forced confinement had a very different flavour for Suu Kyi than for Mandela. His prison became almost a home, bringing him back from his solitary underground role into the warmth of regular social contact.[72] By contrast, Suu Kyi's house arrest turned her home into a prison. After several years in lively cosmopolitan social circles, her Suu Kyi was required to accept a near-solitary existence for months and sometimes years on end. However, house arrest placed her in an urban setting where the charisma of Bogyoke (i.e. General) Aung San was being reinforced daily as people streamed out of Yangon's central railway station and took the short walk to Bogyoke Aung San market on Bogyoke Aung San Road, a few hundred metres from Bogyoke Aung San stadium just south of Bogyoke park. Furthermore, Suu Kyi's place of confinement was only a few hundred yards from Yangon's main university and just half an hour's stroll from the forest of pagodas in Shwedagon Taingotra Park. Aung San's daughter was located close to her most active and vocal supporters: the student body and the Buddhist monastic orders.

Harsh repression was the preferred approach of Than Shwe, the new military leader who emerged in 1992.[73] When Suu Kyi was released in July 1995, she advertised her own very different style. From September till the following April she held regular weekend question and answers sessions over the gate at her house. Suu Kyi's tone was reasonable and humorous, with a constant emphasis on the need for those in authority to listen to the people and explain in a sensible manner what they were trying to do. She spoke like a caring and friendly governess: not ideological, more commonsensical; not hectoring, more encouraging; not Mary Wollstonecraft, more Mary Poppins.[74] However, the regime eventually banned the meetings and imposed tighter restrictions on Suu Kyi's movements. She was imprisoned again in 2000, this time for a year and a half.

Game changers

During the next few years Suu Kyi and the regime were in a situation of stalemate. Neither could achieve their strategic goals. Neither could defeat the other. Meanwhile the Cold War was long over and the name of the game was globalization. Burma's natural resources attracted foreign interest but the military regime could not exploit this without enduring criticism from potential external partners. Where were Burma's human rights and political democracy, and those open, flexible and transparent capitalist institutions that Western eyes looked for? In fact, business within Burma was packaged up nicely for the generals' benefit. The *Tatmadaw*'s interests in, for example, real estate, transport and tourism were coordinated through the Union of Myanmar Economic Holdings (UMEH) founded in 1990. Heavy industry such as steel and cement production was brought under the wing of the Myanmar Economic Corporation (MEC), set up in 1997. The MEC fell under the control of General Tin Aung Myint Oo, one of Burma's richest men. He was well placed in the regime, and a close associate of Burmese business tycoon Zaw Zaw.[75]

The MEC and UMEH were a front for military control of business life. Senior officers enjoyed lucrative returns from Burma's extractive industries such as jade, rubies and teak, mainly based in the fractious borderlands where the military patrolled regularly. They could exploit local profit-making opportunities, including covert trading in opium-based drugs. Having a corrupt judiciary and civilian bureaucracy helped oil the wheels. International sanctions were a drag but did not stop the generals getting very rich. But these arrangements became an embarrassment when the regime edged out into international waters. This was evident after 1997 when Burma joined the Association of South East Asian Nations (ASEAN). External pressure increased further when the so-called Bangkok process started in 2003. Singapore, Australia, Austria, Italy, Germany, France, Japan, China and India began to meet with Burmese representatives in that city.[76] The generals produced a Burmese 'road map for democracy', revived the National Convention originally established after the abortive 1990 election, and slowly resumed the process of consulting interested parties about a new national constitution.

Were such initiatives intended to persuade foreign investors that the Burmese regime was putting on a respectable mask? Was 2003 to be the beginning of a slow trek by the regime towards the vision that inspired Suu Kyi? In other words, towards free and open critical debate, a diverse but politically united country, respect for human rights, a leading political role for Suu Kyi herself, and armed services under the control of a civilian government validated by a parliamentary majority achieved in honestly conducted elections. Not quite. On the contrary, in 2003 a determined effort was made to maim or kill Suu Kyi and her NLD supporters at Depayin. This shocking event, disguised as an unanticipated episode of crowd violence, left about seventy NLD supporters dead. Suu Kyi had a narrow escape. After the massacre, she was imprisoned once more.[77]

If Suu Kyi could not easily be killed could she at least be marginalized? The NLD played its part, unwittingly or not, by marginalizing itself. It refused to participate in the National Convention. This meant that between 2003 and 2008 the political weather was made not by the NLD but by the national minorities, the Shan, the Chin and so on, demanding a federal constitution, devolved assemblies, armed militias and taxation rights.[78] Suu Kyi was not involved in those consultations until 2007.[79] Meanwhile, the NLD's political base was being weakened. Universities were being shifted away from city centres and into distant suburbs and the capital was moved far away from the NLD's stronghold in Yangon. The balance of political advantage seemed to be moving towards the regime.

But globalization and nature intervened. The effects of that powerful combination were not anticipated in 2007 when the government provocatively raised fuel prices by a very large amount. Predictably, perhaps, anti-government street protests began. These grew until they involved several thousands of people. Buddhist monks took the lead in this so-called Saffron Revolution. But this was not a Burmese spring. The regime hit back with force, leaving many dead. In response, the European Union, the United States and Canada increased trade sanctions. Japan cut its aid.

Unexpectedly, a new disaster struck soon afterwards. It was Cyclone Nargis, which hit the Bay of Bengal on 2nd May 2008. It sent a storm surge up the Irrawaddy Delta deep into Burma, killing about 180,000 people. Shockingly, for three weeks the Burmese government obstructed all attempts to bring foreign aid into the country. Astonishingly, a referendum was held just eight days after the cyclone disaster. It endorsed the regime's new national constitution. The regime's paranoia, its obsession with maintaining absolute control, and its prolonged neglect of vulnerable victims generated horrified, aghast interest by outsiders in the behaviour of this peculiar country. What kind of regime did such ghastly things without apparently caring about the human consequences? A Burmese journalist interviewed by Emma Larkin had a useful insight. He said the regime's response was 'something very ancient' left over from 'the age of the old, old kings'. It was as if 'Our senior general is the king and the people are his subjects or slaves.' He thinks 'their death or hardship is not his concern'.[80] Was the regime's behaviour another manifestation of its implied claim to superhuman kingship expressed in the statuary and architecture of Naypyidaw?

The regime's harsh repression of the Saffron Revolution followed by its neglectful approach to the devastation brought by Cyclone Nargis had two consequences. On the one hand, Buddhist monks hostile to the regime learned again, as they had in 1988, that active opposition brought very harsh reprisals. Was this, perhaps, the point when the balance of influence amongst political activists within the monasteries shifted towards the radical racist right, which became more prominent in the following years? On the other hand, the response of the *Tatmadaw* to the events of 2007–8 gave widespread publicity to the unintended message that Burma's military regime was manifestly unfit for purpose in a globalized world.

International humiliation brought the regime's internal struggle to a crisis point. Suu Kyi was released in 2010 but refused to take part in the national election held that year. The key change was the appointment of a new Burmese president, Thein Sein, to succeed Than Shwe who retired in February 2011. Thein Sein was a civilian, albeit a retired general. He released several political prisoners, relaxed media censorship and removed many hardliners from the cabinet. In December 2011, Hillary Clinton, US Secretary of State, visited Burma, met Suu Kyi, and promised increased American support if Burma's liberalizing reforms continued.[81] It seems this was a key moment. Suu Kyi was persuaded that after a decade and a half in total under arrest, and having seen the tide moving against her since 2003, the time and opportunity had finally arrived for her to throw herself back into the swirl of national parliamentary politics. She was sixty-six years old.

Suu Kyi entered the national parliament at a by-election in April 2012. The National Democratic League won a landslide victory in the 2015 general election but Suu Kyi surely realized how weak her political position had become compared to 1988. The NLD had relied on student and monastic support. This coalition had been undermined by two things: Suu Kyi's disagreements with the radical 88 Generation student group; and the demagogic anti-Muslim campaigns led by extremist Buddhists monks such as Wirathu. These campaigns fed, and fed upon, inter-communal violence between Muslim and Buddhist gangs, notably in North Rakhine during 2012. In 2013 religious conflict also came to Meiktila, a town midway between Mandalay and Naypyidaw.

During the run up to the 2015 general election Suu Kyi deliberately presented a moderate profile. She opposed appointing NLD parliamentary candidates who were either Muslims, which she judged would make them virtually unelectable, or from the radical 88 Generation student group with whom she had longstanding disagreements.[82] In both respects she showed herself more a politician than a saint. In line with the 2008 constitution, the *Tatmadaw* held as a right a quarter of all parliamentary seats. This was intended to allow them to block attempts to change the 2008 Constitution, a provision deliberately built into that document. The military also controlled by right three key Cabinet positions: home affairs, borderland affairs and defence.

In the event, Htin Kyaw, one of Suu Kyi's trusted followers, was appointed Burma's national president. Suu Kyi became State Counsellor, minister in the presidential office, minister of foreign affairs, and the president's official spokesperson. Then came a big surprise, an intervention almost as bold and dramatic as Suu Kyi's speech before the Shwedagon Pagoda three decades before. In 1988 Suu Kyi had daringly claimed to speak for the whole Burmese people and roundly chastised the military regime for its cruelties. By 2016 the regime had put on sheep's clothing, offering a quasi-civilian face to the world. But Suu Kyi outbid them by asserting loudly and unexpectedly that she, Suu Kyi, as leader of the largest political party in the national parliament, was now in charge of Burma's government, an outcome that the 2008 Constitution was intended to prevent.[83] This radical claim was a brilliant surprise tactic and may well have caught the Tatmadaw off guard, especially since it came after so many signals of Suu Kyi's caution and moderation immediately before the election. However, the *Tatmadaw* had its own vision for Burma and it held the means of enforcement, both military and budgetary, in its own hands. Perhaps for a short time Suu Kyi's daring claim gave her some additional political space and bargaining power in Naypyidaw. But it was an aspiration, not a reality. However, it was heard globally and believed by many outside Burma.

It is tempting but misleading, to see Suu Kyi's appointment as State Counsellor in 2016 through the lens of Nelson Mandela's election as President of South Africa in 1994. Misleading because standing beside Suu Kyi's new political throne was another government boss, Burma's military commander-in-chief, General Min Aung Hlaing, appointed in 2011. He embodied a rival view of rulership, not democratic but regal rather than feudal. It would be equally misleading to see the *Tatmadaw*'s high command as *shogun*-like figures reminiscent of the all-powerful military chiefs that controlled the emperor of Japan before the Meiji Restoration of 1868.[84] The *Tatmadaw* recognized and valued the political legitimacy that Suu Kyi's reputation for loving freedom and justice brought to the regime. But the military also imposed strict limits on what she could actually do, well aware that Suu Kyi's grandstanding claim, a deliberate and calculated risk on her part, meant she would bear the brunt of foreign criticism, if it came.[85]

Since the *Tatmadaw* would block any proposals to change the 2008 Constitution, Burma's wealthy minority, especially those businesses and families with strong military links, remained in a strong position. Unlike the white Afrikaner elite imposing *apartheid*, which regularly confronted rioting Black South Africans, the generals and their political supporters were demonstrably cut from the same ethno-cultural cloth as the overwhelmingly Buddhist Burman majority population. The *Tatmadaw* could maintain popular support by appealing to the people's prejudices, including widespread hostility to the Rohingya, who were overwhelmingly regarded as intrusive Bengali foreigners.

For her part, Suu Kyi had the freedom to reiterate her vision of Burma's future, articulated in 1988 and largely unchanged since. She could also argue and manoeuvre as shrewdly as possible behind the scenes. But there were two things she could not do publicly if she wished to retain her position and her influence: directly criticize the *Tatmadaw*; or sympathize with and defend any group that was overwhelmingly regarded by ordinary Burmese, rightly or wrongly, as a threat to the nation.

In 2012 Suu Kyi told Christiane Amanpour: 'I've always got on with people in the army; you mustn't forget that my father was the Founder of the Burmese army. This is why I have a soft spot for them even though I don't like what they do – that's different from not liking them.'[86] We hear that Mary Poppins tone again, this time addressed to senior generals, chastised as naughty boys.[87] Suu Kyi's family link with the *Tatmadaw* was her major political asset, but it provided her with a shield, not a sword. In practice, Suu Kyi's weapons for cutting through or bypassing opposition had to be her intelligence, experience, international networks, political instinct and bargaining skills, largely deployed beyond the range of cameras and microphones.

Suu Kyi's other assets were stamina and patience, strengthened during house arrest but sorely tested by the stress of government. In 2012 Suu Kyi sounded like a chiding governess but by 2017 she seemed more like a driven handmaiden. Meanwhile, the military was making a sustained effort to improve its public reputation abroad. In 2016 Liu Yun, a Chinese blogger, reported that diplomats were 'saying that Senior General Min Aung Hlaing has transformed himself from a taciturn soldier into a politician, public figure and statesman.' Liu Yun argued that Min Aung Hlaing 'understands clearly that he needs to try to use Aung San Suu Kyi's peerless legitimacy to fulfill the military's so-called three national causes – non-disintegration of the Union, non-disintegration of national solidarity, and perpetuation of sovereignty.'[88]

In fact, it seems likely that interwoven with those national causes was another agenda, discernable from the military's actions. One objective was evidently to avoid an open conflict with Suu Kyi, if possible. Here is a brief extract of an interview Min Aung Hlaing gave to the Washington Post in November 2015: '*Do you think you can work with [Aung San Suu Kyi]? Why not? Do you trust her?* If we have good results for our country, we can work together. There are so many ways to cooperate.'[89]

Another goal was to defend Burma's rigid hierarchical socio-political order whose norms remained anchored to a considerable degree in the traditional Burmese world that General Prendergast has so rudely disrupted in 1885. Frank criticism that would pass as business as usual in the Western media was easily construed in Burma as a form of heresy, showing culpable disrespect for hallowed institutions, behaviour liable to be met with fines and a jail sentence. This approach was reinforced by aggressive nationalism within Burmese Buddhism, also highly intolerant of disrespectful behaviour.[90]

The heavy censorship of the media, prevailing for over half a century, no longer operated to the same extent. But a freer media became, in many cases, more aggressive, ready to protect the existing socio-political order and attack all perceived threats. To mention one specific instance, in 2017 these formal and informal controls were used to rebuff Phyo Min Thein, chief minister of Yangon, when he spoke critically about the military's preeminence in Burma. Phyo Min Thein was a leading NLD supporter belonging to the 88 Generation movement, and perhaps a possible future presidential candidate.[91]

A third item on this hidden agenda was evidently the desire to defeat the arms embargo and modernize the military's equipment. It was, perhaps, above all this mission that took Min Aung Hlaing on several trips abroad to places such as Thailand, Vietnam, Israel, India, Japan, China and Russia.[92] In November 2016 he addressed the European Union Military Committee (EUMC).[93] The *Tatmadaw*'s foreign contacts also included North Korea, a connection that aroused keen interest in Washington.[94]

Finally, and not least, the *Tatmadaw* devoted great attention to monitoring, containing and, possibly, on occasion, even undermining Suu Kyi's project of bringing peace and harmony to the borderlands.[95] She took responsibility for promoting national reconciliation by setting in motion a successor to the Panglong process of dialogue between warring groups. The original dialogue began in 1947 but was suspended when civil war broke out. Seven decades later official discussions aimed at achieving national reconciliation throughout the borderlands resumed with Suu Kyi in the chair.

On the face of it, Suu Kyi's mission of reconciliation benefitted the military, since the *Tatmadaw* had a terrible reputation for brutality in regions such as the Kayah and Karen (Kayin) states.[96] However, unlike Suu Kyi the military leadership apparently believed that it was preferable to create stability and peace through repression rather than through dialogue. A repressive approach would tend to increase the *Tatmadaw*'s control over actors and events, while an approach through dialogue would undermine the *Tatmadaw*'s claim to exercise autocratic power and unquestionable authority.

Another consideration in the generals' collective mind was possibly that political conditions in the Burmese borderlands were a crucial factor in the global investment decisions of large business corporations in China, India and far beyond. In the spring of 2017 a pipeline opened taking oil across Burma from the port of Kyaukpyu in Rakhine state towards Yunnan in China. The Chinese paid for the lion's share of this development. At the same time, Indian investment capital was developing Sittwe port, also in Rakhine, with a view to exploiting local gas and oil fields and strengthening links between Indian and Southeast Asian markets. Kyaukpyu and Sittwe, both on the Bay of Bengal adjacent to Bangladesh, were chronic inter-communal trouble spots.[97] These facts perhaps made dealing with the disruptive conflicts surrounding the Rohingya in Rakhine a particularly urgent matter for the *Tatmadaw*.

The pipeline not only stretched across Rakhine state with all its troubles but also crossed the turbulent Shan state adjacent to China. Shan state was a stamping ground of the Arakan army, which was also active in Rakhine. Did the *Tatmadaw* fear that Burma's prospective earnings as a key node within China's planned 'one belt, one road' infrastructure plan might be threatened as a result?[98]

Dialogue or repression?

Supporters of democracy and autocracy have been engaged in a long struggle within Burma. Since 2015 this struggle has passed through two phases. The first major exercise of power under the 2008 Constitution by Burma's newly enfranchised voters and its newly unmuzzled mass media occurred during the election in 2015. The result lifted Suu Kyi and her party into government. In sharp contrast, the second major exercise of the newly released popular will in 2017 was directed against the Rohingya in particular and Muslims in general. This time popular opinion was led by demagogic orators, and enacted by vicious mobs and violent police and military action.

In other words, between 2015 and 2017 the Burmese people turned from hope to fear, and from support for a potential benefactor, Suu Kyi, to aggression against a supposed threat, the Rohingya, demonized as an enemy of Burmese Buddhism. These two waves of popular sentiment were equally hard to resist. The *Tamadaw* surely loathed the political rise of Suu Kyi but dared not say so openly for fear of offending Western opinion and frightening off potential investors. Similarly, Suu Kyi surely loathed the wave of intense violence directed against the Rohingya and other Muslims. She apparently dared not say so openly for fear of offending Buddhist opinion, starting a political fight she could not win in Burma, and weakening her own capacity to exert leverage on other matters.

It seems that the larger and more mixed the audience and the more public and formal the event, the more cautious or ambiguous were Suu Kyi's words. For example, on 7th September 2017 she signalled humanitarian intent when she made the unscripted remark to a press conference that 'we have to take care of everybody who is in our country, whether or not they are our citizens'.[99] By contrast, on September 19th, in a televised address to a large audience at Naypyidaw, the Burmese capital and *Tatmadaw* stronghold, she rather robotically asserted that in North Rakhine state, where the Rohingya were being violently expelled from their burning villages, 'The security forces have been instructed to adhere strictly to the code of conduct in carrying out security operations, to exercise all due restraint and to take full measures to avoid collateral damage and the harming of innocent civilians.' As Win Htein, a former military officer high up in the NLD, told the *New York Times*, '"The army, they are watching her every word.... One misstep on the Muslim issue, and they can make their move".'[100]

Suu Kyi's battles with the *Tatmadaw*'s leadership in 2016 and 2017 were apparently being fought mainly behind the castle walls, so to speak, away from the public gaze. We get occasional glimpses of the struggle going on within government. For example, in the by-elections held in April 2017, the NLD campaigned for Burma to be a 'genuine, democratic, federal union', suggesting that if Suu Kyi had the authority and opportunity she would offer more rights and responsibilities to the borderlands than would General Min Aung Hlaing.[101] This difference of approach between the general and Suu Kyi was also expressed in their respective speeches at one of the meetings she chaired aimed at achieving national reconciliation in the borderlands, held at Naypyidaw in May 2017.

The audience included representatives sent by the dissident United Wa State Army from the northern Shan region along with their allies. These rebels had accepted Suu Kyi's invitation to attend the Naypyidaw meeting even though they strongly disagreed with the way that the process of national reconciliation was being organized. Their fragile trust was surely not strengthened when the *Tatmadaw*'s commander in chief deliberately injected the rhetoric of violent repression into this gathering supposedly designed to foster positive peaceful interchange.

Min Aung Hlaing made it clear in his address that he thought those dissident militias were 'grabbing power and splitting from the Union through armed struggle'. The military would take action against 'any organization committing destructive acts'. In very sharp contrast, Suu Kyi's own speech stressed the need for 'political dialogue' to 'identify common ground'. This was better, she said, than having to 'listen from afar to the words and speeches of others and seek to draw conclusions from them'. These remarks implied strong criticism of the *Tatmadaw*'s approach.[102]

Those two speeches, taken together, sum up the struggle in which Suu Kyi was engaged: pressing for sustained, open and mutually-respectful political dialogue, clearing the way for social transformation; and opposing the *Tatmadaw*'s strategy which favoured repressive strictness, silencing competing voices, restricting political freedoms, and seeking utter domination.

Another indication of Suu Kyi's approach is the Annan Report[103] that she commissioned in 2016 on the widespread violence and victimization in North Rakhine, near the Bangladeshi border. A team led by Kofi Annan, one-time UN Secretary-General, carried out a detailed independent investigation over twelve months. It was published in August 2017. The Annan investigation was strongly opposed by the *Tatmadaw*, who wanted instead an in-house inquiry under its control.[104] But Suu Kyi achieved a crucial victory in the national parliament in September 2016 and the independent investigation she had sponsored went ahead.[105]

The Annan Report states that about one tenth of the world's stateless people reside in Burma and 'the Muslims in Rakhine constitute the single biggest stateless community in the world'.[106] The Rohingya include descendants of migrants drawn into the country from India during the British occupation, although some have been in Burma much longer.[107] For decades the Burmese government has refused to recognize the Rohingya as an official Burmese ethnic identity and has denied them Burmese citizenship.[108]

The Rohingya's situation became deadly serious during a bloody round of inter-communal violence in Rakhine state during 2012. Here is the gruesome message given out by the editors of the *Development Journal*, published by Buddhist activists from Rakhine state's largest political party. They told their readers: 'Hitler and Eichmann were the enemies of the Jews, but ... they were probably heroes to the Germans'. They added that 'In order for a country's survival, the survival of a race, or in defence of national sovereignty, crimes against humanity or in-human acts may justifiably be committed.' They concluded: 'We no longer wish to hold permanent concerns about the Bengali in our midst. We just want to get it over and done with, once and for all.'[109] By 'Bengali' they meant the Rohingya.

The Rohingya were made hate objects by extremist Buddhist monks whose leaders were influential enough to secure the overtly anti-Muslim Protection of Race and Religion Laws in 2014.[110] Inter-communal violence in Rakhine between Muslim and Buddhist villagers encouraged the growth of irregular militias. Attacks by the Arakan Rohingya Salvation Army (ARSA) on police and military targets in October and November 2016 brought deaths on both sides. During 2017 there was a punitive response by the *Tatmadaw* and local Rakhine Buddhist activists. The *Tatmadaw* confronted a besieged, politically isolated and socially estranged population stigmatized as the enemy within.

The sustained attack on Rohingya communities resulted in a mass emigration by land and sea. Land mines were planted near the border with Bangladesh on the Burmese side. In early September Jonathan Head, BBC Southeast Asia correspondent, reported that local Buddhist villagers were torching Rohingya villages in North Rakhine state.[111] On 11th September 2017 the

138 *Aung San Suu Kyi*

United Nations High Commissioner for Human Rights described the Burmese military operation against the Rohingya as 'a textbook example of ethnic cleansing'.[112]

This statement both reflected and intensified widespread public opinion, especially in the West and the Muslim world. Understandably, it got far more publicity than Kofi Annan's report,[113] published the previous month, which Suu Kyi had commissioned a year earlier against the *Tatmadaw*'s opposition. The Annan Report clearly identified the human rights crisis and the development crisis lying behind the immediate security crisis. It made several recommendations including the following (with the relevant identifying numbers in brackets): greater investment in local infrastructure, agriculture and business, especially for Muslim entrepreneurs, partly financed by the proceeds of extractive industry in Rakhine state (1–10); rapid movement on implementing effective allocation of national verification cards, as part of a wider effort to clarify residency rights, simplify citizenship regulations, and facilitate naturalization, especially for those threatened with statelessness (11–17); radically reducing barriers to freedom of movement and access to services, closing down camps for internally displaced people as soon as possible, while ensuring dignified and humane treatment for those involved (18–26); improving humanitarian access and access by the media (27–32); extending the availability of education and health care while eradicating the trade in illegal drugs as well as corruption amongst officials (33–50); promoting inter-communal dialogue within civil society, buttressed by democratic election of village leaders and administrators and, at state level, a minister for ethnic affairs and a women's affairs department (51–9); systematic training of community leaders in mediation and dialogue as techniques for promoting reconciliation, and human rights training for security personnel reinforced by clearer identification of individuals through name badges and CCTV (60–71); reinforcing awareness of social justice principles within the judiciary (72–5); cooperation between the governments of Burma (Myanmar) and Bangladesh to facilitate the return of refugees subject to joint verification processes; discussion of the challenges in Rakhine state with neighbouring countries; and the appointment for one year of a Burmese government minister to oversee the implementation of these recommendations (76–88).

The Annan Report helped Suu Kyi to push for a more constructive, humane and accommodating approach to the crises in North Rakhine. In this case, as in Burma's other chronic trouble spots, Suu Kyi's key demand was for dialogue, hopefully leading toward reconciliation and ultimately, socio-political transformation. However, the difficulties Suu Kyi faced were enormous. She had to exert influence on Burmese generals trained over decades to regard all civilians as potential enemies, soldiers whose ethos was most fully expressed when organizing violent military operations in the borderlands. She also needed to enrol and enthuse Burmese citizens, a cautious and conservative population that had voted for her party in 2015 but was accustomed in everyday life to obeying orders from above without question and paying up promptly when bribes were demanded.

More generally, the approach being pursued by Suu Kyi demanded heightened self-awareness by individuals and groups on all sides as well as acute sensitivity by everybody to the needs, character and situation of others. It meant turning away from stereotypical representations that distort perception.[114] As Tom Scheff argues,[115] alienation thrives when self-awareness and consideration for others are absent.[116] Overcoming these obstacles was a considerable challenge for Suu Kyi, as was working in Naypyidaw alongside governmental colleagues some of whom had spent two decades trying to eliminate or disable her as a political operator.

Also highly relevant was the murder in broad daylight of Suu Kyi's close adviser for many years. This was Ko Ni, a brilliant Muslim lawyer, born in Katha, a town 150 miles north of Mandalay. It was Ko Ni who suggested the ingenious device of installing Suu Kyi as State Counsellor when the presidency of Burma was denied her. Ko Ni had plans to alter Burma's constitution and reduce the military's privileged position in government. He spoke openly and bravely about the need to limit the military's power and privilege. But on 29th January 2017 Ko Ni was assassinated in Yangon International Airport as he was getting a taxi.[117]

To summarize, in 1988 Aung San, the military hero, totemic symbol of the *Tatmadaw*, became Suu Kyi's figurehead as she campaigned for political power at the head of the National League for Democracy. In 2016 an ironic reversal took place. Suu Kyi, the democratic hero, totemic leader of the NLD, entered the government and became the *Tatmadaw*'s fig leaf. This became an increasingly uncomfortable situation for Suu Kyi but, crucially, it got her a place at the top table within government, a place where she could seek small and medium-sized victories, salami-style.

In 2016 Suu Kyi's bargaining power and political armoury were substantially reduced by the failure of her main foreign political supporter, Hillary Clinton, to become the US president. As a result, the risk Suu Kyi faced was that instead of instilling her father's vision in the ruling circles of the *Tatmadaw* she might herself become tarred with their brush in the eyes of the world. What could she achieve in her weakened circumstances? Could Suu Kyi effectively exploit her place at the top table without the legal wizardry and daring of Ko Ni and strong diplomatic support from Washington? Could she mobilize the resources needed to implement the Annan Report's recommendations designed to promote peace and prosperity for all in the Rakhine state, including returning Rohingya families? How difficult would it be to organize their return?

There were more questions than answers. Could Suu Kyi push ahead effectively with the process of achieving reconciliation amongst the warring militias in Burma's borderland, in spite of the *Tatmadaw*'s often unhelpful interventions? Could the National League for Democracy's campaign for a more open, humanitarian and democratic Burma overcome the opposing thrust of military authoritarianism and racist propaganda? Above all, how would Suu Kyi play her cards before, during and after the national election in 2020, assuming this took place as planned?

In May 2017 Larry Jagan, a former BBC news editor and Burma specialist, wrote that the Burmese military might be interested in 'strengthening the formal relation between Min Aung Hlaing and Aung San Suu Kyi', perhaps through a 'form of power sharing with the current commander in chief becoming president'. In any case, he concluded, 'Min Aung Hlaing has political ambitions and is forecast to make a bid for the presidency in 2020'.[118] How would Suu Kyi respond to such initiatives, if they were taken? Nobody knows but, as Win Htein, her NLD colleague put it, '"It's always a dance with the generals … She needs to be very quick on her feet."'[119]

Notes

1. Emerson Yuntho, 'Take back Aung San Suu Kyi's Nobel Peace Prize' at https://www.change.org/p/take-back-aung-san-suu-kyi-s-nobel-peace-prize (accessed 19th May 2017). Emerson Yuntho is the Coordinator of the Legal and Judicial Monitoring Division of Indonesia Corruption Watch (ICW).
2. Centre for Peace and Conflict Studies (2010); Kivima and Pasch 2009; Pederson 2007.
3. 'Desmond Tutu condemns Aung San Suu Kyi: "Silence is too high a price"', 8th September 2017, *The Guardian* at https://www.theguardian.com/world/2017/sep/08/desmond-tutu-condemns-aung-san-suu-kyi-price-of-your-silence-is-too-steep (accessed 8th September 2017).
4. 'Oxford college removes painting of Aung San Suu Kyi from display', 30th September 2017, *The Guardian* at https://www.theguardian.com/world/2017/sep/29/oxford-college-removes-painting-of-aung-san-suu-kyi-from-display; 'City of London to debate stripping Aung San Suu Kyi of freedom award', 7th October 2017, *The Guardian* at https://www.theguardian.com/world/2017/oct/07/city-london-debate-stripping-aung-san-suu-kyi-freedom-myanmar-rohingya (accessed 11th October 2017).
5. Zöllner 2012; Leprince de Beaumont 1983.
6. Larkin 2011, 7–65; 'Broken land, broken promises – Myanmar's controversial copper mines', 10th February 2015, *DW.com Media Centre*, at http://www.dw.com/en/broken-land-broken-promises-myanmars-controversial-copper-mines/a-18244246 (accessed 22nd June 2017); Skidmore 2004.
7. On Naypyidaw see 'Burma's bizarre capital: a super-sized slice of post-apocalypse suburbia', 'A New Guide to Burma's Capital City, Naypyidaw', 19th March 2015, *The Guardian* at https://www.theguardian.com/cities/2015/mar/19/burmas-capital-naypyidaw-post-apocalypse-suburbia-highways-wifi (accessed 10th August 2017).
8. 'Suu Kyi adjusts to life in Naypyidaw', 2nd May 2012, *Financial Times* at http://www.ft.com/cms/s/0/78eaf552-93a6-11e1-baf0-00144feab49a.html#axzz44KrJFIuw (accessed 23rd August 2016); Cheesman, Skidmore and Wilson 2012; Dittmer 2010.
9. Quoted in Silverstein 1993, 19–20, 27, 103.
10. Callahan 2003; Egreteau 2016; Egreteau and Jagan 2013; Nakanishi 2013; Rogers 2010; Taylor 2015.
11. Aung San Suu Kyi 1991a; Aung San Suu Kyi 1997; Aung Zaw 2013; Bengtsson 2012; Clements 2008; Lintner 2011; Pederson 2015; Popham 2011; Popham 2016; Smith 2013; Stewart 2008; Wintle 2007; Zöllner 2014; Aung San Suu Kyi 1991b.

12 'Rangoon Journal; A Daughter of Burma, but Can She Be a Symbol?', 11th January 1989, *New York Times*, at http://www.nytimes.com/1989/01/11/world/rangoon-journal-a-daughter-of-burma-but-can-she-be-a-symbol.html (accessed 27th March 2017).
13 Aung San Suu Kyi 1991d, 204.
14 Aung San Suu Kyi 1985; Dittmer 2010; Ho 2015; Lintner 1990; Lintner 1994; Lintner 2015; Orwell 1989; Rogers 2012; Skidmore 2004; Spiro 1970; Steinberg 2010; Thant Myint-U 2007a; Thant Myint-U 2011.
15 Lintner 1994.
16 James Scott suggests that the mountainou of Burma are part of a vast zone whose semi-nomadic residents have avoided or resisted subjection to central government. This zone arguably includes segments of southwest China, northeast India, and parts of five Southeast Asian countries. Scott 2009; Leach 1954; Tambiah 2002, 82–121.
17 Crosthwaite 1912; Nisbet 1901.
18 Lintner 2015; Thant Myint-U 2011; Egreteau, R. and Jagan, L. 2013.
19 Crosthwaite 1912, 188–208, Nisbet 1901, 310–14.
20 Crosthwaite 1912, 20.
21 Crosthwaite 1912, 20.
22 Lord Dufferin, another Anglo-Irishman, served as Viceroy of India between 1884 and 1888. Davenport-Hines 2004; Gailey 2015.
23 Larkin 2011, 43.
24 Thant Myint-U 2001, 186–219, especially 199–200.
25 Spiro 1970; Smith 2015.
26 Adas 1989; Adas 2011; Brown 2014.
27 Orwell 1989.
28 Orwell 1989, viii, xv. George Orwell (1903–50), born Eric Blair, spent five years (1922–27) serving in Burma as a member of the Indian Imperial Police, rising to be an Assistant District Superintendent. *Burmese Days* first appeared in 1934. Larkin 2011.
29 Kuchta 2010, 149–50, 169–78
30 Orwell 1989, 192.
31 Orwell 1989, 209.
32 Orwell's account stands somewhere between social realism and bitter satire. For balance, consider the many good works in Burma of the colonial administrators Vernon Donnison and his wife Ruth; also, the trenchant plain speaking of the colonial magistrate Maurice Collis. Like Orwell's John Flory, they saw the Burmese point of view, as far as they could, and spoke up for it. Donnison 2005; Collis 1945.
33 Aung-Thwin 2011; Collis 1945.
34 Htway 1972. Recent unrest in Ireland and India influenced the Burmese political climate. The thakins' spiritual guide Kodaw Hmaing (1876–1964) wrote about boycotts and *Swaraj*.
35 Lebra 1977, 39–74.
36 Taylor 2015, especially 26–44.
37 Brea 2003.
38 Callahan 2003,13–20, 48–67, 114–16, 161–2, 169–71.
39 Lebra 1977, 70.
40 Lebra 1977, 74.
41 http://www.burmanet.org/news/2014/09/30/the-irrawaddy-tokyo-calling/; Collis 1956; Hla Oo 2011; Journal Kyaw U Chit Maung 2006; Latimer 2005 and Fraser 2000.
42 Hla Oo 2011, 6–11; Carew 2017, 243–5.
43 Carew 2017, 225–30.
44 Silverstein 1993, 39–41.

45 http://www.networkmyanmar.org/images/stories/PDF17/Death-of-Aung-San-rev2.pdf (accessed 21st August 2016). Also Carew 2017, 246–8; Kim Oung 1996.
46 Butwell 1963; U Nu 1954;Tucker 2001.
47 Maung Zarni 2010, 61.
48 Egreteau and Jagan 2013, 71–118; Callahan 2003, 114–207; Lintner 1994, 1–210; Taylor 2015, 107–263.
49 Callahan 2003, 173.
50 Silverstein 1977.
51 Nakanishi 2013.
52 For an insightful analysis of the impact of Buddhism on Burmese politics, and vice versa, see Houtman 1999.
53 'Lieutenant-General Myint Swe, then head of military affairs and security, exhorted me to go and pay homage at the Shwedagon pagoda … to build up my karma' (Maung Zarni 2010, 76, note 27).
54 'Myanmar's ex-president Thein Sein becomes Buddhist monk', 5th April 2016, *The Guardian* at https://www.theguardian.com/world/2016/apr/05/myanmars-ex-president-thein-sein-becomes-buddhist-monk (accessed 23rd August 2016).
55 Taylor 2015.
56 Emma Larkin, 'The Force of a Woman', 4th May 2012, *The New Republic* at https://newrepublic.com/article/103083/lady-peacock-aung-san-suu-kyi (accessed 14th March 2017).
57 Wintle 2007, 204–5; Popham 2011, 214–16.
58 Aung San Suu Kyi 1991c.
59 Aung San Suu Kyi 1991b.
60 Aung San Suu Kyi 1985.
61 Taylor 2015, 259, 287, 289, 312; Callahan 2003, 187, 201; Nakanishi 2013, 129.
62 Aung Zaw 2013, 70; Butwell 1963; U Nu 1954.
63 See Aung Zaw 2013, 68–71.
64 Quotes from Ma Thanegi's diary are taken from Popham 2011.
65 Popham 2011, 108–9.
66 Quoted in Popham 2011, 109.
67 Popham 2011, 110.
68 Thant Myint-U 2007a, 120–1.
69 Wintle 2007, 210–16; Popham 2011, 123–7.
70 Wintle 2007, xxix.
71 Wintle 2007, 384–90; Popham 2011, 332–3.
72 Mandela on Robben Island: 'while it was never a home … it had become a place where I felt comfortable'. Mandela 2003b, 264.
73 Cheeseman, Skidmore and Wilson 2012. Fink 2001; Skidmore 2004; Rogers 2010.
74 Zöllner 2014; Wintle 2007, 5.
75 'Special Report: An image makeover for Myanmar Inc', April 12th 2012, *Reuters* at http://www.reuters.com/article/us-myanmar-cronies-image-idUSBRE83B0YU20120412 (accessed 15th March 2017). Zaw Zaw became chairman of the Max Myanmar Group of Companies, which built a strong conglomerate position in, for example, tourism, transport, energy and banking.
76 'Thoughts on the Bangkok Process', March 2004, *The Irrawaddy* at http://www2.irrawaddy.com/article.php?art_id=918 (accessed 17th March 2017): Kurlantzick and Stewart 2013.
77 Popham 2011, 350–63.
78 International Crisis Group, 'Myanmar's peace process: Getting to a political dialogue' in *ICG Briefing* 149, 19th October 2016 at https://www.crisisgroup.org/asia/south-east-asia/myanmar/myanmar-s-peace-process-getting-political-dialogue (accessed 22nd June 2017).

79 These transactions were bedevilled by a continuing struggle for political advantage between Than Shwe and his chief rival, Khin Nyunt who was excluded from the government in 2004. Brigadier General Aung Kyi was the minister managing official liaison with Suu Kyi. They met nine times between October 2007 and January 2010. Suu Kyi also had three short meetings with Than Shwe, the top general, who reportedly 'Treated her like a niece being addressed by her uncle' (Kyaw Yin Hlaing 2010, 37). *Altsean-Burma* on Aung Kyi at http://www.altsean.org/Research/SPDC%20Whos%20Who/SPDC/AungKyi.htm (accessed 16th September 2017); Maung Zarni 2010, 60–63.
80 Larkin 2010, 204.
81 'Clinton and Aung San Suu Kyi pledge to work together for Burma democracy', 2nd December 2011, *The Guardian* at https://www.theguardian.com/world/2011/dec/02/hillary-clinton-aung-san-suu-kyi-burma-democracy (accessed 8th October 2017). On the Saffron Revolution see Human Rights Watch, 'The Resistance of the Monks: Buddhism and Activism in Burma,' 22 September 2009 at: http://www.refworld.org/docid/4ab87fac2.html [accessed 9 January 2018].
82 'The taming of the NLD…by the NLD', 12th August 2015, *New Mandala*, at http://www.newmandala.org/the-taming-of-the-nld-by-the-nld/ (accessed 22nd June 2017).
83 'Myanmar's Suu Kyi unlikely to take formal role in new government', 21st March 2016, *Reuters* on at http://www.reuters.com/article/us-myanmar-politics-idUSKCN0WM0T2 (accessed 23rd August 2016).
84 See, for example, Hane and Perez 2015. See also Seekins 2007.
85 For background on the military and Suu Kyi, see Egreteau 2016.
86 http://amanpour.blogs.cnn.com/2012/09/21/aung-san-suu-kyi-has-soft-spot-for-the-military-generals/, 21st September 2012 (accessed 27th March 2017).
87 See 'Myanmar: the military-commercial complex', 1st February 2017, *Financial Times* at https://www.ft.com/content/c6fe7dce-d26a-11e6-b06b-680c49b4b4c0?mhq5j=e1 (accessed 3rd March 2017).
88 Liu Yun, 'Civil military relations in Myanmar: legitimacy and political patronage', 21st December 2016, *Tea Circle* at https://teacircleoxford.com/2016/12/21/civil-military-relations-in-myanmar-legitimacy-and-political-patronage/ (accessed 15th March 2017).
89 For the whole interview see 'Burma's top general: "I am prepared to talk and answer and discuss" with Aung San Suu Kyi's government', 23rd November 2017 *Washington Post*, at https://www.washingtonpost.com/opinions/burmas-top-general-i-am-prepared-to-talk-and-answer-and-discuss-with-aung-san-suu-kyis-government/2015/11/23/ddf3ac76-9124-11e5-a2d6-f57908580b1f_story.html?utm_term=.5838c7cf51d6 (accessed 26th May 2017).
90 'A New Zealander Is Facing 4 Years in a Burmese Prison for "insulting Buddhism"', 24th December 2014, *Time*, at http://time.com/3646432/burma-myanmar-new-zealander-insulting-buddhism-vgastro/ (22nd June 2017).
91 In 2017 political and judical manoeuvres were apparently underway to contain or weaken a possible new national political leader from the NLD, Phyo Min Thein, chief minister of Yangon, a radical reformer and an 88 Generation student leader who, like Suu Kyi, has served about fifteen years behind bars. See 'Yangon politician emerges as possible Suu Kyi successor', 7th February 2017, *Nikkei Asia Review*, at https://asia.nikkei.com/Politics-Economy/Policy-Politics/Yangon-politician-emerges-as-possible-Suu-Kyi-successor; 'Myanmar's New Leaders Still Step Softly Around Military', 14th July 2017, *VOA News* at www.voanews.comamyanmar-leaders-step-softly-around-military3943994.html; 'Eurocham networking event with Yangon chief minister in Brussels' (15th June 2017) at www.eurocham-myanmar.orgevent56EuroCham-networking-dinner-with-Yangon-Chief-

Minister-in-Brussels; 'NLD Warns Yangon Chief Minister for Controversial Remarks' 16th July 2017, *The Irrawaddy*, at https://www.irrawaddy.com/news/burma/nld-warns-yangon-chief-minister-controversial-remarks.html; 'Myanmar Army Calls for Action Against Yangon Chief Minister', 11th July 2017, *The Irrawaddy*, at https://www.irrawaddy.com/news/burma/breaking-myanmar-army-calls-action-yangon-chief-minister.html (all accessed 2nd August 2017).

92 Lutz-Auras 2015; Bert Lintner, 'Enter Russia into Myanmar's armed fray', 5th April 2017, *Asia Times*, at http://www.atimes.com/article/enter-russia-myanmars-armed-fray/ (accessed 11th April 2017).

93 'In EU meeting Min Aung Hlaing defends Army's political role', 10th November 2016, *The Irrawaddy*, at https://www.irrawaddy.com/opinion/commentary/in-eu-meeting-min-aung-hlaing-defends-armys-political-role.html (accessed 15th March 2017).

94 'North Korea and Myanmar restore diplomatic ties', 26th April 2007, *New York Times* at http://www.nytimes.com/2007/04/26/world/asia/26iht-myanmar.4.5457138.html (accessed 22nd June 2017). 'North Korea Myanmar Links in the Spotlight Under Trump', 25th July 2017, *The Diplomat* at https://thediplomat.com/2017/07/north-korea-myanmar-links-in-the-spotlight-under-trump/ (accessed 3rd January 2018); 'North Korea: South seizes second ship in oil supply row', 31st December 2017, *BBC News* at http://www.bbc.co.uknewsworld-asia-42527294 (accessed 3rd January 2018). Also Maung Zarni 2010, 67; Seith 2010.

95 'Myanmar military calls for ethnic rebels to join peace talks', 7th March 2017, *New India Express* at http://www.newindianexpress.com/world/2017/mar/07/myanmar-military-calls-for-ethnic-rebels-to-join-peace-talks-1578757.html (accessed 27th March 2017).

96 http://www.burmalink.org/background/thailand-burma-border/overview/ (accessed 27th March 2017).

97 On Kyaukpyu, see 'Burma: New violence in Arakan state', 28th October 2012, *Human Rights Watch*, at https://www.hrw.org/news/2012/10/26/burma-new-violence-arakan-state (accessed 11th April 2017).

98 'A weak plank in Asia's infrastructure drive', 29th March 2017, *Asia Times*, at http://www.atimes.com/article/myanmar-weak-plank-asia-infrastructure-drive/ (accessed 11th April 2017).

99 'Aung San Suu Kyi insists Myanmar trying to 'take care of everybody' in strife-torn state', 7th September 2017 at http://www.scmp.com/news/asia/south-asia/article/2110191/aung-san-suu-kyi-insists-myanmar-trying-take-care-everybody (accessed 9th September 2017).

100 'A Much-Changed Icon, Aung San Suu Kyi Evades Rohingya Accusations', 18th September 2017 at https://www.nytimes.com/2017/09/18/world/asia/aung-san-suu-kyi-speech-rohingya.html?mcubz=0 (accessed 19th September 2017).

101 'National League for Democracy Party presents policy and programmes', 11th February 2017, *Global New Light of Myanmar*, at http://www.globalnewlightofmyanmar.com/national-league-for-democracy-party-presents-policy-and-programmes/ (accessed 27th March 2017).

102 'Union Peace Conference Opens to Military Critique of Ethnic Demands', 24th May 2017, *The Irrawaddy*, at https://www.irrawaddy.com/news/burma/union-peace-conference-opens-to-military-critique-of-ethnic-demands.html and 'State Counsellor Daw Aung San Suu Kyi's speech at the opening ceremony of the Union Peace Conference – 21st Century Panglong 2nd session', 25th May 2017, *Global New Light of Myanmar* at http://www.globalnewlightofmyanmar.com/state-counsellor-daw-aung-san-suu-kyis-speech-at-the-opening-ceremony-of-the-union-peace-conference-21st-century-panglong-2nd-session/ (both accessed 22nd June 2017).

103 Advisory Commission on Rakhine State 2017; henceforth ACRS 2017.

104 The Burmese government set up its own Central Committee on Implementation of Peace, Stability and Development of Rakhine State, which Suu Kyi headed although it also had strong military representation. See 'Formation of Central Committee on Implementation of Peace, Stability and Development of Rakhine State (Notification 23/2016)' at https://myanmar-law-library.org/IMG/pdf/9_formation_of_central_committee_on_implementation_of_peace_stability_and_development_of_rakhine_state_notification_23_2016_.pdf and (accessed 19th September 2017).

105 In early September 2016 an unsuccessful motion in the national parliament to abolish the Annan commission 'was supported by the Arakan National Party (ANP), the Union Solidarity and Development Party (USDP) and all military-appointed lawmakers' (ACRS 2017, 15).

106 ACRS 2017, 9. Advisory Commission on Rakhine State, chaired by Kofi Annan. Sometimes referred to here as the Annan report. Available at www.rakhinecommission.org/app/uploads/2017/08/FinalReport_Eng.pdf (accessed 3rd September 2017).

107 'India plans to deport thousands of Rohingya refugees', 14th August 2017 at Al Jazeera at http://www.aljazeera.com/news/2017/08/india-plans-deport-thousands-rohingya-refugees-170814110027809.html (accessed 9th September 2017).

108 See Wade 2017 for a useful overview and analysis.

109 Quoted in Wade 2017, 134, 277. This is from the November 2012 issue of the *Development Journal*, citing a copy in the personal possession of Francis Wade. A longer version of this quotation is cited on 15th September 2017 in the Dhaka-based newspaper *The Daily Star*. See 'Too little, too late' at http://www.thedailystar.net/frontpage/mayanmar-rohingya-refugee-crisis-too-little-too-late-1462351 (accessed 16th September 2017). See also Frewer 2015.

110 This legislation restricted marriages between Buddhists and non-Buddhists while giving local governments powers to impose limits on the number of children women in their area might produce. See US Library of Congress Global Legal Monitor, 14th September 2015 'Four "Race and Religion Protection Laws" adopted' at http://www.loc.gov/law/foreign-news/article/burma-four-race-and-religion-protection-laws-adopted/ (accessed 13th September 2017).

111 See, for example, Jonathan Head, Twitter @pakhead.

112 'Rohingya seemingly face "ethnic cleansing", says UN rights chief Zeid Ra'ad al-Hussein', 11th September 2017, *The Indian Express* at http://indianexpress.com/article/world/rohingya-seemingly-face-ethnic-cleansing-says-un-rights-chief-zeid-raad-al-hussein-4838750/ (accessed 13th September 2017).

113 ACRS 2017.

114 The Rohingya are seen as Indian or Bangladeshi or, to use the derogatory term often employed in Burma, *kalar*. See, for example, the mocking tone of the comedian Min Maw Kun, and the repeated use of the term *kalar* in 'Rohingya by Min Maw Kun and Nay Min (Director Maung Myo Min)' at https://www.youtube.com/watch?v=AlmBYB8GB4M (accessed 13th September 2017).

115 Scheff 2000.

116 To paraphrase and oversimplify, unhappiness with oneself or with one's group generates hatred of the other. In those circumstances, self-control and humanitarian concern are diminished. Anger and aggression get free rein, unconstrained by feelings of shame, feelings that unsettle the self without being recognized for what they are. In less fraught circumstances shame feelings serve as a moral compass, inhibiting cruel impulses.

117 'Brazen Killing of Myanmar Lawyer Came After He Sparred With Military', 2nd February 2017, *New York Times* at https://www.nytimes.com/2017/02/02/world/asia/myanmar-ko-ni-lawyer-constitution-military.html?mcubz=1; 'U Ko Ni in his own words', 30th January 2017, *The Irrawaddy* at https://www.irrawaddy.com/news/burma/u-ko-ni-in-his-own-words.html; 'Obituary: The "irreplaceable"

U Ko Ni', 31st January 2017, *Frontier Myanmar* at http://frontiermyanmar.net/en/obituary-the-irreplaceable-u-ko-ni; Melissa Crouch, 'A personal tribute to U Ko Ni', 31st January 2017, *New Mandala* at http://www.newmandala.org/personal-tribute-u-ko-ni/; 'A brazen political killing shakes Myanmar already teetering on the path to democracy', 24th March 2017, *Los Angeles Times* at http://www.latimes.com/world/la-fg-myanmar-ko-ni-assassination-2017-story.html;

'Free speech versus hate speech in Aung San Suu Kyi's Myanmar. Media freedom has soared in Asia's new democracy – but so has the language of hatred', 25th March 2017, *Irish Times* at http://www.irishtimes.com/news/world/asia-pacific/free-speech-versus-hate-speech-in-aung-san-suu-kyi-s-myanmar-1.3022211 (all accessed 23rd May 2017).

118 Larry Jagan, 'The lady and the generals are learning to get along', 11th May 2017, *Southasian Monitor* at http://southasianmonitor.com/2017/05/11/lady-generals-learning-get-along-2/ (accessed 4th September 2017).

119 'A Much-Changed Icon, Aung San Suu Kyi Evades Rohingya Accusations', 18th September 2017 at https://www.nytimes.com/2017/09/18/world/asia/aung-san-suu-kyi-speech-rohingya.html?mcubz=0 (accessed 19th September 2017).

Bibliography

Adas, M. (1989). 'Bandits, Monks and Pretender Kings. Patterns of Peasant Resistance and Revolt in Colonial Burma 1826–1941' in R.S. Weller and S.E. Guggenheim (eds) *Power and Protest in the Countryside: Studies of Rural Unrest in Asia, Europe and Latin America*. Durham, NC: Duke.

Adas, M. (2011). *The Burma Delta: Economic Development and Social Change on an Asian Rice Frontier, 1852–1941*. Madison, WI: University of Wisconsin Press.

Advisory Commission on Rakhine State (ACRS) (2017). *Towards a Peaceful, Fair and Prosperous Future for the People of Rakhine*. Geneva: Kofi Annan Foundation at www.rakhinecommission.org/app/uploads/2017/08/FinalReport_Eng.pdf (accessed 3rd September 2017).

Aung San Suu Kyi. (1985). *Let's Visit Burma*. London: Burke Publishing Company; also in Aung San Suu Kyi 1991a, 39–81 under the title *My Country and My People*.

Aung San Suu Kyi. (1991a). *Freedom from Fear and Other Writings*. Edited with an introduction by Michael Aris. London: Penguin Books.

Aung San Suu Kyi. (1991b). *Aung San of Burma*. Edinburgh: Kiscadale Publications; originally published in 1984; also in Aung San Suu Kyi 1991a, 3–38 under the title *My Father*.

Aung San Suu Kyi. (1991c). 'Intellectual Life in Burma and India under Colonialism' in Aung San Suu Kyi 1991a, 82–139; originally published in 1990.

Aung San Suu Kyi. (1991d). 'Speech to a Mass Rally at the Shwedagon Pagoda' in Aung San Suu Kyi 1991a, 198–204.

Aung San Suu Kyi. (1997). *Letters from Burma*. London: Penguin Books.

Aung-Thwin, M. (2011). *The Return of the Galon King: History, Law, and Rebellion in Colonial Burma*. Athens OH: Ohio University Press.

Aung Zaw (2013). *The Face of Resistance. Aung San Suu Kyi and Burma's Fight for Freedom*. Chiang Mai, Thailand: Mekong Press.

Bengtsson, J. (2012). *Aung San Suu Kyi. A Biography*. Dulles, VA: Potomac Books.

Brea, E. J. (2003). *In The Service of the Emperor: Essays on the Imperial Japanese Army*. Lincoln NE: University of Nebraska.

Brown, I. (2014). *A Colonial Economy in Crisis. Burma's Rice Cultivators and the World Depression of the 1930s*. London: Routledge.
Butwell, R. (1963) *U Nu of Burma*. Stanford, CA: Stanford University Press.
Callahan, M.P. (2003). *Making Enemies. War and State Building in Burma*. Ithica, NY: Cornell University Press.
Carew, K. (2017). *Dadland. A Journey into Uncharted Territory*. London: Vintage.
Cheeseman, N., Skidmore, M., and Wilson, T. (eds) (2012). *Myanmar's Transition. Openings, Obstacles and Opportunities*. Singapore: Institute of Southeast Asian Studies.
Clements, A. (2008). *The Voice of Hope. Aung San Suu Kyi. Conversations with Aung San Suu Kyi*. London: Rider Books.
Cockett, R. (2015). *Blood, Dreams and Gold. The Changing Face of Burma*. New Haven and London: Yale University Press.
Collis, M. (1945). *Trials in Burma*. London: Penguin Books.
Collis, M. (1956). *Last and First in Burma (1941–1948)*. London: Faber and Faber.
Crosthwaite, C. (1912). *The Pacification of Burma*. London: Edward Arnold.
Davenport-Hines, R. (2004). "Blackwood, Frederick Temple Hamilton-Temple, First Marquess of Dufferin and Ava (1826–1902)", *Oxford Dictionary of National Biography*. Oxford: Oxford University Press.
Dittmer, L. (ed.). (2010). *Burma or Myanmar? The Struggle for National Identity*. Singapore: World Scientific Publishing Co.
Donnison, D.V. (2005). *Last of the Guardians: A Story of Burma, Britain and a Family*. Newtown: Superscript.
Egreteau, R. and Jagan, L. (2013). *Soldiers and Diplomacy in Burma. Understanding the Foreign Relations of the Burmese Praetorian State*. Singapore: NUS Press.
Egreteau, R. (2016). *Caretaking Democratization. The Military and Political Change in Myanmar*. London: C Hurst & Co.
Elias, N. (1996). *The Germans. Power Struggles and the Development of Habitus in the Nineteenth and Twentieth Centuries*. Cambridge: Cambridge University Press.
Fink, C. (2001). *Living Silence. Burma under Military Rule*. London: Zed Books.
Fraser, G.M. (2000). *Quartered Safe Out Here*. London: HarperCollins.
Frewer, T. (2015). 'A Love of Sovereignty: Borders, Bureaucracy and The Rohingya Crisis – Analysis', *Eurasia Review*, 22nd December 2015 at http://www.eurasiareview.com/22122015-a-love-of-sovereignty-borders-bureaucracy-and-the-rohingya-crisis-analysis/ (accessed 16th September 2017).
Gailey, A. (2015). *The Lost Imperialist: Lord Dufferin, Memory and Mythmaking in an Age of Celebrity*. London: John Murray.
Hane, M. and Perez, L.G. (2015). *Premodern Japan. A Historical Survey*. Philadelphia, PA: Westview Press.
Hla Oo. (2011). *Burma in Limbo*. CreateSpace Independent Publishing Platform (see also http://hlaoo1980.blogspot.co.uk/p/burma-in-limbo.html).
Ho, T.C. (2015). *Romancing Human Rights: Gender, Intimacy, and Power between Burma and the West*. Honolulu: University of Hawai'i Press.
Houtman, G. (1999). *Mental Culture in Burmese Crisis Politics. Aung San Suu Kyi and the National League for Democracy*. Tokyo: Tokyo University of Foreign Studies.
Houtman, G. (2007). 'Aung San's *lan-zin*, the Blue Print and the Japanese occupation of Burma' in K. Nemoto (ed.) (2007) *Reconsidering the Japanese military occupation in Burma (1942–45)*. Research Institute for Languages and Cultures of Asia and Africa (ILCAA). Tokyo: Tokyo University of Foreign Studies, 179–227.

Htway, T. (1972). 'The Role of Literature in Nation-Building (with special reference to Burma)', *Journal of the Burma Research Society*, 1–2, December, 19–46; also at https://mmfreethinker.files.wordpress.com/2009/12/the-role-of-literature-in-nation-building-by-tin-htwe.pdf

Ibrahim, A. (2016). *The Rohingyas: Inside Myanmar's Hidden Genocide*. London: C. Hurst & Co.

Journal Kyaw U Chit Maung (2006). *A Man Like Him. Portrait of the Burmese Journalist Journal Kyaw U Chit Maung*. Ithaca, NY: Cornell University.

Kim Oung (1996). *Who Killed Aung San?* Bangkok: River Books.

Kivima, T. and Pasch, P. (2009). *The Dynamics of Conflict in the Multi-Ethnic Union of Myanmar. Peace and Conflict Impact Assessment*. London: Friedrich Ebert Stiftung

Kuchta, T. (2010). *Semi-Detached Empire. Suburbia and the Colonization of Britain, 1880 to the Present*. London: University of Virginia Press.

Kurlantzick, J. and Stewart, D.T. (2013). 'Burma's Reforms and Regional Cooperation in East Asia'. International Security Research and Outreach Programme, International Security and Intelligence Bureau, Summer 2013. Ottowa: Foreign Affairs and International Trade Canada.

Kyaw Yin Hlaing. (2010). 'Problems with the Process of Reconciliation' in Riefel (2010), 33–51.

Lall, M. (2016). *Understanding Reform in Myanmar: People and Society in the Wake of Military Rule*. London: Hurst.

Larkin, E. (2010). *Everything is Broken. A Tale of Catastrophe in Burma*. London: Penguin.

Larkin, E. (2011). *Finding George Orwell in Burma*. London: Penguin Books.

Latimer, J. (2005). *Burma. The Forgotten War*. London: John Murray.

Leach, E.R. (1954). *Political Systems of Highland Burma: A Study of Kachin Social Structure*. London: Athlone Press.

Lebra, J.C. (1977). *Japanese Trained Armies in Southeast Asia*. New York: Columbia University Press.

Leprince de Beaumont, J.M. (1983). *La Belle et la Bête*. Paris: Gallimard Jeunesse.

Lintner, B. (1990). *Land of Jade. A Journey Through Insurgent Burma*. Edinburgh: Kiscadale Publications.

Lintner, B. (1994). *Burma in Revolt. Opium and Insurgency since 1948*. Chiang Mai, Thailand: Silkworm Books.

Linter, B. (2011). *Aung San Suu Kyi and Burma's Struggle for Democracy*. Chiang Mai, Thailand: Silkworm Books.

Lintner, B. (2015). *Great Game East. India, China, and the Struggle for Asia's Most Volatile Frontier*. New Haven, CT: Yale University Press.

Lutz-Auras, L. (2015). 'Russia and Myanmar – Friends in Need?', *Journal of Current Southeast Asian Affairs*, 34, 2, 165–198.

Mandela, M. (2003b) *Nelson Mandela in his Own Words. From Freedom to the Future*. Edited by K. Asmal, D. Chidester and W. James. London: Abacus.

Maung Zarni. (2010). 'An Inside View of Reconciliation' in Riefel 2010, 52–76.

Nakanishi, Y. (2013). *Strong Soldiers, Failed Revolution. The State and Military in Burma, 1962–88*. Singapore: NUS Press.

Nisbet, J. (1901). *Burma Under British Rule- and Before*. London: Constable.

Orwell, G. (1989). *Burmese Days*. London: Penguin Books.

Pederson, R. (2015). *Aung San Suu Kyi and the New Struggle for the Soul of a Nation*. New York, NY: Pegasus Books.

Pederson, M.B. (2007). *Promoting Human Rights in Burma: A Critique of Western Sanctions Policy.* London: Rowman and Litlefield.
Popham, P. (2011). *The Lady and the Peacock. The Life of Aung San Suu Kyi.* London: Rider Books.
Popham, P. (2016). *The Lady and the Generals. Aung San Suu Kyi and Burma's Struggle for Freedom.* London: Rider Books.
Riefel, L. (ed.) (2010). *Myanmar/Burma. Inside Challenges, Outside Interests.* Washington, DC: Brookings Institution Press.
Rogers, B. (2010). *Than Shwe. Unmasking Burma's Tyrant.* Chiang Mai, Thailand: Silkworm Books.
Rogers, B. (2012). *Burma. A Nation at the Crossroads.* London: Rider.
Scheff, T.J. (2000). *Bloody Revenge. Emotions, Nationalism and War.* Lincoln, NE: Authors Guild Backprint; originally published in 1994.
Scott, J.C. (2009). *The Art of Not Being Governed. An Anarchist History of Upland Southeast Asia.* New Haven, CT: Yale University Press.
Seekins, D.M. (2007). *Burma and Japan since 1940. From 'Co-Prosperity' to 'Quiet Dialogue'.* Copenhagen: NIAS Press.
Seekins, D.M. (2010). *State and Society in Modern Yangon.* London: Routledge.
Seith, A. (2010). 'Myanmar, North Korea and the Nuclear Question' in Riefel 2010, 181–194.
Silverstein, J. (1977). *Burma: Military Rule and the Politics of Stagnation.* Ithaca NY: Cornell University Press.
Silverstein, J. (ed.) (1993) *The Political Legacy of Aung San.* Ithaca NY: Cornell University Press.
Skidmore, M. (2004). *Karaoke Fascism. Burma and the Politics of Fear.* Philadelphia, PA: University of Pennsylvania Press.
Smith, D. (2001a). 'Arendt and Elias' in D. Smith. *Norbert Elias and Modern Social Theory.* London: Sage (2001), 43–70.
Smith, D. (2013). 'Forced Social Displacement: the "Inside Stories" of Oscar Wilde, Jean Améry, Nelson Mandela and Aung San Suu Kyi' in Nicolas Demertsiz (ed.) *Emotions in Politics.* London: Palgrave-Macmillan (2013), 60–83.
Smith, D.E. (2015). *Religion and Politics in Burma.* Princeton NJ: Princeton University Press.
Spiro, M.E. (1970). *Buddhism and Society. A Great Tradition and its Burmese Vicissitudes.* New York, NY: Harper & Row.
Steinberg, D.I. (2010). *Burma/Myanmar. What Everyone Needs to Know.* Oxford: Oxford University Press.
Stewart, W. (2008). *Aung San Suu Kyi. Fearless Voice of Burma,* Bloomington IN: iUniverse.
Tambiah, S.J. (2002). *Edmund Leach. An Anthropological Life.* Cambridge: Cambridge University Press.
Taylor, R.H. (2015). *General Ne Win. A Political Biography.* Singapore: Institute of Southeast Asian Studies.
Thant Myint-U (2001). *The Making of Modern Burma.* Cambridge: Cambridge University Press.
Thant Myint-U (2007a). *The River of Lost Footsteps. A Personal History of Burma.* London: Faber and Faber.
Thant Myint-U (2007b). 'What to do about Burma'. *London Review of Books,* 29, 3, 8th February 2007, 31–33.

Thant Myint-U (2011). *Where China Meets India. Burma and the New Crossroads of Asia.* London: Faber.

Tucker, S. (2001). *Burma: The Curse of Independence.* London: Pluto Press.

U Nu (Thakin Nu). 1954. *Burma Under the Japanese. Pictures and Portraits.* London: Macmillan.

Wade, F. (2017). *Myanmar's Enemy Within. Buddhist Violence and the Making of a Muslim 'Other'.* London: Zed Books.

Wintle, J. (2007). *Perfect Hostage. Aung San Suu Kyi, Burma and the Generals.* London: Arrow Books.

Zöllner, H.-B. (2012), *The Beast and the Beauty. The History of the Conflict between the Military and Aung San Suu Kyi in Myanmar, 1988–2012.* Berlin: regiospectra Verlag.

Zöllner, H.-B. (ed.). (2014). *Talks Over the Gate. Aung San Suu Kyi's Dialogues with the People, 1995 and 1996.* Hamburg, Germany: Abera.

6 Confronting humiliation

The spectre of empire

We have hovered over the British Empire's bumpy trajectory of decline and disintegration, swooping down to track some key struggles.[1] We have traced the inside stories of Oscar Wilde, Jean Améry, Nelson Mandela and Aung San Suu Kyi. This narrative has been intertwined with another: the West's retreat from global power, especially the destructive struggle before, during and after World War I to fill the huge gap in the international order left by the collapse of the old dynastic empires based in Madrid,[2] Berlin, Vienna, Paris, Moscow, Beijing and Constantinople. The contest to fill that gap engaged the ambitions of several regimes who struggled with each other for the territorial prizes on offer. Nazi Germany, Imperial Japan and the British Empire were all big losers in the fight, the first two by 1945, the third a few years later. Three other competitors were big winners in different ways: the United States of America, Stalin's USSR and Mao Zedong's soon-to be-born People's Republic of China; again, the first two by 1945, the third a few years later.

The independence of India and Pakistan was proclaimed in 1947, two years before the foundation of the People's Republic of China. Between 1945 and 1949 the world began to swing on its axis, pivoting towards the East. This process took several decades and its implications did not fully strike home until at least seventy years later. In the interim a battle was fought between the forces of corporate capitalism and state socialism under the banners of the United States and Soviet Russia. China, observing this global struggle between capitalism and communism eventually decided to adopt a hybrid posture, as did the British when confronted with the struggle between autocracy and liberalism in the nineteenth century. The British chose both sides at once. So did the Chinese. Britain followed the path of autocracy with a liberal face. China has given communism a capitalist face.

By the 1990s, Soviet Russia had retired from the field and America was able to complete its historic mission of transmitting its models and methods worldwide. One outcome was an American equivalent of the British World Cup effect. The British invented football in the form of soccer and taught it to a world full of potentially brilliant soccer players. As a consequence, England has not won the World Cup for over half a century. The last time, as almost any English person will be able to tell you, perhaps with a hurt look, was in 1966. Did President Trump have that same hurt look in his eyes when he spoke about the relative weakness of American business in a globalized world?

The two narratives within this book, the individual struggles and the unfolding of socio-historical processes, are woven together, as warp and weft. For example, we have seen that during the mid-1940s Aung San Suu Kyi's father was murdered by enemies within the regime her father had created to replace the departing British and Japanese; and in return Suu Kyi managed to manoeuvre herself into the Burmese government seventy years later, although so far she has failed to loosen the grip of military control very much within that strategically central country. Mandela's high ambitions for himself were ruined by *apartheid*; and in return he played a leading role in ruining *apartheid* itself. Améry was tortured as an anti-Nazi, and sent to the death camps as a Jew; and in return he helped to shape our understanding of humiliation and its transmutations as terroristic dictatorships were displaced by the disciplines and comforts of corporate capitalism. Wilde was lambasted as a cheerleader for Irish nationalism, a friend of the vile French, and a menace to respectable society; and in return he undermined the British imperial spirit by contemptuous mockery, helping to pave the way for future critics such as Gandhi, Kraus and Orwell.

Wilde and Améry both focused on links between: the cruelties and deceptions of high politics; the anger, fear and sorrow of those who faced being victimized; and the egoistical vanity of those with power over others. For example, Améry noticed that in the 1950s that Britain retained its sense, however deluded, of innate global superiority long after the end of World War II. This fact intensified the hurt felt within the British population as it quickly became clear that Britain was a big loser from the war fought for democratic freedom, alongside its enemies in Berlin and Tokyo.

The British Empire exhausted all its resources fighting against fascism during the war and disintegrated soon afterwards. To deepen the irony, after the war the British Empire gave posthumous birth to neo-fascist political establishments in two of its most substantial ex-colonies: the *apartheid* regime in South Africa, and the military dictatorship in Burma. These notoriously anti-democratic regimes drew inspiration from the spirit and tactics of the Nazis and the Imperial Japanese military, respectively. They were less extreme than their fascist mentors, and their motives were defensive rather than expansionist. However, they were routinely murderous and cruel. Each of these regimes, in South Africa and Burma, was able to survive for over half a century before being displaced or partially transformed.

How can we explain the apparent paradox of an empire engaged in an anti-fascist struggle during World War II becoming the step parent of two postwar neo-fascist regimes? A partial answer is found in a well-known nursery rhyme that originated in the nineteenth century. This features a little girl who had a little curl 'right in the middle of her forehead' (pronounced 'forrid').[3] When this little girl was good she was 'very, very good' but 'when she was bad she was horrid'. This depiction of a split personality helps us to understand why the British Empire lasted several decades longer than its rivals based in Berlin, Moscow, Vienna and Istanbul. As just hinted, the point is that the British Empire managed to combine two contradictory attributes: liberalism (being 'very good') and authoritarianism (being 'horrid').

Within Britain itself liberalism and authoritarianism were in conflict during the 1870s and 1880s. Urban industrial society, increasingly educated, organized and opinionated, took shape in the very midst of rural Britain. On one side were politicians like William Gladstone (1809–98) supported by independent-minded Liberal voters: fishing communities, miners, weavers and so on. There were also the likes of Joseph Chamberlain cultivating machine politics in large cities such as Birmingham where citizens learned the benefits of so-called gas and water socialism. These politicians and their followers deployed the rhetoric of freedom, equality and human rights.[4] On the other side was a Tory hierarchy headed by lords and bishops, a rural world where villagers touched their caps as the gentry passed by. This deferential attitude to life was securely rooted in the countryside until railways brought new perspectives and resources to the shires. Occupants of great country houses disconsolately observed the slow disintegration of a deferential social order but could not easily resist it.

But all was not lost for those who valued domineering displays of strength. This spirit thrived in the high Tory social circles of bossy bullies like Lady Bracknell, cutting down rivals and interlopers while looking out for the main chance. Force, determination and blatant opportunism were lauded even more openly in the networks of imperialist entrepreneurs like Cecil Rhodes in South Africa. Rhodes was determined to beat down the indigenous population with an iron fist. In 1894 he told the Cape Colony parliament: 'we are going to be lords of these people and keep them in a subject position'. How was that to be done? 'We must adopt a system of despotism such as works so well in India in our relations with the barbarians of South Africa.'[5] Here is the 'horrid' face of British imperialism.

Lord Salisbury adopted a softer version of the same approach for home consumption. He claimed he could not understand the continuing discontent in Ireland during the 1880s. Salisbury framed Britain's policies towards the Irish as generous benefits provided by a mighty ruler, not a grudging recognition of rights owed to a nation and its citizens demanding to be free. The British had given them so much, said Salisbury, but they did not seem to be grateful. But seen from below, the British were oppressors, keeping the Irish in chains. Ireland, like India, Burma and, indeed, the Boers, demanded liberty and refused to stay quiet in captivity.

The English liberal tradition dedicated to universal human rights and hostile to oppression was strongest in mainland Britain but filtered out into the colonies. This happened in several ways, for example: through educational institutions such as the Methodist high schools, attended by both Mandela and Suu Kyi;

through British legal tradition, imbibed by both Gandhi and Mandela; and through the humane practices, empathetic spirit and sharp critical eye of some British overseas officials, including, for a while, George Orwell. He was thunderous in his condemnation of the autocratic tendency within British authority, both at home and abroad: a dictatorial arrogance that treated those below as intrinsically inferior; at best child-like, at worst contemptible, and in some cases expendable.

Britain's superior technology and firepower enabled its traders and soldiers to infiltrate and govern populations throughout the world during the eighteenth and nineteenth centuries. By contrast, Britain's propertied classes refused to permit or pay for a huge standing army at home. They did not want to risk a revolutionary government using it against them. The French revolution and Napoleon were still present in Lady Bracknell's mind over a century later. Those with wealth preferred instead to yield up legal, political and social rights to members of the working class, as gradually as possible, finally enabling them to become democratic citizens.

Some individuals were in two minds; or, perhaps, had different minds in different places. Joseph Chamberlain began his political life as a vocal opponent of the landlord class but moved towards the Conservative party after the Liberals split in 1886 over the question of whether or not the Irish should have home rule. Meanwhile, some flamboyant imperialists such as Alfred Milner were deeply sympathetic to the plight of the British poor. They supported the work of Arnold J. Toynbee and Samuel Barnett who campaigned against poverty, ignorance and disease in impoverished areas such as East London. Milner, like Oscar Wilde, had been drawn to the humanitarian reformer John Ruskin while at Oxford. Even Lord Cromer, the ruling voice in Egypt for many years, was a convinced Gladstonian Liberal when he began his career.[6]

In World War I it was Britain's liberal credentials that located London within the winning coalition of free nations led, eventually, by the United States. In this war of civilization against barbarism, Britain was counted with the 'good' against the 'horrid'. In World War II Britain survived with massive military help from the empire but was left virtually bankrupt. Liberating the empire after 1945 was an inevitable consequence. Getting a supposedly independent nuclear deterrent after the war gave Britain some cover for the immense humiliation imposed by the empire's loss. It helped dampen down resentment. So did some subtle rewriting of history. Looking back, many British men and women lost sight of the fact that the two world wars had been fought to preserve the British Empire. They remembered them instead as being overwhelmingly caused by the need to prevent invasion by an oppressive dictatorship and, at the same time, secure their voting rights (partially delivered in 1918) and the National Health Service (inaugurated in 1948).

That was, at the very least, an oversimplification, as a glance at Winston Churchill's career would remind us. During the ensuing *pax Americana* the British clung to the national self-image cultivated during two world wars. This was a combination of strength, superiority and entitlement. Again a subtle reworking of sentiment occurred: the object and content of entitlement were redefined. The idea that the British were intrinsically entitled to expect a good living as the masters of a mighty empire shaded into the idea that the Britain's loyal and courageous population had fought for the kind of government that would look after its own people. Specifically, after 1945 overt imperial pride gave some ground before overt pride in the welfare state, which became a sort of national religion, as was commonly remarked. More recently, the hollowing out of the welfare state has hit voters hard at a time when many of them, especially the older ones, were still coping with the belittling of their imperialist pretentions. The sorrow generated by this double bereavement – loss of empire and loss of welfare – has been swirling around British politics, widely unrecognized, looking for release. Brexit provided such as opportunity.

The spectre of empire continued to haunt elite political culture not just in Britain but also in the United States. Jeanne Morefield has seen continuities in the arguments made for British liberal imperialism in the early twentieth century, supposedly spreading freedom and equality, and those made for American global domination a century later. The Round Table movement founded in 1909 by Alfred Milner and his acolytes promoted cooperation between Britain and the white dominions based on a shared Anglo-Saxon spirit. Morefield argues this spirit was echoed in Niall Ferguson's call for the United States to be more imperial in its international dealings. She also sees a strong similarity between Jan Christian Smuts's idea of turning the British Empire into an enlightened Commonwealth of independent nations headed by the British crown and Michael Ignatieff's promotion of so-called Empire lite.[7] We have seen the brutalizing effect of Milner's civilizing mission in South Africa. The disastrous results of more recent civilizing missions by the West are likewise visible in Afghanistan, Iraq, Syria, Iraq, Libya and across the Mediterranean Sea.

Saboteur, soldier, saint and sage

Let us draw together the inside stories of Oscar Wilde, Jean Améry, Nelson Mandela and Aung San Suu Kyi. In all four cases their careers brought threats of humiliation counterbalanced by declarations of intense admiration. They have all been both pariahs and icons. Their experiences and responses, and the actions of the regimes they opposed, provide us with valuable evidence that help us to understand the dynamics of forced social displacement.

Oscar Wilde, born in Dublin, acted as a cultural saboteur, the role to which his revolutionary mother aspired in her younger days. Wilde's political stance was a mixture of advanced liberalism, which strongly supported oppressed nationalities such as Ireland, and utopian socialism allied with anarchism and aestheticism: in other words, he stood for individual freedom, national sovereignty, universal citizenship, and unrestricted access to all forms of beauty. He saw that the British Empire with its selfish and corrupt establishment stood in the way. Wilde's deadliest sabotage weapon was the poison of existential doubt, administered to perpetrators, beneficiaries and hapless victims of imperialist autocracy. This poison was laced with the tantalizing sweetness of ferocious wit and daring imagination. Looked at another way, the poison was a kind of antidote, meant to kill off autocracy so liberalism and socialism might breathe more freely, and expand their sphere of influence. Wilde's success was mainly posthumous but real. He eased the way for others.

Jean Améry, born in Vienna, wanted to be a soldier fighting for human freedom against imperialism's heir, fascism, and all other oppressors of human freedom. His father fought in the Austrian army, and did not return home from the front. The son spent his life looking for the front line: in the streets of Vienna, with the anti-Nazi resistance in Belgium, and later, in the struggle against three apparently unrelenting foes. One was the German people whose implacable self-righteousness, as he saw it, was reinforced by their ignorance of the harm they had perpetrated on Jews and others. Another was international corporate capitalism, which stifled human imagination and imposed humiliating disciplines upon the population, limiting human freedom in order to maximize profit for a few. Finally, there was the human condition itself, which imposed a brave but ultimately fruitless struggle on individuals who tried to make themselves free and noble.

Nelson Mandela, born in Mvezo in South Africa's Eastern Cape, had a feisty father who defended his chiefly status against the colonial authority. His deeply religious mother built a Methodist church in her African village. His father nudged him towards the wider political sphere by getting him into the Thembu ruler's royal court. His mother blessed his later move to the big city when she knew he was marrying a devout Christian woman. Mandela, who was his own man, took it from there. He aimed for the top, politically. He knew the tactical value of violence but did not relish bloodshed. Instead, he allowed himself to be portrayed as an imprisoned martyr until an opportune time came for him to make his mark as a political saint. This analogy is apt since saints can only be canonized if they perform miracles. The secular near-miracles Mandela performed were two: he persuaded the deeply aggrieved and highly mobilized Africans in the townships to restrain their desire for revenge against the white population; and he persuaded the Afrikaner Nationalist government that giving up their monopoly on political power was a viable option, that their supporters would be safe. He did not do this alone but his voice was crucial. Secular sainthood was his reward.

Aung San Suu Kyi was born in Yangon, then Burma's capital. Her highly political mother, a Burmese diplomat, made sure her daughter accepted the authority of her father's vision of a modern independent Burma. Aung San had been assassinated, his career cut short. Aung San Suu Kyi's very name conveyed her destiny: to find a way of fulfilling her father's unfinished task of uniting Burma, achieving national reconciliation. During her long political campaign she gave evidence of soldierly bravery, once challenging the military to shoot her. She also displayed public piety whenever the opportunity arose.

However, Suu Kyi's most distinctive claim to charismatic authority was based on her close kinship to the departed national hero, Aung San, and her confident proclamation of the strategic vision she had inherited from her father. This vision described the kind of Burmese constitutional order that would, in her view, work best for the Burman majority as well as the many national minorities in the borderlands. Her skills in *realpolitik* eventually helped Suu Kyi's party into government. The title of State Counsellor that she acquired in April 2016 institutionalized her role as a sage, one whose task was, in effect, to convey authoritative guiding wisdom to the principal agent of state power, the *Tatmadaw*.[8] It turned out to be, in some respects, a poisoned chalice.

In practice Suu Kyi's most recent function has been to take the blame internationally for the Burmese government's most blatant cruelties. This situation is the opposite of Mandela's final role, which was to take the credit internationally for the South African state's avoidance of a bloodbath. Each of these politicians has been given roles in two plays: a morality play enacted on the world stage contained within a larger play, the discreet drama of *realpolitik*. World opinion in the media has moralized about both politicians, promoting Mandela and demoting Suu Kyi. But public opinion only has a bit part in the largely hidden drama of *realpolitik*, dominated by the interests and wishes of wealthy business corporations, and powerful governments. As pragmatic politicians, Suu Kyi and Nelson Mandela have each been able to handle their roles, whether enjoyable or painful, in both these dramas. They have each been well aware of the limits and potentialities offered by such roles.

At first sight, Mandela the political saint and Suu Kyi, the worldly-wise sage, both Nobel prize winners, seem cut from the same cloth.[9] Both endured long prison sentences but emerged from incarceration to find high government office awaiting them. Both have highly elegant profiles and could almost be co-stars.[10] But this impression is highly misleading. As we have seen, it vastly underplays their differences. By contrast, Wilde the smooth saboteur and Améry the frustrated soldier seem far apart in their character and mission. In fact they are very close. Let us take these two comparisons further, beginning with Oscar Wilde and Jean Améry before turning to the two politicians.

Oscar Wilde and Jean Améry

Wilde and Améry both had many objectives: to understand their own lives, discover how human beings work, analyse the dynamics of society and culture, assess the issues at stake in contemporary politics, and resist oppression. They gave everything they had to all these ambitious tasks and ended up exhausted and disillusioned. There are three evident differences between them. Firstly, Wilde was on the scene when the British imperial engine of domination was fully stretched and moving beyond the peak of its vigour in the late Victorian era. Almost a century later, Améry was keeping watch when that imperial engine finally ran out of steam in the early 1960s. Wilde levered aside the arrogant masks of London Society to mock the corruption he saw beneath. Améry found postwar British men and women still wearing out-dated imperial masks and feeling thoroughly estranged from themselves and the world.

Secondly, Wilde and Améry were displaced in different ways. Wilde's family from the Anglo-Irish gentry had something in common with Mandela's close kin from African royalty. They both came from the top rank of a social order that felt it has been elbowed aside by the imperialist power, pushed away from the action. Each of those elite social groups resented the way its job description had been changed, taking away real powers even though their dignity was officially respected. Each was touchy regarding its own importance, looked with suspicion on polite but insincere compliments, and learned to fight hard and dirty to keep the privileges it still had.

By contrast, Améry, like Suu Kyi, came from a family displaced not sideways but downward. The assassination of Suu Kyi's father, and the virtual exile and deliberate humiliation of Suu Kyi's mother were later followed by the sustained vilification of Suu Kyi herself when she returned to Burmese politics. Améry's parents had been moving upwards into the solid middle of highly respectable, piously Catholic, Viennese society. The death of Améry's father rapidly pushed mother and son down into a far less prestigious place in society, keeping a provincial tavern, paying court to prosperous guests from the big city. Later, the rise of Hitler shoved Améry down towards an even worse prospect.

Thirdly, they have different orientations to the arena of culture. Jean Améry, who left school at fourteen without his *baccalaureate*, was much more in awe of Culture with a capital C than Oscar Wilde had ever been. Améry was a supplicant seeking admission. By contrast, Wilde, a graduate of Trinity and Oxford, assumed the cultural realm belonged to him by right, as a highly educated person. He treated the work of other writers and artists as a well-stocked larder of delights he could plunder at will. Wilde reached down into culture 'from above', picking and choosing what he wanted to borrow. Améry reached up 'from below', hoping to be allowed to enter the hall of fame.

But some other apparent differences dissolve on closer acquaintance. For example, on the face of it, the Austro-German and the Anglo-Irishman represent the two classic masks, respectively, of tragedy and comedy: from Améry the bitter groan, from Wilde the witty grin. Reading Jean Améry's reports on his own life, he appears to be a real misery, a stark contrast with Oscar Wilde. But, in fact, the contrast is less pronounced than it seems. After all, Wilde certainly groaned hard in Reading Gaol. His last published work, *The Ballad of Reading Gaol*, the story of a hanging, was originally signed with his cell number C33, a symbol of the writer's alienation just as telling as the prison camp number recorded on Améry's gravestone.[11]

Wilde and Améry appear at first to be dissimilar – bisexual vs straight, gregarious vs loner, gentile vs Jew, comedic vs tragic, and confident vs insecure– but both are experts in exploring the challenge posed by humiliation. We have already noticed the convergence between Wilde's story of Dorian Gray, the amoral abuser, and Améry's tale about Lefeu, the vehement victim. Both men destroy pictures that graphically depict their state of being. Both then die. In these works Wilde and Améry address similar issues from complementary perspectives. Améry's main preoccupations, the indignity of aging, the prospect of death, and the pain of humiliation, are all key themes in Wilde's work.

Miserable Jean and amusing Oscar are brothers under the skin. They both enjoy making us worry. Wilde dissolves some false but comforting certainties we hate to lose. Améry exposes some repressed truths we hate to hear. They both have a touch of ghoulishness. Améry always seems to have an inner graveyard smile. He is a master of irony and relishes its contradictions. In his best-known works during the 1960s and 1970s Améry poses one insoluble existential puzzle after another. His central theme, ever recurring, is that the prospects offered by human conditions such as humiliation, aging and death are completely unacceptable but at the same time totally inescapable.

Améry does not turn his eyes away from these terrible and impossible scenes. How hilarious, he, almost, says but straightens his face before we catch him grinning. Like a perverse Houdini in reverse, Améry conjures himself and his readers into tightly fastened padlocks and chains. Such skill. But he does not spring us out of our manacles like a decent fellow should; instead, he leaves us there. Améry does not discard his Sartrian dreams of freedom but he knows that in the end they cannot be realized. Like Dante he takes us into Hell to wander among its trapped and tormented victims: ourselves.

Like Wilde, Améry wants to pass on what life has taught him. For both the main technique is to set a trail of intellectual surprises and emotional shocks leading towards the same two conclusions: we are made and make ourselves through our experiences; but we should not be surprised if we end up broken. Wilde gathered his material by gaining entry to the haunts of the mighty, discovering their corrupt and destructive habits. He noticed the different ways that disillusioned *roués* like Lord Darlington or compromised libertines such as Dorian Gray tried, often without success, to escape, adapt or fight back.

Améry, likewise, tried to enter Europe's intellectual aristocracy, targeting first Vienna, and later, Paris. Both attempts ended in disillusionment. In between times, Améry was forced onto an assembly line for disposable rejects from the human race. The cruel curriculum in this hellish finishing school made a powerful impact on him. Améry experienced the threat of being brutally snuffed out. He also observed the thrill of domination enjoyed by the maestros of cruelty. He began to search out the internal switches that trigger resistance, retreat or acquiescence in the face of such challenges. Between them, Wilde and Améry provide us with very handy notes for a route map around the dynamics of humiliation.

Both men had difficult relationships with their reputations in the wider world. Wilde worked hard to acquire his image as a notorious fop poised precariously between the sensational and the ridiculous, and then worked equally hard to get rid of it when it became a barrier to greater success. By the early 1890s he had remade his persona and was widely known both sides of the Atlantic as a brilliant storyteller whose narratives and dialogues challenged prevailing power structures, moral codes and the conventional wisdom that protected them. That was the reputation Wilde wanted. Ironically, his fame and the threat he posed to powerful interests made him vulnerable, a target for sensation-seeking tabloid journalism.

Following his conviction for gross indecency in 1895 Wilde's name and face became notorious around the world. He was narrowly depicted as a supposedly clever fellow who failed to live up to gentlemanly standards, a dirty beast that offended against morality in a dangerous and disgusting way. After the First World War Wilde's reputation recovered almost in parallel with the collapsing prestige of imperialism, his lifetime foe. Today throughout Eurasia and beyond Wilde is revered as a fabulous wit, a humanitarian socialist, and a gay martyr.

Améry's reputation has never been global. But it blossomed throughout Europe from the early 1960s when he wrote about his time in Auschwitz and its effect upon his life. The publication dates of Améry's writings in various languages tell us when and where his impact was felt: in Germany during the late 1960s and through the 1970s; spreading to English-speaking countries during the 1980s; France during the 1990s; and then Spain and Italy after the turn of the century. Améry worked hard for his badge of recognition. But like Wilde he became disappointed with how he was recognized. Améry was annoyed that critical attention to his work focused narrowly on his feelings of resentment about how he was treated as a Jew rather than his larger message about the challenge of being human. His critics saw the wronged victim. He wanted them to see the engaged rebel.

After all, Améry achieved an enormous amount. He not only lived an amazing life, full of terror and excitement. He also turned a great deal of that life into superb art. In his writings he painstakingly mapped out two related terrains of human struggle. One was the arena of political struggle shaping post-war Europe and its relations with the United States and the Soviet Union. The other was the tumultuous zone of emotional struggle where he and others had wrestled with feelings such as despair and the desire for release from feelings of abandonment. Améry did not want to be misunderstood as an icon representing vengefulness. He wanted to be recognized by the world as a literary warrior pursuing a noble cause, someone who refused to bow down before overpowering social injustice, who tried to discover how to achieve a meaningful and satisfying existence, for himself and for others.

In some obvious respects Améry's life was uniquely horrible. But in other ways it was one version of a much larger world story, a bumpy ride of aspiration, hope, disappointment, suffering, renewed hope then quiet despair. Améry was one of life's foot soldiers, like most of us. He never felt secure in the saddle, able to gaze down at others from above. Nor could he emulate Wilde who rose and fell like the 'remarkable rocket' that figures in one of his short stories, enjoying his own high sky ride for over two decades.[12] Améry felt much more like a scuttling rabbit than a soaring rocket. His experience was close to the ground throughout his life.

Nelson Mandela and Aung San Suu Kyi

By contrast, Mandela and Suu Kyi launched their careers from royal or ambassadorial households and later won even more prestigious platforms. Aung San Suu Kyi in 1988 and Nelson Mandela in 1990 both arrived on the national political scene with dramatic suddenness after an absence of over a quarter of a century. Mandela had been in prison, kept away from reporters, cameras and microphones. Suu Kyi had been abroad, keeping her promise to remain a private and non-political person while outside Burma. In both cases, hardly anyone knew what they looked like until they suddenly appeared in the full glare of publicity, potential saviours arriving amongst the oppressed.

The intense processes of familiarization that followed their respective debuts were, politically, solid gold. They brought a special excitement right into the very heart of the political arena. This experience was much more intense and personal than admiring an icon. It was akin to seeing a much-desired newborn baby for the first time. In 1988 the Burmese learned a new name to go with a familiar face. In 1990 South Africans discovered a new face to go with a familiar name. Everyone in South Africa knew about Mandela but what did he look like? Everybody discovered the answer at more or less the same time. They shared the birth. Every Burmese person knew Aung San's face but suddenly here was a great novelty, the hero's daughter, his spitting image. Her audience, like Mandela's, witnessed together the springing into being of a new political life.

Mandela's reputation became global during his quarter of a century of incarceration but it remained controversial and divided until the collapse of *apartheid*. However, after Mandela's release his authority became quasi-papal. It gave legitimacy to the South African peace process. On some key occasions, as we have seen, it quelled popular anger and reduced the likelihood of violence in the townships. But Mandela's charisma would surely have become a diminishing asset if he had not reduced his direct involvement in contentious political conflicts and controversial decision-making after just two years as national president. An iconic figure cannot afford to be seen getting too deeply involved in the ignoble work of political or business-related wheeler dealing.

In the early phase of her political career in Burma Suu Kyi benefited enormously from the previous iconization of her father, Aung San, whose image was ubiquitous throughout the land. She captured this image from the hands of the military regime that had made Aung San into its patron saint.

Suu Kyi converted her iconic father into the presiding spirit of her own democratic movement during her political campaigns throughout Burma. Later, during Suu Kyi's long years under house arrest, it was very useful to be a highly recognizable figure that could be depicted as the symbol of a country being martyred by its oppressive government. However, since achieving governmental office, Suu Kyi has tried to shrug off her iconic status. It is no longer useful. It does not fit her style as a pragmatic politician: 'I have always said I don't like to be called an icon, because icons do nothing except sit on the wall. And I have had to work very hard.'[13]

Both rebels entered the fray with an immense store of political capital but their regime opponents were at very different stages in their own careers, and this is where the most important differences between Suu Kyi and Mandela may be seen. By 1988, the year of Suu Kyi's return to Burma, Ne Win's plans for Burmese socialism had fallen flat but the Burmese military were still confident China would give them backing. The repressive response of Beijing to the Tiananmen Square demonstrations in 1989 surely reassured them. In Burma the generals continued to treat political dissidents, indeed all citizens, as potential enemies of the state. They managed to keep themselves in power for at least another quarter of a century. Compare the South African government in 1990, the year Mandela was released. The regime knew the game was up for *apartheid*. The Soviet Bloc in Eastern Europe had collapsed, to be quickly followed by the Soviet Union's dissolution. The United States no longer regarded South Africa as a key stronghold in a global Cold War. This situation radically weakened the *apartheid* regime, which came under American pressure to abolish racist institutions. It also meant that the ANC was no longer able to rely on support from Moscow.

These very dissimilar contexts dictated the options open to Mandela and Suu Kyi during the 1990s and beyond. After 1989, Mandela, like many ANC colleagues, judged that the fruits of negotiation and compromise would be greater than any gains from further violent conflict. So Mandela's immense popular appeal was heavily invested in the urgent task of defusing the anger of South Africans trapped in poverty within the townships. He was the peacemaker. By contrast, Suu Kyi played the warrior, especially in the early phase of her long campaign. She dared to accuse the government of sustained criminal violence against the people, brazenly naming Ne Win as the chief perpetrator. Suu Kyi encouraged her followers to stand up against the army and police, not run away. Her objective was not to quell her followers' anger but to help them overcome their fear.

As politicians, both calculated the odds, pragmatically. For survival's sake their antennae had to be highly sensitive and multi-directional but in speech and action they deliberately narrowed themselves down to a hard sharp point. Like sea captains, they looked at the stars not to speculate about cosmology but to plan the best route to their projected anchorage. At the top of their agenda was the goal of achieving governmental power for themselves, preferably the position of national president, or the equivalent. Both Suu Kyi and Mandela were absolutely committed to overthrowing the existing political order. Both were totally determined to be at the top of the successor regime. Both decided early on they wanted to lead their countries. Mandela told his ANC colleagues in the mid-1950s that he would be the first Black president of South Africa.[14] Suu Kyi was haunted from adolescence with the feeling that she was destined to try and complete her martyred father's unfinished business.

Mandela and Suu Kyi both played key roles in easing the transition away from overtly neo-fascist political regimes. However, Mandela had a much easier task. Global big business was deeply embedded in South Africa before and after 1994 and could adjust fairly easily to the dismantling of *apartheid*, providing prosperity not just for the South African white business community but also for a new Black elite. By contrast, the *Tatmadaw* in Burma had used its power to maintain control over the governmental apparatus and the country's exploitable resources. It did this to ensure that a large share of the business profits made in that country continued to be directed into the hands of leading generals and their associates. The military, in effect, hired out Burma's productive resources for a substantial cut or rent.

Despite the opening up of Burma to outside influences, by the early twenty-first century the institutional infrastructure of the capitalist market and the practices and standards of modern business organizations were scarcely developed in that country, much less so than in South Africa. How could capitalism and democracy advance further in Burma without major transformations in the military? But how could the military be persuaded to transform without major advances in democratic organization and business infrastructure? The challenge facing Suu Kyi and her most important negotiation partner, military commander-in-chief, Min Aung Hlaing – or, perhaps, in time, their successors – was even more daunting and globally significant than the immense demands made upon Nelson Mandela and F.W. De Klerk in South Africa over twenty years before.

Judo, chess and poker

More generally, what has our adventure in comparative biography told us about the dynamics of forced displacement and humiliation? As we know well, humiliation at its most severe brings threats of death and physical destruction. More generally, the victim survives but in a thoroughly shaken state. For a vivid physical image of what it is like to be humiliated, imagine being grabbed by the scruff of the neck, forced onto your knees, kicked in the stomach then tossed aside. That horrid scene sums up three aspects of humiliation which imposes: *subjection* on those who used to run free; *relegation* on those who had been raised above others; and *exclusion* on those who previously had a sense of belonging within specific groups, networks or hierarchies. More generally, humiliation brings a forcible reordering of statuses, along with a demeaning recasting of social identities.[15]

The initial reaction to being at the receiving end of attempts to impose humiliation is shocked protest. But what happens next? As in judo, people tend to make two types of response. One is to step back or step away from the incoming aggression. An example of this *yielding* response is Oscar Wilde's acceptance of his own guilt and shame in *De Profundis*, the long letter he composed in Reading Gaol. The other type of response involves standing one's ground or advancing towards the point of attack to defy it, deflect it or disable it. An example of this *challenging* response is Nelson Mandela's public destruction of his passbook, an act of defiance against the *apartheid* regime.

Whether you challenge or yield when faced with attempted humiliation, what is your objective? At this point the options are more reminiscent of chess than judo. It is a matter of weighing up the relative attractiveness of two different approaches: either short-term self-protective tactics reducing the impact of attacks or long-term strategies intended to reduce the likelihood of attacks occurring at all. To illustrate this distinction let us consider another yielding response made by Wilde: not acceptance as in *De Profundis*, but escape, a move he rejected before his trial but adopted after being released from prison. Wilde crossed the English Channel and spent his last years abroad under an assumed name. This was an emergency measure. He needed to avoid the torment of being constantly recognized, pursued and abused in England. But Wilde also had a long-term goal that he confided in *De Profundis*.

He hoped that by finding some secluded place close to nature he might nurture the creative insights he had gained from his sorrowful sojourn behind bars. Wilde's optimistic vision was that by escaping from society for a while he could concentrate on finding a remedy for human cruelty and suffering, driving humiliation out of human affairs. He memorably depicted some of those evils in his *Ballad of Reading Gaol* but Wilde could not bring his remedial project to completion. There were too many distractions and, finally, illness and death intervened. In other words, escape alleviated the worst effects of being publicly humiliated in England but did not enable Wilde to compete his self-appointed task of finding a remedy for human suffering by exposing its causes in the realm of human behaviour. In other words, for Wilde escape abroad was an *alleviative* response but did not become a *remedial* one, in spite of his hopes.

To summarize the distinction just made: *alleviative* responses seek to make the *effects* of humiliation more bearable or avoidable, temporarily at least; and more radical *remedial* responses try to eradicate completely the condition of humiliation by eliminating or modifying its *causes* in some way. The notion of escape can be refined a little further, using this distinction. Escape's alleviative form is *avoidance*. This involves getting away, creating a protective barrier of distance between the agent of humiliation in one's old place of residence or occupation, and the escaped victim, who is no longer located there, for the moment at least.

As we have seen, Améry in 1938 and Suu Kyi in 1960 each adopted this approach, leaving their homeland in order to alleviate pressures upon themselves. However, both also kept in mind the possibility that they might well return to the struggle later in a more challenging spirit. Both Améry and Suu Kyi examined in depth the societies they later tried to influence. Suu Kyi researched the main countries of Southeast Asia, including her homeland, before returning to Burma in 1988. Améry studied the key societies of Western Europe, both before and after the war.[16] He made two returns to the fray: one in 1943 when he joined the anti-Nazi resistance, the other in 1964 when he opened up a sustained artillery barrage against the complacency and self-willed ignorance of the German people who had, in his view, caused or permitted his own suffering.

Avoidance, the alleviative form of escape, works by absenting the self or the group from the threatening place. By contrast, *replacement*, a remedial form of escape, becomes possible if escapees find a new dwelling place that suits them well for the long term in a different location. For Wilde, as we have seen, that place was the imagined utopia set out in 'The Soul of Man under Socialism', a promised land that he failed to reach. The point is that successfully finding a satisfactory new place to live, utopian or not, reduces any residual sense of connection with the old home, as well as any leftover feelings of humiliation associated with that previous location.

Escapees who find a replacement for their old home may build up a new network of relationships in their chosen environment. If so, they may become liberated not simply from the effects of the humiliation they suffered in their original location but also from fears related to the country, group, individuals or condition that caused it. They may progress from immediate alleviation to a longer-term remedial response, one that does not just make things feel better, so to speak, but also makes the world right for them. But things do not always work out that way. Consider for example, Europeans who found their way to the American continent, South Africa, and Israel. Three driving forces typically push forward such escapees seeking a lasting replacement for the miserable situation left behind; a desire that the new place should be perfect, a promised land; a sense of self-righteousness, perhaps validated by religious belief, that may feed a spirit of impunity; and, not least, a deep anxiety that they might be hurt or trapped once again. This clearly applied to many Afrikaner *Voortrekkers* and early American pioneers. It is striking that both groups symbolized themselves in terms of the wagon train circle deployed against surrounding threats.

Let us move away for a moment from these scenarios inspired by judo (challenge or yield) and chess (alleviative tactics or remedial strategy) to the realm of poker. That is because dealing with the threat of humiliation also draws on skills and attributes that are useful in poker games. In both cases, it is advantageous to be self-aware, flexible and coolly detached when handling relationships between the self and what might be labelled the *inner*, the *outer* and the *other*. In other words, the following relationships: firstly, between the persona that one presents to the world and the inner self (the *inner*), typically kept hidden within; secondly, between the self and the *outer*, that is, the circle of players, spectators and other interested parties that may influence one's behaviour and be affected by it; and, thirdly, between oneself and the *other*, which refers to those particular individuals or groups that are the source of humiliation.

We can explore this further by looking at another potential yielding response by those suffering humiliation, which is *acceptance*. Some people in conditions of humiliation may conclude that the best move for them is to try adapting themselves to their new situation, especially if they do not seem to have any choice. Unlike escapees, accepters stay put. They do not try to change the places they occupy, nor their subordinate situation. However, they may well deliberately alter their behaviour and even their beliefs. The idea is to make themselves less offensive, and hopefully less vulnerable, to those with the power to damage them.

Améry encountered many examples of this accepting behaviour when he returned under cover to Belgium during the Nazi occupation. He tells us, rather sarcastically, that he was impressed by how well the Belgians had adjusted to being an occupied country, how skilfully they operated the black market, how easily they assumed that the Jews were getting what they deserved, and how compliant they were with the dominance of the German language rather than Flemish or French.[17] Later, in Auschwitz, Améry had a different perspective. He rapidly came to realize that compliance with the commands of those who could implement an instant death sentence was a shrewd option.

However, like escape (avoidance vs replacement), acceptance takes at least two forms. Its alleviative form is *deception*. This means carefully managing the inner self, shielding it with a false reflecting mirror. This response involves disguising the sufferer's feelings and behaving as if the degradation they truly feel is wrongly imposed upon them is, in fact, legitimate and acceptable. That is the attitude that Améry and others determined to survive adopted in Auschwitz, especially when standing in line to be assessed on their fitness and suitability for useful work rather than being sent for disposal in the gas chamber.

However, there is also a remedial form of acceptance, which tries to eliminate the threat of humiliation confronting potential victims. This remedial form is *conversion*, becoming wholeheartedly committed to the worldview of the individual or group that threatens those potential victims. When conversion occurs, the perceptions and attachments of those who have been humiliated are reconfigured. They stop believing their suffering is due to degradations outrageously forced upon them. Instead, like Wilde in jail, they come to believe, rightly or wrongly, that the discomfort they feel is an expression of intense shame, the result of their own failings for which they must take responsibility. Shame is felt when someone breaks worthy and valid rules they believe should be obeyed. These rules derive from a consensus shared between all concerned about values and behaviour. Infringements lead to sanctions that express legitimate and righteous outrage at culpable moral weakness.

So far we have looked at two types of yielding response by those who step back in the belief that it is too difficult, risky or costly to challenge the humiliation being threatened. But what about those challenging responses that involve standing one's ground or stepping forward in order to undermine humiliation by taking decisive action? Again there are two main options, and at this point a glance at Table 6.1 will help us see how these cases fit in to the bigger picture.

One type of challenging response to humiliation is *rejection*. This involves initiating action to achieve one or both of two things. One is to diminish the likely force or ferocity of any attack or threat. The other is to strengthen the capacity of the individual or group to withstand the impact of an attack or a disaster with minimum loss or diminishment. An example of attempted rejection is Améry's nocturnal distributions of subversive literature in wartime Belgium, which were part of an effort to undermine the occupying army's morale.

Another type of challenging response is to work for a *transformation* of the damaging relationship. In this case the idea is to enable all parties concerned to manage down, so to speak, the incidence of humiliation, reducing its effects and, if possible, eliminating its causes. That is how Mandela and De Klerk tried to deal with each other. It was also the philosophy of the Convention for a Democratic South Africa (CODESA). For her part, Suu Kyi has tried, with limited success but in that spirit, to transform relations between the Burmese military and the people, and between the majority Burman population and the national minorities in the borderlands.

Returning to rejection, it's most prominent alleviative form is seeking *revenge*. This may feel visceral, emotional rather than rational, but it does have an implicit logic. The implicit intention is to moderate or repair the effects of being at the receiving end of humiliation after the event has occurred. It is an act of striking back that provides a layer of protection around a bruised self-identity by refurbishing the victim's honour or self-esteem. It puts a salving bandage on the wound. Revenge inflicts counter-humiliations upon

Table 6.1 Responses to the Threat of Forced Social Displacement

THREAT-RESPONSE MODEL			
YIELDING		CHALLENGING	
I ACCEPTANCE	II ESCAPE	III REJECTION	IV TRANSFORMATION
Alleviative			
I Deception	II Avoidance	III Revenge	IV Conciliation
Remedial			
I Conversion	II Replacement	III Resistance	IV Emancipation

the attacker or tormentor. It is a way to even up the score, to diminish the opponent's self-esteem and sense of honour while restoring the self-regard of the victims who are striking back.

For his part, Améry went out of his way to insist that his own intense aversion to the Germany that permitted Nazism did not stem from a thirst from revenge. Instead, he wanted those responsible for his own humiliation and the humiliation of millions of others to understand and share in some way his own experience of being a victim in a meaningful and visceral way. In other words, to be jolted into the zone of horrified awareness that a massive and inhumane outrage had occurred, one that remained central to the lives and moral existence of all concerned, victims and perpetrators alike.

Rejection's remedial form is *resistance*, which is basically self-strengthening, equipping the threatened individual or group so it can mount effective counter-pressure against attempts at humiliating forced displacement. Resistance typically takes such forms as increasing muscle power, brainpower, organizational capacity, stamina, or whatever enhances the ability of an individual, group or institution to withstand hostile assaults and mount self-preserving or self-enhancing initiatives of its own. This is what Mandela called for when he spoke to his followers after finally being released from prison. He urged them to give up their revenge feuds and return to school, making themselves assets for the new South Africa.

As we have seen, the other challenging response to humiliation is *transformation*. In this case the alleviative form is *conciliation*, damage-limiting negotiations that increase the range and depth of communication, and divert energies from more destructive forms of mutual engagement. This might involve a negotiated agreement to limit the level of harm produced by potential confrontations between opposed parties. Agreed mutual reductions of nuclear stockpiles is one example. Another is the current process of dialogue between the Burmese central government and the discontented nationalities in the borderlands. Of course, such dialogue may produce periods of truce but conciliation does not by itself eliminate the causes that trigger conflict and mutual humiliation.

This turns our attention to the other transforming option which is the remedial approach of *emancipation*. This is grounded in a shared recognition that the painful or deeply irksome relationship at issue is damaging for all and that it is worth trying to restructure it in mutually agreed ways that will, hopefully, diminish or even eliminate the causes of humiliation. This might entail reducing sources of tensions, eradicating misunderstandings, making comparable sacrifices on both sides, and beginning new, shared projects in which all have an investment. The object of this kind of transformation is to diminish radically any inclinations towards humiliating behaviour among participants.

This is a project that would enthuse the author of 'The Soul of Man under Socialism',[18] the passionate campaigner that presented her programme for a better Burma at the Shwedagon pagoda in 1988, the South African president who presented the Rugby World Cup to the Springbok captain in 1995, and the young Austrian idealist who in 1934 inaugurated a new literary journal named *Die Brücke* (*The Bridge*) dedicated to encouraging people from all backgrounds to get along well with each other. A major precondition for a viable transformation of this kind is that those involved should be prepared to *restructure* their inner selves (the *inner*), be willing to help alter the socio-political and cultural environment (the *outer*) and be ready to rethink their relations with their enemies, rivals and oppressors (the *other*).

But where are such people likely to spring from? Chronic revenge seekers are unlikely candidates. They tend to get institutionalized by the revenge cycle itself. It freezes their assumptions and attitudes, making them tough without being flexible. The same applies to escapees committed to the remedial option of replacement, who have found a promised land and are determined to defend it. They may have great courage, but little interest in radically changing or renewing their attitudes and beliefs. These escapees have found a new place that suits them better and most of them do not want to waste their energy wrestling with the old socio-political environment or the old oppressors that caused their initial humiliation. Members of these two groups, committed emigrants and fully engaged merchants of vengeance, may be largely ruled out of the game of progressive transformation leading towards emancipation. So who else is available?

A provisional working proposition is that attempts at socio-political transformation leading from humiliation to emancipation may benefit if they get support from among the following groups that already have experience of working on the inner self in order to transform themselves, and therefore are capable of changing further. These are: firstly, *charismatic returnees* including long-term political prisoners who have, in effect, suffered prolonged internal exile, and escapees who have accepted the challenge of re-engagement with the struggle they earlier left behind; secondly, *disillusioned accepters* who, in order to survive, have developed increased flexibility in their relationships with the inner, outer and other; and thirdly, *visionary resisters* who have strengthened themselves sufficiently to envisage engaging in an effort to help create a shared non-humiliating future.

Charismatic returnees committed to the vision of an emancipated future may play a catalytic role in transforming conditions that reproduce humiliation. These returnees may include some that have been forcibly excluded or marginalized and others who have made a temporary escape. The former group includes Mandela, back from internal exile as a long-term political prisoner. The latter category includes Suu Kyi, a long-term but temporary escapee. Each made a spectacular comeback at the end of the 1980s. Both were highly honoured late-coming returnees without the emotional and political baggage that comes from prolonged day-to-day engagement on the streets. Both returned to the front line having spent years preparing for that moment.

Such returnees are likely to need validation and support from old campaigners who did not leave the scene but have been through the many torments brought, in different ways, by taking the stances of acceptance, rejection and all shades between. Suu Kyi turned to ex-generals who had been worsted in the *Tatmadaw*'s internal struggles, students who had pursued their degree courses under intolerable conditions, Buddhist monks plagued with government spies, and the Burmese people generally, resentful and hoping for a saviour. All those mentioned surely spent much of their lives trying to find a viable emotional resting place somewhere between angry rejection and resigned acceptance of the conditions of Burmese life under the military regime. Mandela had support both from South Africa's long-suffering and intermittently rebellious cities, and also from ANC exiles. In both cases their support includes some who were weary of the continual demeaning compromises required in their daily lives (disillusioned accepters) and others keen to mobilize their strength not just to defend themselves and damage their opponents but also to create a more just society (visionary resisters).

For another example of this three-way coalition in favour of transformation, let us turn to Europe during and after World War II. The Americans, veterans of the previous war, imbued with democratic values, were a high profile example of highly honoured late-coming returnees to the front line they left in 1918. Viewed from within an even larger historical framework they were escapees from the old world who had persuaded themselves it would be both worthy and advantageous to make the return journey to Europe, for a while at least. When the Americans arrived in 1942 they were, indeed, charismatic returnees. They had a well-advertised noble heritage, coming from 'the land of the free', and they quickly won their spurs in the struggle.

After the war the United States strongly encouraged a Europe-wide peace movement committed to eliminating the humiliations of tyranny and war. This movement eventually led to the formation of the European Union (EU). This was another product of the pragmatic alliance mentioned earlier. The Americans, still glowing with their charismatic reputation, worked very closely with two groups of politicians: visionary supporters of the resistance, for example from France, Belgium and the Netherlands; and disillusioned accepters of humiliating fascist tyranny in Germany and Italy, who had acquiesced in an alleviative spirit, making the best of an outrageous situation.

Stepping back, let us recall the three interconnected historical processes we are investigating: the West's retreat from global power, the British Empire's decline, fall and aftermath, and, not least, Britain's proposed retreat from the European Union. Each one tracks through various options mentioned here. Washington has recently found it more difficult to get its way internationally, so it has made several shifts: from the global *transformation* strategies it adopted from a position of strength in the late 1940s and again, briefly, in the early 1990s; through *resistance* and *revenge* postures during the Cold War and after 9/11; towards a shrewdly managed combination of *rejection* and *acceptance* under Obama; followed by a shift under Trump towards possible *escape* in the form of isolationism interspersed with threats of *revenge* against chosen enemies. The British Empire tried: initially, *transformation*, for example Smuts's inter-war Commonwealth schemes;[19] followed by *rejection* for example in Burma after 1944, in Malaya (1940–60), in Cyprus (1955–9) and again during the 1956 Suez campaign; and, finally, reluctant *acceptance* in South Asia, Africa[20] and East of Aden.

Brexit combines both *escape* and *rejection*, as we will see in the final chapter. This occurred after a decade during which the EU had been weakened by the sharp transition away from the promise of Social Europe cultivated during the 1990s, when the social rights of European citizens were heavily promoted, towards the sustained imposition of austerity during the 2010s, when those rights were overridden. This was a classic example of humiliating forced displacement, most intensively displayed in the suffering imposed on Greece and the violent response.[21] Populist leaders such as Marine Le Pen, Beppe Grillo and Nigel Farage have done their best to undermine the EU, operating in a spirit that dances between *rejection* and *escape*. Such speakers are experts at mobilizing deep feelings of resentment. One outcome of this populist wave was Brexit but this needs to be understood as part of the big picture.

Notes

1 *On Oscar Wilde*: Ellmann 1988, Eltis 1996, Friedman 2014, Wilde 2013. *On Jean Améry*: Améry 1980b, Améry 1999, Heidelberger-Leonard 2010, Zolkos 2011. *On Nelson Mandela*: Bundy 2015, Lodge 2006, Mandela 2002, Mandela 2003a. *On Aung San Suu Kyi*: Aung San Suu Kyi 1991a, Clements 2008, Lintner 2011, Popham 2011. *On mid and late Victorian Britain*: Collini 1991, Jones 1971, Smith 2016a, Webb 1980. *On the Third Reich*: Bukey 2001, Evans 2009, Gehl 1963, Lorenz and Weinberger 1994. *On South Africa*: Johnson 2015b, Plaut and Holden 2012, Thompson and Berat 2014, Welsh 2000. *On Burma (Myanmar):* Larkin 2010, Lintner 1994, Rogers 2012, Thant Myint-U 2007a. *On the European Union (EU):* Cockfield 1994, Duchêne 1980; Middlemas 1995; Milward 1992. *On the British Empire*: Darwin 1988, Darwin 1991, Darwin 2009, Darwin 2013, Gott 2012, Kwarteng 2012, Price 2008.
2 In the ten-week Spanish-American War of 1898, the Americans destroyed much of the Spanish fleet, and gained the Philippines, Guam and Puerto Rico from Spain as colonies. Cuba became a US protectorate until 1902 when it gained its independence with the United States retaining a perpetual lease on Guantanamo Bay.
3 http://www.bartleby.com/360/1/120.html (accessed 22nd June 2017). 'There was a little girl' was composed by Henry Wadsworth Longfellow (1807–82).
4 Smith 2016.
5 Adedeji,Teriba and Bugembe 1991, 337.
6 Baring 1908; Ellmann 1988; Nimocks 1968; O'Brien 1979; Owen 2004; Reid 2004.
7 Morefield 2014; Ignatieff 2004; Meyer 2000.
8 Aung San Suu Kyi 1991a; Aung San Suu Kyi 1997; Clements 2008.
9 https://drkokogyi.wordpress.com/2011/10/20/daw-aung-san-suu-kyis-international-awards-honors-appointments/; and https://en.wikipedia.org/wiki/List_of_awards_and_honours_bestowed_upon_Nelson_Mandela (both accessed 25th August 2016).
10 'Nelson Mandela's family launches House of Mandela wines', 22nd February 2013, *Associated Press*, at https://www.thestar.com/business/2013/02/22/nelson_mandelas_family_launches_house_of_mandela_wines.html (accessed 15th September 2016).
11 Wilde 2013, 263.
12 Wilde 1994, 310–18.

172 Confronting humiliation

13 'Aung San Suu Kyi vows to lead Myanmar if her party wins election', 7th October 2015, *The Guardian* at https://www.theguardian.com/world/2015/oct/07/aung-san-suu-kyi-vows-to-lead-myanmar-if-her-party-wins-election (accessed 15th September 2016).
14 Carlin 2008, 57.
15 For some previous research and writing that have fed into this approach see, for example, Smith 2001b; Smith 2002; Smith 2006a; Smith 2010; Smith 2012; Smith 2013; Smith 2014a; Smith 2016a.
16 Améry 1964; Aung San Suu Kyi 1985; Aung San Suu Kyi 1991b; Aung San Suu Kyi 1991c.
17 *Lugares*, 37–81; *OK*, 28–69.
18 Wilde 1891b.
19 For example, Hancock 1968, 36–49.
20 Although the white settler government of Southern Rhodesia led by Ian Smith briefly resisted decolonization.
21 Smith 2001, 134–47; Smith 2014; Smith 2015.

Bibliography

Adedeji, A., Teriba, O., and Bugembe, P. (1991). *The Challenge of African Economic Recovery and Development*. London: Frank Cass.
Améry, J. (1964). *Preface to the Future. Culture in a Consumer Society*. New York, NY: Frederick Ungar; originally published in 1961 as *Geburt der Gegenwart: Gestalten und Gestaltungen der westlichen Zivilisation seit Kriegsende*. Olten: Walter (*Birth of the Present*).
Améry, J. (1980b). *At the Mind's Limits. Contemplations by a Survivor on Auschwitz and its Realities*. Bloomington, IN: Indiana University Press; originally published in 1966 in German as *Jenseits von Schuld und Sühne* (*Beyond Crime and Punishment*). München: Szczesny.
Améry, J. (1999). *On Suicide. A Discourse on Voluntary Death*. Bloomington and Indianapolis: Indiana University Press; originally published in 1976 in German as *Hand an Sich legen. Diskurs über den Freitod*. Stuttgart: Klett-Cotta.
Aung San Suu Kyi. (1985). *Let's Visit Burma*. London: Burke Publishing Company; also in Aung San Suu Kyi 1991a, 39–81 under the title *My Country and My People*.
Aung San Suu Kyi. (1991a). *Freedom from Fear and Other Writings*. Edited with an introduction by Michael Aris. London: Penguin Books.
Aung San Suu Kyi. (1997). *Letters from Burma*. London: Penguin Books.
Aung San Suu Kyi. (1991b). *Aung San of Burma*. Edinburgh: Kiscadale Publications; originally published in 1984; also in Aung San Suu Kyi 1991a, 3–38 under the title *My Father*.
Aung San Suu Kyi. (1991c). 'Intellectual Life in Burma and India under Colonialism' in Aung San Suu Kyi 1991a, 82–139; originally published in 1990.
Baring, E. (Lord Cromer). 1908. 'The Government of Subject Races'. *The Edinburgh Review*, January 1908, reprinted in Baring 1913.
Baring, E. (Lord Cromer). 1913. *Political and Literary Essays, 1908–1913*. London: Macmillan.
Bukey, E.B. (2001). *Hitler's Austria: Popular Sentiment in the Nazi Era, 1938–1945*. Chapel Hill, NC: University of North Carolina Press.
Bundy, C. (2015). *Nelson Mandela*. Stroud: The History Press.

Carlin, J. (2008). *Playing the Enemy. Nelson Mandela and the Game that Made a Nation.* London: Atlantic Books.
Clements, A. (2008). *The Voice of Hope. Aung San Suu Kyi. Conversations with Aung San Suu Kyi.* London: Rider Books.
Cockfield, A. (Lord Cockfield) (1994). *The European Union. Creating the Single Market.* London: Wiley Chancery Law.
Collini, S. (1991). *Public Moralists. Political Thought and Intellectual Life in Britain 1850–1930.* Oxford: Oxford University Press.
Darwin, J. (1988). *Britain and Decolonisation. The Retreat from Empire in the Post-War World.* London: Palgrave.
Darwin, J. (1991). *The End of the British Empire.* London: Basil Blackwell.
Darwin, J. (2009). *The Empire Project. The Rise and Fall of the British World System 1830–1970.* Cambridge: Cambridge University Press.
Darwin, J. (2013). *Unfinished Empire. The Global Expansion of Britain.* London: Penguin.
Duchêne, F. (1980). *Jean Monnet. The First Statesman of Interdependence.* London: W.W. Norton.
Eltis, S. (1996). *Revising Wilde: Society and Subversion in the Plays of Oscar Wilde.* Oxford: Clarendon Press.
Evans, R.J. (2009). *The Third Reich at War. How the Nazis Led Germany from Conquest to Disaster.* London: Penguin.
Friedman, D.M. (2014). *Wilde in America. Oscar Wilde and the Invention of Modern Celebrity.* New York: W.W.Norton.
Gehl, J. (1963). *Austria, Germany, and the Anschluss, 1931–1938.* Evesham, UK: Greenwood Press.
Gott, R. (2012). *Britain's Empire. Resistance, Repression and Revolt.* London: Verso.
Hancock, W.K. (1968). *Smuts. vol 2. The Field of Force.* Cambridge: Cambridge University Press.
Heidelberger-Leonard, I. (2010). *The Philosopher of Auschwitz. Jean Améry and Living with the Holocaust.* London and New York: I.B.Taurus.
Ignatieff, M. (2004). *Empire Lite. Nation-building in Bosnia, Kosovo and Afghanistan.* London: Penguin.
Johnson, R.W. (2015b). *How Long Will South Africa Survive?* London: C. Hurst.
Jones, G.S. (1971). *Outcast London. A Study of the Relationship between Classes in Victorian Society,* Oxford: Oxford University Press.
Kwarteng, K. (2012). *Ghosts of Empire: Britain's Legacies in the Modern World.* London: Bloomsbury Paperbacks.
Larkin, E. (2010). *Everything is Broken. A Tale of Catastrophe in Burma.* London: Penguin.
Lintner, B. (1994). *Burma in Revolt. Opium and Insurgency since 1948.* Chiang Mai, Thailand: Silkworm Books.
Lintner, B. (2011). *Aung San Suu Kyi and Burma's Struggle for Democracy.* Chiang Mai, Thailand: Silkworm Books.
Lodge, T. (2006). *Mandela. A Critical Life.* Oxford: Oxford University Press.
Lorenz, D.C.G. and Weinberger, G. (eds) (1994). *Insiders and Outsiders. Jewish and Gentile Culture in Germany and Austria.* Detroit, MI: Wayne State University Press.
Mandela, N. (2002). *Long Walk to Freedom. The Autobiography of Nelson Mandela. Volume One. 1918–1962.* London: Abacus.
Mandela, N. (2003a). *Long Walk to Freedom. The Autobiography of Nelson Mandela. Volume Two. 1962–1994.* London: Abacus.

Middlemas, K. (1995). *Orchestrating Europe. The Informal Politics of the European Union 1973–95*. London: Fontana Press.

Milward, A.S. (1992). *The European Rescue of the Nation-State*. London: Routledge.

Nimocks, W. (1968). *Milner's Young Men: The "Kindergarten" in Edwardian Imperial Affairs*. London: Hodder and Stoughton.

O'Brien, T.H. (1979). *Milner. Viscount Milner of St James's and Cape Town 1854–1925*. London: Constable.

Meyer, K.E. (2000) 'An Edwardian Warning: The Unraveling of a Colossus', *World Policy Journal*, 17, 4, Winter, 47–57.

Morefield, J. (2014). *Empire without Imperialism. Anglo-American Decline and the Politics of Deflection*. Oxford: Oxford University Press.

Owen, R. (2004). *Lord Cromer: Victorian Imperialist, Edwardian Proconsul* Oxford: Oxford University Press.

Plaut, M. and Holden, P. (2012). *Who Rules South Africa?* London: Biteback Publishing.

Popham, P. (2011). *The Lady and the Peacock. The Life of Aung San Suu Kyi*. London: Rider Books.

Price, R. (2008). *Making Empire. Colonial Encounters and the Creation of Imperial Rule in Nineteenth-Century Africa*. Cambridge: Cambridge University Press.

Reid, D. (2004). 'Review of Lord Cromer: Victorian Imperialist, Edwardian Proconsul (review no. 414)' in *Reviews in History*, July 2004 at http://www.history.ac.uk/reviews/review/414 (accessed 13 August 2016).

Rogers, B. (2012). *Burma. A Nation at the Crossroads*. London: Rider.

Smith, D. (1999c). 'Making Europe. Processes of Europe-Formation Since 1945' in D. Smith and S. Wright, (eds) *Whose Europe? The Turn Towards Democracy*. Oxford: Blackwell, 235–256.

Smith, D. (2001b). 'Organizations and Humiliation: Looking Beyond Elias', *Organization*, 8, 3, 2001, 537–560.

Smith, D. (2002). 'The Humiliating Power of Organizations: A Typology and a Case Study' in A. van Iterson, T. Newton, , W. Mastenbroek, and D. Smith (eds) *The Civilized Organisation*, Amsterdam: Benjamin, 41–57.

Smith, D. (2006a). *Globalization. The Hidden Agenda*. Cambridge: Polity.

Smith, D. (2009c). 'The Dynamics of Domination and Displacement in Global Politics' in M. Gornostaeva (ed.) *Sociology: History, Theory and Practices vol 10*, Moscow: Institute of Socio-Political Research, Russian Academy of Sciences, 122–144.

Smith, D. (2010). 'Social Fluidity and Social Displacement', *Sociological Review*, 58, 4, November, 680–688.

Smith, D. (2012). 'Dimensions of World Making: Thoughts from the Caspian Sea' in D. Kalekin-Fishman and A. Denis (eds) *The Shape of Sociology*, London: Sage, 113–133.

Smith, D. (2013). 'Forced Social Displacement: The 'Inside Stories' of Oscar Wilde, Jean Améry, Nelson Mandela and Aung San Suu Kyi' in Nicolas Demertsiz (ed.) *Emotions in Politics*, London: Palgrave-Macmillan, 60–83.

Smith, D. (2014a). 'Coping with the Threat of Humiliation: Contrasting Responses to the Crisis of the Eurozone in Greece and Ireland' in N.P. Petropoulos and G.O. Tsobanoglou (eds) *The Debt Crisis in the Eurozone: Social Impacts*, Newcastle-upon-Tyne: Cambridge Scholars Publishing, 84–108.

Smith, D. (2015). 'Not just singing the blues: Dynamics of the EU crisis' in H.-J. Trenz, C. Ruzza and V. Guiraudon (eds) *Europe's Prolonged Crisis. The Making or the Unmaking of a Political Union*, London: Palgrave Macmillan, 23–43.

Smith, D. (2016a). *Conflict and Compromise. Class Formation in English Society 1830–1914. A Comparative Study of Birmingham and Sheffield*. London: Routledge.
Smith, D. and Wright, S. (eds) *Whose Europe? The Turn Towards Democracy*. Oxford: Blackwell.
Thant Myint-U (2007a). *The River of Lost Footsteps. A Personal History of Burma*. London: Faber and Faber.
Thompson, L. and Berat, L. (2014). *A History of South Africa*. New Haven and London: Yale University Press.
Webb, B. (1980). *My Apprenticeship*. Cambridge: Cambridge University Press; originally published 1926.
Welsh, F. (2000). *A History of South Africa*. London: HarperCollins.
Wilde, O. (1891b). 'The Soul of Man under Socialism', *Fortnightly Review*, 49, Feb 1891, 292–319.
Wilde, O. (1994). *The Complete Plays, Poems, Novels and Stories of Oscar Wilde*. London: Parragon.
Wilde, O. (2013). *De Profundis and Other Prison Writings*. London: Penguin.
Zolkos, M. (ed.) (2011). *On Jean Améry. Philosophy of Catastrophe*. Lanham, MD: Lexington Books.

7 The big picture

War and freedom

The retreat of the West from global power has so far been examined through the perspectives provided by the lives and careers of four civilized rebels: Oscar Wilde, Jean Améry, Nelson Mandela and Aung San Suu Kyi.[1] These lives offer distinctive takes on the decline, fall and aftermath of the British Empire and its entanglements with rivals in Europe, Asia and the Americas. Making sense of these visionary dissidents meant looking at the national and international contexts in which they operated. Now we examine that bigger Western and global picture more directly, isolating some key vectors of recent transformations. Then we focus briefly on Brexit as a case study that nicely illustrates the threat-response model set out in the previous chapter. Brexit illuminates the dynamics of a world somewhat out of joint.

The world in the early twenty-first century is still being shaped by the effects of two prolonged carnivals of slaughter, World War I and World War II, and four moments of national rebirth through revolution and independence movements: the American Declaration of Independence (1776), the French Revolution (1789), the creation of the Republic of India (1947) and the Chinese Revolution (1949). Highlighting these four moments does not diminish the significance of the Bolshevik revolution (1917) or the Third Reich (1933) since both these historical landmarks were to a great extent, major aftershocks of the earthquakes that occurred in 1776 and 1789. The Russians and the Germans both drew inspiration from revolutionary France and American capitalism. These four moments of rebirth were all profoundly liberating and helped create conditions for greater national prosperity, at least in the long run. However, the wars and the national rebirths were intimately connected, which provides a challenge for those seeking ways to combine advancing prosperity with increasing pacification of the world.

World War I triggered a decisive dismissal of the feudal thinking that had underpinned monarchy and aristocracy in Europe's great imperial dynasties in St. Petersburg, Vienna, Berlin and Constantinople. If you read *The Good Soldier Svej*[2] you will quickly see the depth of contempt in which the old regime was held by that time. The confident absolutist spirit in which during four centuries the dynasts had cheered and rewarded aggressive Western imperial expansion finally drained away.

World War I was the point when the French Revolution finally struck home across Europe; not least in Turkey during the 1920s and beyond as the Kemalist regime learned the value of a vigorous secular state acting as a decisive instrument of modernization. Dynastic influence and clientelism lost much of their legitimacy but remained powerful.[3] Between the wars the French revolutionary mechanism of the terror, praised by Robespierre for delivering rapid and robust justice, found ample exercise and was brought to a high pitch by Stalin and Hitler.[4] Meanwhile, the British Empire sailed on for another half century, maintaining imperial pomp and circumstance while making continual liberalizing compromises: giving away its sovereign powers to the dominions, and promising the colonies they would eventually come into their inheritance.

While World War I finally brought the lessons of the French Revolution to millions in Europe, World War II took the American Revolution and its aftermath, the American Dream of contented consumers, deep into the lives of billions worldwide, followed by even more billions after 1989. The unacknowledged presiding genius of World War I was the ghost of Maximilien Robespierre, the revolutionary leader whose insurgent movement brought the French monarchy and aristocracy to the guillotine. By contrast, one particular military figure did very well out of America's victory in World War II. The reference is not to General Eisenhower but to Colonel Sanders.[5] He and others made food and drink on demand a regular treat for all, not just the aristocracy.

During the 1930s Sanders sold fried chicken to his neighbours in Kentucky. By the 1950s and 1960s he was franchising his KFC brand nationally, then worldwide. The demand for fast food was met by a host of such products, all highly marketable, available, affordable, transportable and disposable. The stomach, too, was democratized. Sadly, we cannot test the views of Robespierre on Coca Cola, McDonalds, Burger King, KFC and so on.

During and immediately after World War II the United States came into its own across Eurasia and Africa. The Americans were gloriously and justifiably centre stage. Apart from the atomic bomb, which certainly commanded attention, the Americans' main assets were their wealth, efficiency, belief in science, profit-mindedness, and, not least, their promotion of private domestic happiness. With typical American generosity they shared these assets and values with the rest of the world over the next half-century.

The key mechanisms of the American Way were not just the militarized state with its long reach,[6] but also the market and its seductive promises conveyed via television. Those flickering screens showed countless potential consumers the delights of nice homes, motorized transport and fast food. Ironically, the Americans effectively trained up their allies and clients throughout the world so well that some of them became very effective competitors. Japan and South Korea are prime examples, a fact that now turns our attention towards Asia.

Delhi and Beijing both saw decisive events during the late 1940s. The Republic of India in 1947 and the People's Republic of China in 1949 finally flickered into life, having won long struggles to be their own masters. Like the French Revolution and American independence, revolutionary China and independent India will take several more decades to make their impact fully felt across Asia and beyond. That future is riddled with unknown unknowns. However, by the early twenty-first century Asia's impact was already beginning to gather pace and strength, although both were liable to be exaggerated by Westerners.

For example, two things are becoming clear regarding not just Burma but also North Korea, where the regime has been rapidly developing its capacity to deploy nuclear arms. One is that China has much more influence on those countries than have either the United States or the EU. The other is that China's ability to control the governments of either North Korea or Burma is limited. North Korea is an important buffer state and Burma a major gateway state for the Chinese. This gives both Pyongyang and Naypyidaw significant bargaining power with Beijing. Such complexities make the unfolding politics of Southeast Asia very difficult to read from outside. In fact, rather than trying to discern the future, it is more useful to consider some apparent tendencies that are already becoming discernable in the current state of global affairs.

For example, the retreat of the West from its previous condition of global dominance during the past few decades does not in itself seem to signal a rapid rise of the East to an equivalent position. Instead we are probably set for a prolonged period during which no particular power or region is in charge, consistently able to exact compliance from all others. Meanwhile, the contest for access to energy, land, water and other resources has intensified, with more players in the game. The equalizing effect of the global tendency towards multi-polarity is undermining the legitimacy and acceptability of hierarchical relations at all societal levels. Complex political federations have become more likely to fragment and their populations less willing to trust leaders from outside their cultural group. In turn, this has encouraged populist insurgencies whose leaders emphasize their close bonds with the people they claim to represent.

A fabric of rules and institutions for global governance including the International Labour Organization (ILO), the United Nations (UN), the North Atlantic Treaty Organization (NATO) and the World Trades Organization (WTO), has been inherited from the periods when the British Empire and the United States, in turn, acted as global referee. This fabric has been bulked out by other bodies such as: the African Union, the European Union, the Association of South East Asian Nations (ASEAN), the Conference on Interaction and Confidence Building in Asia (CICA), and the Shanghai Cooperation Organization (SCO).

However, as global power relations become increasing complex, global rules depend more than ever on an infrastructure of trust relations. Diplomats, politicians, secret service agents, businesses, and professionals, including the media, are continually laying down hidden wiring, holding the whole thing together. This pattern disguises and alleviates the increasing disjunction between business globalization, which continues to thrive in spite of the systemic failure of the banking system in 2007–8, and political globalization, which has gone into reverse since the collapse of the Soviet Union and the end of the Cold War, as has just been mentioned.[7]

Maintaining global cohesion increasingly depends on states being clubbable. This means that critical situations arise when some potential club members, such as North Korea, refuse to join and obey club rules, or when powerful and highly networked members make a move that gestures towards leaving the club, as President Trump did over the climate change agreement and as the UK did over Brexit. What can we learn from the United Kingdom's referendum vote to leave the European Union, and its aftermath?

Brexit and Britannia

In 1597 Francis Bacon, philosopher, statesman and life coach *avant la lettre*, pronounced: 'This is well to be weighed; that boldness is ever blind; for it seeth not danger, and inconveniences.'[8] Or, in the language of almost any British senior civil servant: 'That is a very brave of you, minister. Have you thought it through?' The politicians and business folk who backed having a referendum on Britain's EU membership in June 2016 should have done some basic research by checking out the video of *The Italian Job*, a film released in 1969.

This film stars two typical British characters. One of them is a civilized rebel spending time behind bolted gates, as the main characters in this book have done. This is Mr Bridger played by Noel Coward. He is an expensively educated toff, contemptuous of everyone around him but ready to invest in dodgy deals if they seem likely to give him a big return. Bridger is the banker for the Italian job, which is going to be a sensational exercise in grand larceny.

The other well-observed British type is the man in charge of the robber gang. He is Charlie Croker, played by Michael Caine: a more primitive rebel, sharp as a tack, an experienced East End thief with cockney charm and an eye for the main chance. Croker is taking his gang to Turin to steal several million pounds worth of gold. It's going to be straight in, straight out. No messing. The plan is clear. Get into Turin. Foul up the traffic lights. Grab the gold. Get out in a fleet of minis. Transfer the gold to a bus. Come back through the Alps. Then it's straight back to dear old England for fish and chips and whatever. Especially whatever. Then bury Bridger's share of the loot in a field till he gets out. What could possibly go wrong?

But what actually happened? The plan was faulty. Lady Luck was unfriendly. It was difficult to get off the mainland. Not easy to get out of Europe with all those winnings. Instead, where did the bus end up? On a cliff edge, precariously swinging out over a dangerous ravine. What a laugh, unless, of course, you happened to be inside the bus. This allegorical comparison certainly applied during the late summer of 2017 when the state of Brexit negotiations was uncertain and precarious. By the time you read this the bus may have fallen into the ravine, be back on the road, or even be still swaying on the cliff edge.

The following analysis tries to rise above the intense passions of the debate surrounding the project of extracting the United Kingdom from membership of the European Union: i.e British Exit, typically shortened to Brexit. It explores certain aspects of why the British electorate backed Brexit, if only narrowly, and how competing politicians have pursued this project, which, at the time of writing, remains unfinished business. We also explore what these events tell us about Britain, Europe and the West.

Opponents of Brexit stressed its potential economic disadvantages as compared with material benefits that flowed from the EU, especially to deprived regions of the UK. However, it was English working-class senior citizens from many of those deprived regions in the Midlands and the North that helped to tip the leave vote into the lead. They were crucial swing voters. Leave campaigners promised them increased funding for the National Health Service but these voters' motivations did not seem to be primarily material. More important, many of them had a strong sense of their own national and ethnic superiority that was just as deeply ingrained as the class-based *hauteur* of Prime Minister David Cameron. He was the old Etonian who engineered the referendum, presumably expecting to persuade voters to stay within the EU. But for many elderly voters the world the British Empire made was fundamentally still in existence. In their own minds they were at the top of a global hierarchy of merit. They took it for granted that so-called Anglo-Saxons were better than all other Europeans. All Northern Europeans were superior to all Southern or Eastern Europeans. All Europeans were a cut above all Asians and Africans.

Many of these voters had no etiquette for treating individuals from these other groups on equal terms. They rarely encountered them as friends or neighbours. In their eyes, it was horrifically unbelievable that Europe should be dictating to the British. It was ghastly that strange people from all over the world were muscling in on British jobs, houses and schools. It was disgusting that the government was letting such things happen instead of looking after much more deserving people who had lived and worked their whole lives in Britain. In other words, their own rights and dignity were being trampled on. It was insufferable.

Thick seams of resentment lay just below the surface of Britain's post-imperial culture and could be mined to fuel a whole range of antagonisms. Political credibility and artistic recognition had been given to this strong sense of dissatisfaction by the group of so-called 'angry young men' such as John Osborne[9] who burst onto the English literary scene during the 1950s. According to Jean Améry these British writers shared 'something absolutely negative, a universal, all-embracing, and well-reasoned rejection fed by deep emotional springs'.[10] Their work 'produced a national myth. It was a myth of negation ... The angry young men performed an act of comprehensive nay saying'.[11] They expressed the resentment of the generation that lived through World War II and became parents in the first post-war decade. These men and women passed their feelings on to their children, many of whom became those elderly voters who opted for Brexit in the EU referendum.

A young German woman fundraising for my old college gave me her opinion over the telephone that the Brexit vote was 'political suicide' by Britain. There may be something in that idea. The Chancellor of the Exchequer, George Osborne, certainly made it clear that Brexit would be the 'most extraordinary self-inflicted wound'.[12] As we have seen, Améry thought suicide was in many case a way of reasserting sovereignty over the self. It was a reaction to the feeling of being overwhelmed by life conditions that seemed disgusting; and often a response to some great setback that challenged a person's established social or socio-political identity, radically reducing their status, and diminishing their sense of self-worth.[13]

We should note that a key message of the campaign to leave the EU was: let us take back control; in other words, let us reclaim our sovereignty. Some leave campaigners placed heavy emphasis upon the upsetting idea that large numbers of unwelcome strangers, some allegedly with deeply unpleasant habits and intentions, were overwhelming Britain. The predictable reaction was a feeling of disgust. The great setback was, of course, the loss of empire, an enterprise that had implanted elevated expectations in the heads and hearts of many British people. They asked: why do top dogs have to live in dingy kennels?

George Osborne, a leading member of the government and the principal architect of its austerity programme, was one of the biggest political losers in the Brexit struggle.[14] After all, along with Cameron, he had invested considerable effort in wooing the German political and business establishment.[15] The referendum put all that at risk.

But the referendum vote was, for many voters, the chance to toss the advice of austerity's most enthusiastic advocate right back in his face, even at the cost of potential national self-harm. With their Brexit vote they were able to shake the British political, business and cultural establishments to their foundations. The vote administered the kind of penetrating shock to those high-ups that Améry wanted his own oppressors to feel. In other words, a shock whose impact was equivalent to the humiliation those oppressors had inflicted on the communities they had neglected, and treated as worthless.

Améry went to his grave regretting he had been unable to strike back. By contrast, in the Brexit vote many ordinary citizens trapped at the wrong end of key distribution curves for income, education, health, housing, and so on seized the chance to do exactly that. By striking back at the ballot box they forced the British establishment to experience that sense of being dismissed and cast aside that had been the daily diet of many ordinary citizens for years, indeed decades. From Améry's perspective, that counts as a positive outcome, especially if it makes the establishment realize what humiliation it had inflicted on others and how much repair work was required. That is, of course, a big if. Was the establishment listening? Did it realize what was happening? The costs of not paying attention to human feelings are high.[16]

In this context Norman Angell's *The Great Illusion* (Angell 1911) is relevant.[17] This author carefully explained over several pages why complex and extensive trading links freely established would definitely make war in Europe and elsewhere irrational, futile, redundant and irrelevant. In Angell's view, the institution of war was virtually extinct. Unfortunately, he did not take into account the dynamics of political humiliation, not least the vengeful rivalry between Germany and France. In 1914 Angell's thesis was discredited by the outbreak of World War I. The point is that free trade *alone* does not, in fact, abolish war and make people universally content.[18] Nor does wealth alone guarantee safety. The recent Syrian, Iraqi and Libyan civil wars destroyed many prosperous households along with much poorer abodes amid the general devastation. Similar carnage happened across South-East Europe during the 1990s. The implication is that free trade has to be accompanied by stable political institutions, well tended international alliances, effective military defences and, now we must add, cybersecurity.[19]

In Europe, the North Atlantic Treaty Organization (NATO) needed support from a strong underpinning of trust and familiarity between the societies it was defending. The main force responsible for creating those bonds of peaceful exchange and cooperation was the European Union, the outcome of a peace movement based on economic integration. Step by step, a coherent and viable inter-governmental and supra-governmental framework was created to keep market transactions as transparent, honest and fair as possible, not just within member states but also between them.[20] At its centre were four freedoms of movement, relating to goods, services, capital and people. Then out of the blue in 2016 the United Kingdom voted to leave.

Although unexpected, Brexit was consistent with other happenings in the European Union's near neighbourhood. It was part of a bigger picture. Traumatic events had been occurring since the 1980s in regions closely adjacent to the EU such as the Soviet Bloc, South-East Europe, North Africa and the Middle East. In every case there has been a dramatic and devastating collapse of regional socio-political arrangements. Each cataclysm made headlines for a few weeks or months but was then quickly assimilated as a partial shift of the landscape. However, these disasters should be considered together. They represent the destruction of a major part of the West's immediate hinterland over a mere quarter of a century. In the wake of Brexit and Donald Trump's election it was not clear whether that process was complete, nor how strong the political appetite was for rebuilding or replacing those shattered structures.

This accumulation of national and international tragedies showed that when complex political arrangements began to rip and tear it was very difficult to repair them, even though they had previously endured for decades. Such rips and tears accumulate and worsen. Old hostilities flare up, exacerbating the damage. It is far from impossible that Brexit might trigger such a sequence of progressive and increasingly disorderly fragmentation within the EU, echoing what happened in the Soviet Union and Yugoslavia. That would make everybody less safe. The most important underlying issue across the whole of Europe, as in the other cases mentioned, was the damage being inflicted upon long-established bonds and carefully cultivated relationships.

A politically peaceful and happy Brexit was probably not envisaged by many people who researched the matter, whatever their public statements. A politically contentious and painful Brexit seemed much more likely. But, in spite of this, a detached approach was surely able to recognize that the Brexit vote was a remarkable expression of the power and deeply grounded character of British democracy, albeit a power exercised by a *demos* rendered half-blind by Delilah-like advocates on both sides. The referendum produced an assertion of popular will that contradicted the clearly expressed wishes of the UK government, whose allegiance to the most powerful section of the national and global business establishment was not in doubt.

The UK establishment overwhelmingly wanted to remain within the EU. But the unwelcome and unexpected Brexit vote gave parliamentarians at Westminster and their associates in the corporate world a slap in the face. Impressively, most of them dutifully treated this as the democratic voice of the people. Then a year later, in the snap general election in June 2017, the voters struck again. Once more they denied the government what it wanted. Prime Minister Theresa May asked for a much larger majority so that she could govern in a strong and stable way, as she repeatedly put it. Instead, the voters did exactly the opposite. They took away her existing majority, leaving her heading a weak and potentially unstable government. Jeremy Corbyn's Labour party argued strongly that the balance of influence in Britain had swung too heavily towards business interests and too far away from citizens as a whole. Many people evidently agreed, enabling him to increase his party's share of seats and the popular vote in the 2017 election.

To summarize: the Brexit vote showed there were important limits to capitalism's ability to get its own way. In Britain at least, the people could say no to what big business wanted and make it stick. They were able to make their point, good and hard. But the British people, having made their point, became seriously concerned about collateral damage. The 2017 UK general election produced a hung parliament. It sent a message across Europe from the rebellious British people. Let us call them civilized rebels. This message declared that the British refused to be dictated to from above by the political and business establishments. Rebelliously, they had decided to reserve their position. Rebelliously, they were going to wait and see.

Rebellion, risk and revenge

What might the British people learn from our four civilized rebels about the costs and benefits of insurgency? In terms of the threat-response model explored in the previous chapter, those four dissidents sought remedial solutions not temporary alleviations. They all had successes. But they also suffered enormously, enduring pain and misery on behalf of great causes: socialism, anarchism and artistic freedom (Wilde), the right to choose how to live and die (Améry), human freedom and equality (Mandela), and, finally, democracy and freedom from fear (Aung San Suu Kyi). Were the British people making a conscious decision to accept a degree of suffering, if necessary?[21]

In fact, there is little sign that voters on the winning side in the EU referendum expected to suffer much if at all as a result of their actions. Their vote was alleviative, seeking both avoidance and revenge. It signalled their wish to remove themselves from the pain and anxiety the EU allegedly brought. That was the avoidance element. Winning the referendum was like booking a plane ticket. It enabled voters to imagine and symbolically enact their hopefully imminent escape from the EU. The leave vote was also alleviative in another way. It was an act of revenge upon the British establishment for imposing several years of sustained austerity. The voters got the satisfaction of saying to those who had been spoiling their lives 'Take that. See how it feels.

But once the victory party was over, how could those short-term alleviative effects be translated into beneficial and achievable long-term remedial outcomes? Two prominent attempts were made to give answers to that question by competing teams of politicians. These were the free-trade Brexiteers on the one side and the Labour party leadership under Jeremy Corbyn on the other side.

The free-trade Brexiteers proposed that a longer-term remedy for Britain's ills could be found by pursuing a national future trading freely around the globe. By implication, the United Kingdom did not need to change its character. It just needed a better place to express that character. This was a remedial strategy moving beyond avoidance towards replacement, substituting a wide-open globe for a highly regulated continent. By contrast, Jeremy Corbyn and the leadership of the Labour party suggested building up the politico-economic strength of the British citizenry, enhancing its ability to achieve a better life for itself. In other words, Labour under Corbyn offered an alternative remedial pathway, one that moved beyond revenge towards resistance against capitalist exploitation or neglect (see page 167).

Both groups, Corbynites and free-trade Brexiteers, thought, like Oscar Wilde, that a map of the world without utopia was not worth having. In effect, the choice being offered was between a socialist utopia offering social justice delivered through state action and a capitalist utopia promising creative freedom to be exercised by ambitious entrepreneurs trading across the world's oceans. A disinterested observer might notice that these two utopias, when merged together, were the very basis of the EU as it developed during the 1990s and early 2000s: in other words, free trade combined with social justice. In that case was Brexit really necessary? A moderate sort of person might reflect that each of these two utopias had very desirable aspects but neither would be very comfortable for their inhabitants if taken to extremes. This disinterested moderate citizen might even ponder that a pragmatic balance between these two ideals might be achieved within the EU, the largest free-trade block in the world. She might even reflect upon the potential role of British diplomats in achieving this, renowned as they were for being expert and experienced at managing such compromises. However, the British were arranging to leave, turning the EU-28 into the EU-27, a significantly smaller, weaker, poorer, and less stable union.

Revolt and retreat

In fact, Brexit, the election of Donald Trump and the European populist upsurge were all moments in the long retreat of the West from global power. They swirled together at the confluence of two unwinding relationships, both ripe for reframing: one between the very rich and the rest within the West; the other between the West as a whole and the rest of the world.

The contract forged during the Thatcher–Reagan era in the 1980s between the West's very rich and powerful minority with their massive holdings in stocks and shares and the weaker, poorer majority with their democratic votes lost its legitimacy during the early twenty-first century. Neo-liberalism's appeal to private greed was increasingly being seen by the people at large as a recipe for, at best, static living standards combined with widespread and advancing public squalor.

The establishment and the citizenry became deeply estranged from each other. Corporate profit-seeking seemed to be increasingly self-centred and inward-looking. Greed drove out other considerations. Political and business establishments paid less attention than before to the needs, wishes and feelings of ordinary people. But in capitalist democracies the *demos* had a powerful lever in its hands: the vote. When the people's discontent with being neglected and taken for granted became sufficiently intense they were able to use the ballot box to deliver big surprises such as Brexit, Trump and the election of Emmanuel Macron as French president in 2017.

Meanwhile, Asia, Africa and Latin America were asserting themselves. The West was presented with a mountain of evidence about the damaging consequences of its victimizing behaviour during previous centuries. Intellectuals such as Edward Said, Kishore Mahbubani, Shintaro Ishihara and Pankaj Mishra busily put Europeans and North Americans in their place, usually with eloquence, erudition and justice on their side.[22] But the West responded badly as these chickens came home to roost, complain, moralize and correct. Citizens in the US and across Europe who were being ignored by their own national governments, were themselves, in turn, largely deaf to the demands of the world's poor and nearly-poor millions outside their own borders.

One reason was that many people in the West began defining themselves as victims too, blaming globalization rather than imperialism. The debt crises plaguing Asia, Russia and Latin America in 1997–8 struck the West a decade later. A similar story can be told about the Washington Consensus. Its Western agents, mainly the International Monetary Fund (IMF) and World Bank, habitually imposed harsh conditions on the tax-and-spend strategies of indebted governments in Asia, Africa and Latin America in return for loans with tight repayment conditions. But the Washington Consensus came back to the West with a vengeance. The EU's so-called *troika* commissions, including the IMF, regulated the distribution of emergency loans to states such as Greece and Ireland during the Eurozone crisis. They imposed similarly harsh humiliating conditions on those governments and peoples.[23]

It became difficult for Westerners who were angry about their own recent humiliations to recognize how outrageous it had been for their predecessors to plunder the rest of the world. Imperialism had been exhilarating and rewarding at the time.[24] But now imperialism's victims were confidently asserting their rights. How should the West and its historical victims deal with each other? A mature and detached approach to these issues might favour the pursuit of survivors' justice, as interpreted by Mahmood Mamdani. This eschews essentialist talk of victims and perpetrators, since resentment and revenge make all of us liable to wound others. Instead, Mandani suggests, we should all find ways of working together to make things better for everyone, seeking long-term remedies, not instant alleviations.[25]

But who was listening? Complaining about one's own hurts took precedence over caring for others' problems. Many Westerners rejected involvement in the concerns of the wider world they had once claimed and controlled. Enthusiasm for Brexit was part of this. It offered many Britons a convenient rabbit hole down which to scurry, leaving behind the complexities of globalization, imperialism and Europe's past. Likewise, President Trump offered fellow citizens a safer and more comfortable America behind walls and barriers. How realistic or realizable these escape projects might be is something we will all discover soon enough. For now let us notice that Brexit and Trump both pointed in the same direction: away from global concerns and towards the particular demands of 'our' people.

Populist movements of both left and right were in denial. The radical left habitually said that many wicked things had been done but, as their slogan went, 'not in our name'. For their part the radical right told the rest of the world: we will look after ourselves in our own country, and we will not help anyone else. Don't expect us to share ownership of your problems. On all sides the yielding spirit of retreat, the search for an escape route, lurked behind the rhetoric of revolt, evading responsibility and trying to avoid the resentment of others.[26] Can this damaging trend in the West's political culture be diverted towards more beneficial objectives?

Challenge for the West

In fact, the West remains immensely influential in the world and will continue so. However, a great deal depends on how it acts now, in the early twenty-first century. The shrewdest move it could make at this point would be to take the global lead in confronting the most fundamental challenge facing us across the globe, including the West's hinterland and, following Brexit, its heartland. That challenge is to reverse the current historical trend towards socio-political breakdown, which is the classic breeding ground for humiliation. This will be expensive, complex and time-consuming but the West can certainly afford to promote this mission and make a substantial contribution, one commensurate with its share of aggregate global wealth. It will be cheap at the price, especially considering the enormous costs of the disastrous alternative.

This is a challenge no less important than coping with climate change, fighting global poverty, controlling and eliminating nuclear weapons, cleaning up the oceans, defeating cancer and fighting AIDS. In fact it is intimately related to those other challenges, all of which confront conditions that threaten to undermine and restrict the opportunities for individuals and communities to live healthy and civilized lives in peace and relative comfort.

Most of us, women and men, old and young from all continents, know from our own experience, however slight or intense, that being humiliated entails having our social identity and social position spat upon, leaving us feeling degraded and discarded. We know the potential causes of humiliation: poverty, sickness, chronic disorder and uncertainty, bigotry, corruption, exploitation, cruelty and culpable neglect. We know the symptoms of humiliation: anger, fear, sorrow and deep unease. We also know the prognosis of humiliation: if untreated, the result is excessive and persistent emotionality, irrationality, hatred, and restlessness. This often culminates in action, either upon the self or others, to alleviate personal or group tension, often without rational consideration of its wider consequences. Untreated humiliation breeds unending war: inside the self, inside families, inside communities, inside nations, and within continents. That is the real inside story told here.

Studying the struggles of our four civilized rebels has led us towards two conclusions. One is that in many lives the pursuit of success and happiness takes second place to another challenge: how to cope effectively with the threat of failure and forced social displacement, being pushed down, knocked back and kicked out. The other conclusion is that a distinct pattern of alleviative and remedial responses to such threats applies across a wide range of situations. The pathways potentially available range from the drastic escape route eventually taken by Améry, who ended his own life, to the emancipatory route recommended and followed by Mandela, which involved working to eliminate degradation in human relationships,

These and other routes leading into, through, and out of humiliation are being followed, day in, day out, by individuals, groups and even nations. The more we know and understand about these processes, the more we can act upon them, seeking not just alleviations but also remedies that are life enhancing.[27] The West has accumulated centuries of diverse historical experience through its long engagement with peoples on all continents. Its embarrassing and often shameful history of imperialist oppression and exploitation has, paradoxically, given its governments, traders and professionals a strong sense of fellow-feeling with people in all parts of the world. But to be taken seriously as a force for global good the West must demonstrate systematically and repeatedly that it is willing to make a major contribution to rebuilding communities and enhancing regional infrastructures not only within the West but beyond. This is a challenging task because it means making the difficult transition from alleviative to remedial thinking. This transition is complicated by the fact that alleviative responses – such as avoidance, deception, revenge and conciliation – are largely motivated by self-protective distrust. By contrast, remedial responses – such as replacement, conversion, resistance and emancipation – make a radical switch from the negative to the positive. They are driven by a commitment to fulfilling a vision of a better future condition of the self, the group, relationships with others, and the broader socio-political and ecological context.

We must counteract the energy of collapse that is all around us with the energy of creation. The best way to outmanoeuvre those who recommend the virtues of killing, conquest and the pursuit of humiliation is to offer as many people as possible the means of life, liberty and the pursuit of happiness. The West has the means to do this and must rediscover the will to do it. Some strategic altruism drawing on the highest moral standards of Western culture would come in very handy right now. This entails recognizing the human needs of others and responding generously to them, doing this with a caring rather than a controlling intention. This is the moral and emotional colouring that our political life both at home and with our global neighbours needs if we are all to be fully civilized in the best sense. It is the key to surviving with dignity, self-respect and satisfaction. Gandhi was supposedly once asked what he thought of Western civilization. He said he thought it would be a good idea. He was right. Perhaps there is still time.

Notes

1 Here is a summary of some source materials that provide background for prominent topics in this chapter. There are further references on some of these topics in other chapters. *On Oscar Wilde*: Ellmann 1988. *On Jean Améry*: Heidelberger-Leonard 2010. *On Nelson Mandela*: Lodge 2006. *On Aung San Suu Kyi*: Popham 2011. *On the European Union (EU) and Eurozone crisis*: Cockfield 1994; Duchêne 1980; Middlemas 1995; Milward 1992; Smith 2014; Smith 2015; Smith and Wright 2000. *On the City of London, Wall Street and the financial world*: Geithner 2014, Henwood 1997; Hertz 2001; Klein 2000; Mayer 2016; Meek 2015; Palan 2003; Shaxson 2012; Streek 2013; Tett 2009. *On populism and neo-liberalism*: Alinsky 1971: Kirkchick 2017; Mishra 2017, Luce 2017.. *On Brexit*: Ashcroft and Culwick 2016; Banks 2016; Bennett 2016; Cato the Younger 2017; Farage 2015; Gibbon 2016; Shipman 2016; Smith 2014a; Smith 2014b; Smith 2015. *On globalization*: Davis 2001; Davis 2006; Frankopan 2016; Giddens 2000; Holton 2008; Huntington 1997; Keen 2012; Klare 2001; Klare 2008; Noreng 2005; Petersen 2011; Robertson 1992; Sands 2005; Scheff 2000; Smith 2006b; Stiglitz 2010. *On British post war policy and politics*: Aldrich 2010, Annan 1990, Hennessy and Jinks 2015; Middlemas 1986; Middlemas 1990; Middlemas 1991; Moore 2013; Moore 2015; Schofield 2013; Seldon and Snowdon 2015; Singer and Friedman 2014. *On humiliation, rebellion and*

emancipation: Alexander 2012; Bailey 2001; Lindner 2006; Mamdani 2004; Mamdani 2009; Sassen 2014; Scheff 2000; Schivelbusch 2003; Smith 2010; Smith 2013; Smith 2014a. *On the British and their empire*: Barr 2012; Churchill 2007 [1931]; Colley 2004; Dietrich 2017; Elkins 2005; Smith 2016a; Smith 2016e; Von Tunzelman 2007.
2 Hašek 2016; originally published in 1923.
3 The practices of the court society examined by Norbert Elias also remained vigorous wherever rulers, hierarchies and the potential for favours and favouritism persisted. See Elias 1983; Smith 2001a.
4 Linton 2006.
5 See Ozersky 2012.
6 See, for example, Blum 2014.
7 See Smith 2006a; Holton 2008. For examples of the cultural approach to globalization see Huntington 1997 and Robertson 1992. The economic perspective includes, for instance, both Wallerstein 1974–2011 and Kennedy 1983. Michael Mann's approach is multi-dimensional, as are those of Barrington Moore and Gary Runciman. See Mann 1986–2013; Moore 1991; Runciman 1989; Runciman 2009; Smith 2016c. For a comparison of Mann, Wallerstein and Runciman, see Smith 1991; Smith 2016b.
8 http://www.literaturepage.com/read/francis-bacon-essays-24.html (accessed 23rd August 2016).
9 Osborne 2015.
10 Améry 1964, 223.
11 Améry 1964, 234.
12 'Brexit an "extraordinary self-inflicted wound" which will cost households £4,300 says George Osborne', 18th April 2016, *International Business Times* at http://www.ibtimes.co.uk/brexit-extraordinary-self-inflicted-wound-which-will-cost-each-household-4300-says-george-1555319 (accessed 25th August 2016).
13 Améry 1999.
14 'Cameron pressing leaders for EU deal by Christmas, says Tusk', 2nd December 2015, *The Guardian* at http://www.theguardian.com/politics/2015/dec/02/cameron-pressing-leaders-for-eu-deal-before-christmas-says-tusk
15 'UK and German economies "the beating heart of Europe", says George Osborne', 2nd November 2015, *The Guardian* at http://www.theguardian.com/world/2015/nov/02/uk-and-german-economies-are-the-beating-heart-of-europe-says-osborne; 'UK premier fights to put US-EU trade talks back on track',17th December 2014, *ft.com* at http://www.ft.com/cms/s/0/59ea62c8-8601-11e4-a105-00144feabdc0.html#axzz3pr8O4anR; 'TTIP: David Cameron attempts to rally support for controversial international trade deal', 18th December 2014, *The Independent* at http://www.independent.co.uk/news/world/europe/ttip-david-cameron-attempts-to-rally-support-for-controversial-international-trade-deal-9934330.html (accessed 24th August 2016).
16 Tom Scheff identifies links between mutual estrangement, competitive humiliation and destructive conflict. See Scheff 2000.
17 Angell 1911.
18 For an insightful discussion see Rodrick 2011.
19 Aldrich 2010; Singer and Friedman 2014.
20 See, for example, Smith 2014, Smith 2015, Smith and Wright 2000. See also Middlemas 1995.
21 See, for example, Banks 2016; Oliver 2016; Shipman 2016.
22 Ishihara 1991; Kupchan 2012; Mahbubani 2008; Mishra 2013; Said 1994.
23 Geithner 2014; Smith 2014; Smith 2015b; Tett 2009
24 Baden-Powell 2004; Churchill 2007; Kipling 2010.
25 Mamdani 2004; Mamdani 2009.
26 For example, Mishra 2017; Kirkchick 2017; Luce 2017
27 See Kagan 2003; Kant 1983; Saurette 2005; Senghaas 2007; Smith 2006, 132–5.

Bibliography

Aldrich, R.J. (2010). *GCHQ. The Uncensored Story of Britain's Most Secret Intelligence Agency.* London: Harper Press.
Alexander, J.C. (2012). *Trauma. A Social Theory.* Cambridge: Polity Press.
Alinsky, S. (1971). *Rules for Radicals. A Pragmatic Primer for Realistic Radicals.* New York NY: Random House.
Améry, J. (1964). *Preface to the Future. Culture in a Consumer Society.* New York, NY: Frederick Ungar; originally published in 1961 as *Geburt der Gegenwart: Gestalten und Gestaltungen der westlichen Zivilisation seit Kriegsende.* Olten: Walter (*Birth of the Present*).
Améry, J. (1980b). *At the Mind's Limits. Contemplations by a Survivor on Auschwitz and its Realities.* Bloomington, IN: Indiana University Press; originally published in 1966 German as *Jenseits von Schuld und Sühne.* Munich: Szczesny (*Beyond Crime and Punishment*).
Améry, J. (1999). *On Suicide. A Discourse on Voluntary Death.* Bloomington and Indianapolis: Indiana University Press; originally published in 1976 in German as *Hand an Sich legen. Diskurs über den Freitod.* Stuttgart: Klett-Cotta.
Angell, N. (1911). *The Great Illusion. A Study of the Relation of Military Power in Nations to their Economic and Social Advantage.* New York: G.P. Putnam's & Sons.
Annan, N. (1990). *Our Age. The Generation that Made Post-War Britain.* London: Fontana.
Ashcroft, M. and Culwick, K. (2016). *Well, You Did Ask... Why the UK Voted to Leave the EU.* London: Biteback Publishing.
Baden-Powell, R. (2004). *Scouting for Boys. A Handbook for Instruction in Good Citizenship.* Edited with an Introduction and Notes by Elleke Boehmer. Oxford: Oxford University; originally published 1908.
Bailey, F.G. (2001). *Stratagems and Spoils. A Social Anthropology of Politics.* Boulder CO: Westview; originally published 1969.
Banks, A. (2016). *The Bad Boys of Brexit. Tales of Mischief, Mayhem and Guerilla Warfare in the EU Referendum Campaign.* London: Biteback Publishing.
Barr, J. (2012). *A Line in the Sand: Britain, France and the struggle that shaped the Middle East.* London: Simon and Schuster.
Bennett, O. (2016). *The Brexit Club. The Inside Story of the Leave Campaign's Shock Victory.* London: Biteback.
Cato the Younger (pseud.). (2017). *Guilty Men.* London: Biteback Publishing.
Churchill, W.S. (2007). *London to Ladysmith via Pretoria.* Teddington: Echo Library; originally published in 1900.
Churchill, W.S. (2007). *The World Crisis 1911–1918.* London: Penguin; originally published 1931.
Cockfield, A. (Lord Cockfield) (1994). *The European Union. Creating the Single Market.* London: Wiley Chancery Law.
Colley, L. (2014). *Acts of Union and Disunion.* London: Profile Books.
Davidson, C. (2016). *Shadow Wars. The Secret Struggle for the Middle East.* London: Oneworld.
Davis, M. (2001). *Late Victorian Holocausts: El Nino Famines and the Making of the Third World.* London: Verso.
Davis, M. (2006). *Planet of Slums.* London: Verso.

Duchêne, F. (1980). *Jean Monnet. The First Statesman of Interdependence*. London: W. W.Norton.
Eisenstadt, S.N. (2000). 'Multiple Modernities', *Daedalus*; Winter 2000, 1–29.
Elias, N. (1983). *The Court Society*. Oxford: Blackwell.
Elkins, C. (2005). *Britain's Gulag. The Brutal End of Empire in Kenya*. London: Jonathan Cape.
Ellmann, R. (1988). *Oscar Wilde*. London: Penguin.
Emerson, R.W. (1876). *English Traits*. Boston, MA: Houghton, Mifflin and Company.
Farage, N. (2015). *The Purple Revolution. The Year That Changed Everything*. London: Biteback Publishing.
Ford, R. and Goodwin, M.J. (2014). *Revolt on the Right. Explaining Support for the Radical Right in Britain*. London: Routledge.
Frankopan, P. (2016). *The Silk Roads. A New History of the World*. London: Bloomsbury Publishing.
Geithner, T.F. (2014). *Stress Test. Reflections on Financial Crises*. London: Penguin Random House.
Gibbon, G. (2016). *Breaking Point. The EU Referendum on the EU and its Aftermath*. London: Haus Curiousities.
Giddens, A. (2000). *Runaway World. How Globalization is Reshaping Our Lives*. London: Routledge.
Godwin, M. and Milazzo, C. (2015). *UKIP: Inside the Campaign to Redraw the Map of British Politics*. Oxford: Oxford University Press.
Gorman, D. (2012). *The Emergence of International Society in the 1920s*. Cambridge: Cambridge University Press.
Hancock, W.K. (1968). *Smuts. vol 2. The Field of Force*. Cambridge: Cambridge University Press.
Hašek, J. (2016). *The Good Soldier Švejk*. London: Penguin; originally published in 1923.
Heidelberger-Leonard, I. (2010). *The Philosopher of Auschwitz. Jean Améry and Living with the Holocaust*. London and New York: I.B.Taurus.
Hennessy, P. and Jinks, J. (2015). *The Silent Deep. The Royal Navy Submarine Service since 1945*. London: Penguin.
Henwood, D. (1997). *Wall Street. How It Works and for Whom*. London: Verso.
Hertz, N. (2001). *The Silent Takeover. Global Capitalism and the Death of Democracy*. London: William Heinemann.
Holton, R.J. (2008). *Global Networks*. Basingstoke: Palgrave Macmillan.
Huntington, S.P. (1997). *The Clash of Civilizations and the Remaking of World Order*. London: Penguin.
Ikeberry, G.J. (2001). *After Victory. Institutions, Strategic Restraint, and the Rebuilding of Order After Major Wars*. Princeton, NJ: Princeton University Press.
Ishihara, S. (1991). *The Japan That Can Say No*. New York, NY: Simon & Schuster.
Johnston, D.J. (2017). *Missing the Tide. Global Governments in Retreat*. Montreal: McGill-Queen's University Press.
Kant, I. (1983). *Perpetual Peace and Other Essays*. Cambridge: Hackett Publishing Company; originally published in 1784–1795.
Keen, D. (2012). *Useful Enemies. When Waging Wars is More Important than Winning Them*. New Haven CT: Yale University Press.
Kennedy, P. (1987). *The Rise and Fall of the Great Powers. Economic Change and Military Conflict from 1500 to 2000*. New York, NY: Random.
Kipling, R. (2010). *Kim*. London: Vintage Classics; originally published 1901.

Kirkchick, J. (2017). *The End of Europe. Dictators, Demagogues and the Coming Dark Age*. New Haven CT: Yale University Press.
Klare, M.T. (2001). *Resource Wars. The New Landscape of Global Conflict*. New York: Owl Books.
Klare, M.T. (2008). *Rising Powers, Shrinking Planet. How Scarce Energy is Creating a New World Order*. Oxford: OneWorld.
Klein, N. (2000). *No Logo. Taking Aim at the Brand Bullies*. London: HarperCollins.
Kupchan, C. (2012). *No One's World. The West, the Rising East and the Coming Global Turn*. Oxford: Oxford University Press.
Lindner, E. (2006). *Making Enemies. Humiliation and International Conflict*. Santa Barbara CA: Praeger.
Linton, M. (2006). 'Robespierre and the Terror', *History Today*, 56, 8, 23–29.
Lodge, T. (2006). *Mandela. A Critical Life*. Oxford: Oxford University Press.
Luce, E. (2017). *The Retreat of Western Liberalism*. London: Little, Brown.
Mahbubani, K. (2008). *The New Asian Hemisphere. The Irresistible Shift of Global Power to the East*. New York, NY: Publicaffairs.
Mamdani, M. (2004). *Good Muslim, Bad Muslim. Islam, the USA and the Global War Against Terror*. Hyderabad: Orient Black Swan.
Mamdani, M. (2009). *Saviours and Survivors. Darfur, Politics and the War on Terror*. London: Verso.
Mann, M. (1986–2013). *The Sources of Social Power*, 4 vols. Cambridge: Cambridge. University Press.
Mayer, J. (2016). *Dark Money. How a Secretive Group of Billionaires is Trying to Buy Political Control in the US*. London: Scribe Publications.
Meek, J. (2015). *Private Island. Why Britain Now Belongs to Someone Else*. London: Verso.
Middlemas, K. (1986). *Power, Competition and the State. Vol 1: Britain in Search of Balance, 1940–61*. London: Macmillan.
Middlemas, K. (1990). *Power, Competition and the State. Vol 2: Threats to the Postwar Settlement, 1961–74*. London: Macmillan.
Middlemas, K. (1991). *Power, Competition and the State. Vol 3: The End of the Postwar Era: Britain Since 1974*. London: Macmillan.
Middlemas, K. (1995). *Orchestrating Europe. The Informal Politics of the European Union, 1943–95*. London: Fontana.
Milward, A.S. (1992). *The European Rescue of the Nation-State*. London: Routledge.
Mishra, P. (2013), *From the Ruins of Empire. The Revolt against the West and the Remaking of Asia*. London: Penguin.
Mishra, P. (2017). *The Age of Anger. A History of the Present*. London: Little, Brown.
Moore, B. (1991). *Social Origins of Dictatorsbip and Democracy*. London: Penguin.
Moore, C. (2013). *Margaret Thatcher. The Authorized Biography. Vol 1: Not For Turning*. London: Allen Lane.
Moore, C. (2015). *Margaret Thatcher. The Authorized Biography. Vol 2: Everything She Wants*. London: Allen Lane.
Oliver, C. (2016). *Unleashing Demons. The Inside Story of Brexit*. London: Hodder & Stoughton
Osborne, J. (2015). *Look Back in Anger*. London: Faber & Faber.
Ozersky, J. (2012). *Colonel Sanders and the American Dream*. Austin, TX: University of Texas Press.
Palan, R. (2003). *The Offshore World. Sovereign Markets, Virtual Place, and Nomad Millionaires*. Ithaca, NY: Cornell University Press.

Petersen, A. (2011). *The World Island. Eurasian Geopolitics and the Fate of the West.* Santa Barbara CA: Praeger.
Popham, P. (2011). *The Lady and the Peacock. The Life of Aung San Suu Kyi.* London: Rider Books.
Robertson, R. (1992). *Globalization. Social Theory and Global Culture.* London: Sage.
Rodrick, D. (2011). *The Globalization Paradox. Why Global Markets, States and Democracy Can't Coexist.* Oxford: Oxford University Press.
Runciman, W.G. (1989). *A Treatise on Social Theory. Vol 2: Substantive Social Theory,* Cambridge: Cambridge University Press.
Runciman, W.G. (2009). *The Theory of Cultural and Social Selection.* Cambridge: Cambridge University Press.
Said, E. (1994). *Culture and Imperialism.* London: Vintage Books.
Sands, P. (2005). *Lawless World. Making and Breaking Global Rules.* London: Allen Lane.
Sassen, S. (2014). *Expulsions. Brutality and Complexity in the Global Economy.* Cambridge MA: Belknap Press of Harvard University Press.
Saurette, P. (2005). *The Kantian Imperative. Humiliation, Common Sense, Politics.* Toronto: Toronto University Press.
Scheff, T.J. (2000). *Bloody Revenge. Emotions, Nationalism and War.* Lincoln, NE: Authors Guild Backprint; originally published in 1994.
Schivelbusch, W. (2003). *The Culture of Defeat. On National Trauma, Mourning and Recovery.* London: Granta.
Schofield, C. (2013). *Enoch Powell and the Making of Postcolonial Britain.* Cambridge: Cambridge University Press.
Scholte, J.A. (2000). *Globalization. A Critical Introduction.* London: Palgrave.
Seldon, A. and Snowdon, S. (2015). *Cameron at 10. The Inside Story 2010–2015.* London: William Collins.
Senghaas, D. (2007) *On Perpetual Peace. A Timely Assessment.* Oxford: Berghahn Books
Shaxson, N. (2012) *Treasure Islands. Tax Havens and the Men who Stole the World.* London: Vintage.
Shipman, T. (2016). *All Out War. The Full Story of How Brexit Sank Britain's Political Class.* London: William Collins.
Singer, P.W. and Friedman, A. (2014). *Cybersecurity and Cyberwar. What Everyone Needs to Know.* Oxford: Oxford University Press.
Smith, D. (1990a). *Capitalist Democracy on Trial. The Transatlantic Debate from Tocqueville to the Present.* London: Routledge.
Smith, D. (1991). *The Rise of Historical Sociology.* Cambridge: Polity.
Smith, D. (2001). *Norbert Elias and Modern Social Theory,* London: Sage.
Smith, D. (2006a). *Globalization. The Hidden Agenda.* Cambridge: Polity.
Smith, D. (2010). 'Social Fluidity and Social Displacement', *Sociological Review*, 58, 4, November, 680–688.
Smith, D. (2012a). 'Dimensions of World Making: Thoughts from the Caspian Sea' in D. Kalekin-Fishman and A. Denis (eds) *The Shape of Sociology.* London: Sage, 113–133.
Smith, D. (2013). 'Forced Social Displacement: the 'inside stories' of Oscar Wilde, Jean Améry, Nelson Mandela and Aung San Suu Kyi' in Nicolas Demertsiz (ed.) *Emotions in Politic.* London: Palgrave-Macmillan (2013), 60–83.
Smith, D. (2014a). 'Coping with the threat of humiliation: Contrasting responses to the crisis of the Eurozone in Greece and Ireland' in N.P. Petropoulos and G.O.

Tsobanoglou (eds) *The Debt Crisis in the Eurozone: Social Impacts.* Newcastle-upon-Tyne: Cambridge Scholars Publishing, 84–108.
Smith, D. (2014b). 'Making sense of the EU crisis' in D. Smith et al *Dennis Smith in Ljubljana.* Ljubljana: University of Ljubljana, 2014, 89–109.
Smith, D. (2015). 'Not just singing the blues: Dynamics of the EU Crisis' in H.-J. Trenz, C. Ruzza and V. Guiraudon (eds) *Europe's Prolonged Crisis. The Making or the Unmaking of a Political Union.* London: Palgrave Macmillan, 23–43.
Smith, D. (2016a). *Conflict and Compromise. Class Formation in English Society 1830–1914. A Comparative Study of Birmingham and Sheffield.* London: Routledge.
Smith, D. (2016b). 'The Return of Big Historical Sociology' in R. Schroeder (ed.) *Global Powers. Michael Mann's Anatomy of the Twentieth Century and Beyond.* Cambridge: Cambridge University Press, 39–61.
Smith, D. (2016c). 'Barrington Moore' in *International Encyclopedia of the Social and Behavioral Sciences,* 2nd edition, 768–774.
Smith, D. (2016d). 'Coping with Captivity. The Social Phenomenon of Humiliation Explored Through Prisoners' Dilemmas' in E. Halas (ed.) *Life-World, Intersubjectivity and Culture. Contemporary Dilemmas.* Warsaw: Peter Lang, 147–165.
Smith, D. (2016e). 'Englishness and the Liberal Inheritance after 1886' in P. Colls and P. Dodd (eds) *Englishness. Politics and Culture 1880–1920.* London: Bloomsbury, 279–306.
Smith, D. and Wright, S. (2000). *Whose Europe? The Turn Towards Democracy.* Oxford: Blackwell.
Singer, P.W. and Friedman, A. (2014). *Cybersecurity and Cyberwar.* Oxford: Oxford University Press.
Stiglitz, J. (2010). *Freefall. Free Markets and the Sinking of the Global Economy.* London: Penguin Books.
Streek, W. (2013). *Buying Time. The Delayed Crisis of Democratic Capitalism.* London: Verso.
Tett, G. (2009). *Fool's Gold. How Unrestrained Greed Corrupted a Dream, Shattered Global Markets and Unleashed a Catastrophe.* London: Little Brown.
Von Tunzelman, A. (2007). *Indian Summer. The Secret History of the End of an Empire.* London: Penguin Books.
Wallerstein, I. (1974–2011). *The Modern World System,* 4 vols. New York: Free Press.
Zarakol, A. (2011). *After Defeat. How the East Learned to Live with the West.* Cambridge: Cambridge University Press.

Index

abuse, 75, 79, 99, 104, 159, 164
acceptance, 156, 159, 164, 166–71, 178, 184, 187
acquiescence, 159, 170
Adorno, Thedor, 71
Adour river (France), 67
advocacy, 80, 94, 127, 181, 183
Afghanistan, 33, 38, 155
Africa, 3, 90–1, 94, 96, 99, 107; *see also* South Africa
African National Congress (ANC), 15–16, 88–91, 95–109, 162–3
African Union (AU), 178
Afrikaners, 11, 13, 88, 90–9, 102, 106–7; *see also* Dutch, Boers
aging, 76–8
Alaungpaya, king (Burma), 118
Albemarle club (London), 39
Alexander II, czar, 40
Alexander, George, 17
alienation, 11, 79, 139, 158
alleviation, 164–8, 170, 179, 183–4, 186–7
Alps, 12, 64, 103
altruism, 188
Altstätten (Switzerland), 15
Amanpour, Christiane, 133
Amarapura, king (Burma), 117
Ambühl, Johann Ludwig, 15
Améry, Jean, 61-81; *family*: father (Paul Mayer), 63–4; mother (Valerie Mayer née Goldschmidt), 64–5; paternal grandfather, 64–65; 63–5; wife, first (Regina Mayer née Berger), 66–7, 70; wife, second (Maria Leitner), 67, 69, 75; *life and career*: after World War II, 69–71; analyzing the human condition, 74–80; avoiding the Nazis, 67–8; childhood, youth and early adulthood, 65–6; in the Nazis' hands, 68–9; reputation, 69–70, 77, 79–81, 160; suicide, 61, 80–81; surveying the West, 71–4; *works*: *At the Mind's Limit*, 12, 18–19, 72–5; *Die Schiffbrüchigen (The Shipwrecked)*, 66, 75; *Dornenkrone Der Liebe (Love's Crown of Thorns)*, 70; *Karrieren und Köpfe (Careers and Leaders)*, 71; *Lefeu*, 78–9; *Preface to the Future*, 72–4, 180–1; *On Aging*, 76–8; *On Suicide*, 5, 61, 76, 79–81; *see also* Hans Mayer
Amis, Kingsley, 73
Amritsar (India), 53
Amsterdam (Netherlands), 8
anarchism, 12, 17, 33, 40–47, 117, 155, 184
Anawrahta, king (Burma), 118
Andromedid meteor shower, 1
Angell, Norman, 182
Anglicanism, 12, 47
Anglo-Burmese wars, 34, 42, 128
Anglo-Irish, 10, 35–6, 48, 158
Annan, Kofi, 137–8, 145n105, 145n106
Annan Commission (Advisory Commission on Rakhine state), *see* Annan
Anschluss, 63
anthropology, 13, 45, 97
anti-fascism, 124
Antigone, 14
anti-Semitism, 64
Antwerp (Belgium), 2, 67
anxiety, 11–13, 38, 62, 67, 73, 165, 184
apartheid, 3–4, 10–16, 19, 21, 88–107, 124–5, 133, 152, 161–4
Apennines (Italy), 6
Arakan (Burma), 120, 135, 137, 144n97, 145n105

architecture, 8, 71, 118, 131
A Rebours (Huysmans), 42; *see also* Huysmans
Arendt, Hannah, 18, 51–3, 87
Arnold, Matthew, 45
Assam (India), 119
Association of South East Asian Nations (ASEAN), 130, 178
Athenaeum club (London), 39
Aung San Suu Kyi, 115–40; *family*: father (Aung San), 20–1, 116, 118–20, 122–5,127, 129, 139; husband (Michael Aris), 126, 128; mother (Khin Kyi), 15, 116, 123, 126; *life and career*: childhood and early youth, 126; imprisoned, 128–9; in exile, 126; in government, 132–40; political campaigning, 127–8; reputation115–6; writings, 126
austerity, 171, 181, 184
Australia, 37, 130
Austro-Hungarian empire, 51, 63, 65
authority, 4, 8, 11, 16, 19, 40–1, 97–102, 129–36, 154–61
autocracy, 2, 51, 53, 117, 135, 154
Auschwitz (Poland), vii, 10–19, 61, 68–80, 103, 160, 166
Austria, 10–15, 61–67, 69–70, 78, 81n9, 102–3, 130, 156, 169
autonomy, 97, 101, 124
avoidance, 157–67, 184, 186

Bacon, Francis, 179
Bad Aussee (Austria), 64
Bad Gastein (Austria), 64
Bad Ischl (Austria), 61, 63–4
Baldwin, James, 66
Bandula, general (Burma), 128
Bangkok (Thailand), 130, 142n76
Bangladesh, 114, 117, 135, 137–8, 145
Bantustans, 16, 100, 106
Baring, Evelyn (Lord Cromer), 52, 154
Barlas, John, 34–5, 49, 120–1
Barnett, Samuel, 154
Bavaria (Germany), 18
Bayinnaung, king (Burma), 118
Bayonne (France), 67
Beijing (China), viii, 6, 116, 151, 162, 178
Belgium, 7, 10, 12, 59, 67–9, 78, 156–70
Benson, Edward Frederic, 50
Berchtesgaden (Germany), 64
Bergen-Belsen (Germany), 69

Berlin (Germany), vii, 4, 8–9, 63, 77, 88, 151–3, 177
Bhutan, 126
Biko, Steve, 89
Bingham (UK), 39, 47
bird of misfortune, 78; *see also* Schmid
Black consciousness movement, 89, 99
Blunt, Wilfrid Scawan, 34
Boehmer, Elieke, 96
Boers, 4, 21, 42, 51–2, 87–107, 153; *see also* Afrikaners, Dutch
Bombay (Mumbai), 52
Bo Min Yaung, 120
borderlands (Burma), 13, 16, 63–4, 98, 117, 119–124, 130–39
borders, 8, 12, 15, 116, 124, 185
Bosie, 34, 45, 48–50; *see also* Douglas
Botha, Louis, 94
Botha, Pieter, 88
Botswana, 98
Bovary, Charles, 77, 79, 80
Bovary, Emma, 77, 79, 80
boycotts, 15, 95, 98, 141n34
Boyne, battle of, 35
Bracknell, Lady, 2, 33n3, 43–4, 47, 121, 153
Braine, John, 73
Brasenose College, Oxford, 38
Brexit, 22n9, 155, 171, 176, 179–87
British South Africa Company, 93
Broadway (New York), 45
Broch, Hermann, 65
Broederbond, 95, 124
Brücke, Die, 65, 75, 169; *see also* Améry
Brussels (Belgium), 2, 11, 67–71, 75, 144, 184
Buckingham Palace, 8, 35, 102
buddhism, 4, 13, 20, 116–37, 170
Buffalo City (South Africa), 89
Bunthorne (Gilbert and Sullivan), 39, 41, 45, 47
Burlington Magazine, The, 41
Burma (Myanmar), 116–46
Burma Defense Army (BDA), 123
Burma Independence Army (BIA), 123
Burma Socialist Programme Party (BSPP), 124–5
Burman people (Burma), 16, 119–20, 122, 133, 157, 167
Buthelezi, Wellington, 15

Caine, Michael, 179
Cairo (Egypt), 41

Calcraft-Kennedy, Bennet Christian Huntingdon, 52–3; *see also* Carthill
Callahan, Mary, 122
Calvin, Jean, 15
calvinism, 52
Cameron, David, 180–1
Camus, Albert, 70
Canada, 37, 131
Canetti, Elias, 65
Cape Town (South Africa), 91–2, 103
Carew, Tom, 123
Carlson, Joel, 90
Carnap, Rudolf, 65
Carroll, Lewis, 41–3
Carson, Edward, 36, 48, 158
Carthill, Al, 52, 55n83; *see also* Calcraft-Kennedy
catholicism, 12, 35, 42, 62, 64
Cavalleria rusticana (Pietro Mascagni), 47
celebrity, 11, 33, 36, 39, 71
censorship, 125, 132, 134
Central Intelligence Agency (CIA), 124
Cervantes, Miguel, 76
Chamberlain, Joseph, 42, 62, 93, 153–4
Chamberlain, Neville, 62
Champion, Henry Hyde, 33
Chancellor House Trust (South Africa), 105
charisma, 11, 89, 104–8, 122–9, 157, 161, 169–70
Charlemagne, 6
charm, 11–15, 37, 39, 46, 103, 115, 179
Chelsea (London), 34, 39, 41, 43, 47
Cheltenham (UK), 33
Chiang Kai-shek, 122
Chin (Burma), 119, 130
China vi, 37, 74, 117–52, 162, 176, 178
choice, 61–2, 70, 76, 127, 156, 166, 184
christianity, 8, 13, 52, 64, 88–107, 125, 156
Churchill, Winston, 19, 94, 107, 154
cigarettes, 12, 17–18, 44
circumcision, 97, 121
civilization, 8, 12–14, 74–94, 154, 179, 183, 188
Clinton, Hillary, 131, 139
collapse, 151, 161, 163, 182, 188
Collins, Michael, 94
Collis, Maurice, 141n32
Cologne (Germany), 47
Commonwealth, 3, 194, 55, 171
communism, 19, 74, 89–91, 97–124, 151
compliance, 7, 10, 75, 166, 178

concentration camps, 10, 19, 51, 61, 68–72, 93, 152
conciliation, vii, 50, 65–6, 102–3, 134–9, 156, 167–8; *see also* Truth and Reconciliation Commission
Conference on Interaction and Confidence Building in Asia (CICA), 178
Congress of South African Trade Unions (COSATU), 104–5
Congress of Vienna, 33
conquest, 7, 40, 53, 119–20, 188
conscience, 40, 52, 73–4, 80, 119
consciousness, 17, 68, 72, 89, 99
Constantinople, 8–9, 151, 176; *see also* Istanbul
constitutions, 104, 130–1; Austria 1938 (*Anschluss*), 62; Burma 1947, 128; Burma 1974, 124: Burma 2008, 132–3, 135, 139, 157; Ireland 1937, 62; South Africa 1996, 101; Transvaal (South Africa), 1907, 107
consumption, 71, 79, 89, 177–8, 177–8
Convention for a Democratic South Africa (CODESA), 103–4, 167
Coppola, Francis Ford, 47
Corbyn, Jeremy, 183
corruption, vi, 11, 46–51, 70, 89, 100–6, 130, 138, 155–9, 187
cosmology, 120, 126, 162
courts, royal, 14, 39, 47–8, 156, 189n3; judicial, 15, 19, 35–7, 53, 80, 95–8, 103–4
Coward, Noel, 179
Crabbet Park, 34
Crimean War, 21
criticism, 39–41, 46, 66, 77–80, 108, 115–16, 128–36, 152–4, 160
cronyism, 105–6
Crosthwaite, Charles (chief commissioner, Burma), 120
cruelty, 50–1, 73–4, 91, 99, 159, 164, 187
Cuba, 98, 101, 171n2
culture, 125–6, 155–8, 180, 186, 188
Curzon, George, 34
Cyclone Nargis (Burma), 131
Cyprus, x, 7, 171
Cyrillic alphabet, 8
Czechoslovakia, 62

dacoit (bandit), 16–17
dams; *see* hydropower
Dante Alighieri, 158
Danubyu (Burma), 128

Davies, Thomas Arthur Harkness, 33
Davitt, Michael (Ireland), 15–16, 36
De Beauvoir, Simone, 70
deception, 18, 34, 50–1, 77, 152, 167
decline, viii, 2–3, 11, 21, 62, 76, 151, 170, 176
defiance, 12, 53, 72, 80, 97, 164
De Gaulle, Charles, 72
Delhi (India), 116, 126, 178
Depayin (Burma), 130
De Valera, Eamonn, 10, 127
Dickens, Charles, 18
dictatorship, 3–16, 53, 88, 152, 183–4
disintegration, vii, 2, 21, 40, 66, 133, 151–3
displacement, 73–4, 119, 128, 138, 152–71, 187
Disraeli, Benjamin, 8
Dobama Asiayone (We Burmans Association), 122
Dollfuss, Englebert, 66
dominions, 93, 95, 177
Don Quixote, 76; *see also* Cervantes
Dora-Mittelbau (Germany), 69
Douglas, Lord Alfred (Bosie), 10, 34, 44–5, 48–50
D'Oyly Carte, Richard, 39
Dracula, 37; *see also* Stoker
Drakensberg mountains (South Africa), 96
drug trafficking, 16, 117, 119
Drumlanrig, Lord, 49
Drury Lane Theatre (London), 18
Dublin, 2, 11–12, 35–8, 42, 127, 155
Dufferin, Lord, 120
Dumas, Alexander the younger, 18
Durban (South Africa), 18, 89, 92, 96, 105, 108
Dutch, 52, 87, 90–1; *see also* Afrikaners, Boers
Dutch Reformed Church, 89
Dyer, Reginald, 53

Eagleton, Terry, 12
Egypt, 44, 52, 154; *see also* Suez, Cairo
Eichmann, Adolph, 18, 137
Eighty Club (UK), 43
Einstein, Albert, 71
Eisenhower, Dwight, US general, US president, 177
elephants, 1, 6, 120
emancipation, 122, 167–9

emotions, vii, 5, 14, 22, 73–79, 100, 128, 159–60, 181–8; *see also* feelings
empires, 8–9, 22, 37, 51, 63, 65, 118, 151, 153
engagement, 1, 14–15, 48–79, 91–9, 135–6, 151–69, 187
escape, 10, 49–67, 69, 75, 78, 80, 101, 104, 130, 159–66
Eurasia, vii, 21, 160, 177
European Union (EU), 178–86
Eurozone, 186
exclusion, 39–40, 64, 106, 169
exile, 2, 10, 39–43, 98–104, 124, 158, 169–70
existentialism, 3, 61–2, 70, 102, 156
exploitation, 13, 35, 79, 87, 184, 187–8

Fackel, Die (The Torch), 65; *see also* Kraus
Farage, Nigel, 171
fascism, 87–90, 118, 152, 156; *see also* nazism, neo-fascism
Fashoda, 51
Federmann, Moritz, 66
feelings ix, 14, 62–64, 76–80, 128, 146, 160–6, 171, 181; *see also* emotions
feminism, 12, 42
Fenians, 9–10, 38
Ferguson, Niall, 155
feudalism, 15, 176
Feuermann, 78
Feuerreiter, 78–9
Freemasons, 38
Flaubert, Gustave, 77, 80
Flory, John, 121
Fort Breendonk (Belgium), 68, 70, 74, 79
Franks, 6
Freemasons, 38
Freud, Sigmund, 56

Gadla Henry, 97
Gandhi, Mohandas, 4, 50–1, 95–98, 108, 127, 152–4, 188
Gasthaus zur Stadt Prag (Bad Ischl), 63
Geneva (Switzerland), 15
Genoa (Italy), 7
Gestapo, 68, 70, 78
Gide, André, 50
Gilbert and Sullivan, 45
Ginsberg (South Africa), 89, 105
Gladstone, William, 40, 53, 153

Glasgow (Scotland), 7, 34
Gliwice (Poland), 69
globalization, 129–30, 179, 185–6, 189n7
Goethe, Johann Wolfgang, 64
Good Soldier Svej, The (Jaroslav Hašek), 176
Gossau (Switzerland), 15
Gounod tavern (Antwerp), 67
Grass, Günter, 18
Greece, 8, 14, 18, 37, 39, 171
Grillo, Beppe, 171
Gupta family (South Africa), 105
Gurs (France), 67

Haggard, Rider, 50
Hainan island (China), 122
Hani, Chris, 98, 102
Hapsburg dynasty, 21, 63
Haringey (London), 98
Hastings, Warren, 51
Hauptmann, Gerhart, 71
Heidegger, Martin, 70
herrenvolk, 88
Hertzog, Barry, 91, 96
Het Volk (South Africa), 94
High Organ, 99, 101; *see also* Robben Island
Hirohito, emperor, 124
Hiroshima (Japan), 21
Hitler, Adolf, 3–4, 8–11, 51–3, 62–6, 73, 87–8, 137, 159, 177
Hobsbawm, Eric, 15
Hohenems (Austria), 15, 64
Holden, Paul, 108
Hölderlin, Friedrich, 19
Holocaust, 12, 78
homosexuality, 12, 48–51
Horkheimer, Max, 71
Houdini, 159
Htin Kyaw, 132
Huddleston, Trevor (bishop), 88
humanitarian, 13, 53, 136–9, 145–54, 160
humiliation, vii, ix, 5–11, 49, 79–87, 131, 151–75, 181–4, 186–8
Huysmans, Joris-Karl, 42; *see also A Rebours*
hydropower, 16, 119

icons, 13, 18, 88, 126, 155, 160–1
ideology, 8, 91, 100, 124, 129
Ignatieff, Michael, 155
Indian Institute for Advanced Studies, 126

Inkatha Freedom Party (South Africa), 102
inner, vii, 72, 75, 116, 159–69
insurgency, 2–4, 15, 90–1, 123–4, 178, 183
intellectuals, 13–4, 19, 43, 62, 66–7, 73–4, 97, 126
International Labour Organization (ILO), 178
International Monetary Fund (IMF), 185–6
Iraq, ix, 63, 155, 182
Ireland, 2–3, 9, 11–12, 15, 34–62
Irish-Americans, 43
Irrawaddy river (Burma), 17, 117, 119, 120–1, 127, 131
Ishihara, Shintaro, 185
Islam, 7; *see also* muslims
Israel, 18, 103, 134, 165
Istanbul, 8, 153; *see also* Constantinople
Italy, 7, 9, 50, 78, 130, 160, 170

Jagan, Lary, 140
Jameson, Leander Starr, 93
Jameson Raid, 49, 93
Japan, 62, 74, 117–18, 131, 133–4, 152, 178
Jews, vii, 10–15, 43, 62–75, 95–103, 137, 152–66
Joffe, Joel, 20
Johannesburg (South Africa), 2, 19, 66, 88–9, 92, 97, 102
Johnson, Boris, 2
Johnson, R.W., 105–6
journalism, 17, 36, 43, 69–75, 107, 131, 160
judo, 163–5
justice, 3, 18, 103–4, 133–38, 160, 177–86

Kachin (Burma), 119, 127
Kalvarienberg (Mount Calvary), 63
Katha (Burma), 139
Katlehong (South Africa), 102
Khin Gyi, 123
Ko Ko Gyi, 127
Kyi Maung, 127

Langtry, Lillie, 39
Laos, 117, 119
Larkin, Emma, 131
Latin America, 7, 185–6
Lebra, Joyce, 123

legitimacy, 36–7, 66, 103, 133–38, 167–78, 185
Le Pen, Marine, 171
Lesotho, 96, 98
Levant, 7, 23n15
Levi, Primo, 19
liberalism, 40, 42, 52–3, 64, 80, 131, 151–7
Libya, 155, 182
Lisbon (Portugal), 8
Liu Yun, 133
Liverpool (UK), vii, 7
Lombards, 6
London (UK), 2, 7–17, 34–50, 54n3, 72, 92–98, 107–26, 154–58
Lueger, Karl (mayor of Vienna), 64
Lusaka (Zambia), 100
Lyceum Theatre (London), 36
Lyons (France), 78

Macron, Emmanuel, French president, 185
Madame Bovary (Flaubert), 79–80
Madikizela family, 97, 107
Madrid (Spain), 7, 152
Magdalen College, Oxford, 11, 37, 111n62
Mahaffey, John Pentland, 37–8
Mahbubani, Kishore, 185
Majuba Hill (South Africa), 92
Malan, Daniel, 87
Malaya, 122, 171
Mamdani, Mahmood, 103–4, 186
Mandalay, 1–2, 9, 13, 17, 42, 117–21, 139
Mandela, Nelson, 87–109; *family*: father (Gadla Henry), 97; kin network, 100–101; mother (Nonqaphi Nosekeni), 96; wife, first (Elizabeth Mase), 97; wife, second (Winnie Madizikela-Mandela), 97–101, 107; *life and career*: at the Thembu royal court, 96–7; childhood, 96; education, 96–7; ending apartheid and after, 101–107; in the ANC, 96, 98–103; going underground, 98; lawyer in Johannesburg, 97–8; reputation, 88, 107–8; Robben Island, 99–100
Manipur (India), 20
Mann, Thomas, 12, 77
Maoris, 37
Mao Zedong, 122
Marikana (South Africa), 105
Maritz rebellion (South Africa), 94

Mary Poppins, 129, 133
marxism, 71, 98–99
masks, vi, 44, 47, 49, 51, 158–63
Matabeleland, 52
Matanzima, Kaiser, 100
Ma Thanegi, 127–8
Maughan, Somerset, 50
Maung, Shu; *see* Ne Win
Maxim gun, 2, 52
Maxse, Violet, 41
Maxwell, Elsa, 71
Mayer, Hans, vi, 10, 12, 62, 69; *see also* Jean Améry
Mayfair (London), 47
Mbeki, Govan, 91, 98–100
Mbeki, Thabo, 98, 100–1
McDonalds, 177
Meiktila (Burma), 132
Mein Kampf, 53
Merchant Taylors' School, 33
Merleau-Ponty, Maurice, 70
Merrion Square (Dublin), 35
Mers-el-Kébir (Algeria), 51
methodism, 13–14, 96, 153, 156
Mignolo, Walter, 4
migration, 7, 35, 90, 92, 121, 137
Miles, Frank, 39
Military Intelligence (Burma), 125, 127
Milner, Alfred, 41, 52, 91, 93, 154–5
Minami Kikan, 122
Min Aung Hlaing, Burmese senior general, 116, 132–6, 140, 163
Mingaladon (Burma), 123
Min Yaung, 120
Mishra, Panjak, 185
missionaries, 13, 96
monks, 4, 8, 20, 117–137, 170
Morefield, Jeanne, 155
Mörike, Eduard, 78
Moscow (Russia), 7–8, 17, 151, 153, 162
Mountbatten, Louis, 123
Mount Katrin (Austria), 63
Mozambique, 98
Munich (Germany), 18, 62
muslims, 4, 8, 115, 132, 135, 138–9; *see also* Islam
Mussolini, Benito, 87
Mvezo (South Africa), 96, 156
Myanmar, *see* Burma
Myanmar Economic Corporation (MEC), 129–30

Nagasaki (Japan), 21
Namibia, 90

Napoleon Bonaparte, 8, 37
Natal (South Africa), 37, 95, 108
National Convention (Burma), 130–1
National League for Democracy (NDL, Burma), 117–19, 127–32, 134–40
Naypyidaw (Burma), vii, 117–19, 125, 131–39, 140n7, 178
nazis, vii, 4–5, 9–15, 51, 53–91, 102–3, 152–68
Ndebele, 52
neo-fascism, 3–4, 89, 152, 163
neo-liberalism, 185
Nepal, 126
Netherlands, 7, 170
Newfoundland, 7
New York (USA), viii, 7, 14, 39–40, 45, 115
New Zealand, 37
Nietzsche, Friedrich, 5
nihilism, 40
Nkandla (South Africa), 89
Nordhausen (Germany), 69
Normans, 7
North Atlantic Treaty Organization (NATO), 178, 182
Novgorod (Russia), 7
Nuremberg (Germany), 66, 103

Obama, Barack, US president, 170
Old Bailey (London), 48
opium, 16, 37, 119–20, 130
Orange Free State (South Africa), 90, 91–4, 106
Orange river (South Africa), 91
Origins of Totalitarianism, The, 51; *see also* Hannah Arendt
orthodox christianity, 8
Orwell, George, 50, 52–3, 121, 152, 154
Osborne, George, 181
Osborne, John, 73, 180
Ossewabrandwag (South Africa), 87
Ottoman empire, 6, 8; *see also* Turkey
outsiders, viii, 4, 39, 131
Ovambo, 90
Oxford, 11–14, 33–39, 93, 115, 126–8, 140n4, 154, 158

Pakistan, 151
Pall Mall Gazette, 41
Pan-Africanist Congress (PAC), 91, 99
Panglong (Burma), 120, 134
Panthéon (Paris), 78

Paris (France), 4, 7, 11, 14, 42–4, 70, 78, 159
Parnell, Charles Stewart, 10, 15, 35–6, 38, 43
Parnell Commission, 43
passbooks, 96, 164; *see also* Gandhi, Mandela
Pater, Walter, 38
Patience (Gilbert and Sullivan), 40
Pearl Harbor (Hawaii), 122
Pearson, Charles, 38
Pentonville prison (London), 10
Père Lachaise cemetery (Paris), 50
Pirow, Oswald, 88
Plaut, Martin, 108
poker, 163, 165
Pollsmoor prison (South Africa), 101
Pondo people (South Africa), 16, 96–7, 100, 107
Portugal, 7
Pretoria (South Africa), 19, 88–9, 95, 105
Prussia, 37
Punch, 17–18, 45–7
Punjab (India, Pakistan), 53
Pyongyang (North Korea), 178

Queensberry, Marquess of, 34, 48
Qunu (South Africa), 88, 96

Raddatz, Fritz, 75
Rakhine (Burma), 19, 88–9, 95, 105
Ramaphosa, Cyril, president of South Africa, 108
Rangoon, 33, 53, 55n83, 117, 122; *see also* Yangon
Reagan, Ronald, US president, 185
realpolitik, 157
reconciliation, vii, 13, 138–9, 156
referendum, in Burma 20, 131; in UK, 179–85
Regent (Thembu royal guardian), 96–7
rejection, 10, 35, 39–40, 62–78, 128, 159–71, 181, 186
replacement, 165–7, 169, 184
repression, 4, 119, 129, 131, 134, 136
resentment, 2, 4–5, 10, 35–40, 62–75, 103–6, 125, 154–86
resistance, ix, 7–19, 50, 67–78, 90–1, 98, 104–8, 119–23, 156–71
respect, 1, 5, 29, 36–48, 67, 77, 80, 96–117, 130–36, 152–8, 188
revenge, 6, 10, 38–49, 104, 149, 156, 168–71, 183–4

Rhodes, Cecil, 41, 49, 51, 91–3, 154
Rhodesia, 92–3, 171
Rhymers' club (London), 34–5, 39
rice, 124–5
rioting, 15, 122, 133
Rivonia trial (South Africa), 19, 98
Robben island (South Africa), 10, 14–15, 98–9, 101
Robespierre, Maximilien, 177
Rohingya, 4–5, 115–6, 133–9
Rome (Italy), 6
Rooi Hell prison (South Africa), 91
Roosevelt, Franklin Delano, 93
Rosebury, Lord, 48
Rothschilds (financiers), 92
rugby football, 102–3, 169
Ruskin, John, 38, 154
Russia, 3, 6–8, 21, 34–40, 51, 68, 72, 135, 151, 176, 185; *see also* Soviet Union

sabotage, 10, 19, 87, 101, 156
Said, Edward, 185
sainthood, 5, 115, 132, 155–7, 161
St. Hugh's College, Oxford, 14
St Petersburg (Russia), 8
Saki (Hector Hugh Munro), 50
Salisbury, Lord (Gascoyne-Cecil, Robert), 21, 41, 52, 153
Salzburg (Austria), 61–2, 64
Salzkammergut (Austria), 63
sanctification; *see* sainthood
Sanders, Harland David (Colonel Sanders), 177
Sangha, 121; *see also* monks
Sartre, Jean-Paul, 69–70, 74–7, 80
satyagraha, 96; *see also* Gandhi
Savile club (London), 39
Saya San, 122
Scandinavia, 6
Scheff, Thomas, sociologist, 139
Schiller, Friedrich, 16, 63
Schladming (Austria), 64
Schlick, Moritz, 65
Schmid, Eric, 78
Schoenberg, Arnold, 65
Schreiner, Olive, 42, 44, 93
Schreiner, William, 93
Scotland, 3, 21, 107
Seeley, John Robert, 2
segregation, 87, 89, 95, 107
shame, 46–51, 80, 145n116, 164, 167, 188
Shan (Burma), 120–36
Shanghai, 178

Shanghai Cooperation Organization (SCO), 178
Sharpeville (South Africa), 98, 101, 105
Shepherd's Bush (London), 34
Sheridan, Richard, 18
Shimla (India), 50, 126
Shu Maung; *see* Ne Win
Shwedagon pagoda (Burma), 2, 129, 132, 142n53, 169
Siam, 8; *see also* Thailand
Siberia, 8
Sicily, 7
Singapore, x, 122, 130
Sisulu, Walter, 97
Slim, Joseph ('Bill'), field-marshal, 123
Slovo, Joe, 97
Smuts, Jan Christian, 4, 91, 93, 107–8, 155, 171
Sonnenschein, Jacques, 67
Sophiatown (South Africa), 89
South African Communist Party (SACP), 90, 98, 100, 104–5
Soviet Bloc, 163, 182
Soviet Union, 4, 6, 9, 19, 67–8, 91, 101, 151
Sowetan, The, 89
Soweto (South Africa), 89, 99
Spain, 7, 9, 67, 160, 171n2
Spectator, 43
Speranza, 36, 65; *see also* Wilde
Stalin, Josef, 151, 177
Stalingrad (Soviet Union), 87
Stepniak, Sergei, 34
Stoker, Bram, 36
Strijdom, Hans, 88
Strobl, Gerwin, 51, 87
students, 20, 37, 94–9, 117–32, 170
Sturgeon, Nicola, 21, 24n53
Stuttgart (Germany), 18
subversion, 10, 20, 39, 44, 52, 68, 121, 167
Sudan, 38
Sudetenland (Czechoslovakia), 62
Suez, 2, 46, 171
suicide, 5, 11, 21, 49, 61–77, 83–9, 181
Supreme Court, Pretoria, 19–20
Sussex, 50–1
Swabia (Germany), 18
Swaziland, 98
Switzerland, 15, 69, 99
Syria, 55, 182
Syriam (Burma), 18

Tambo, Oliver, 97–8
Tamil Nadu (India), 121

Tasmania (Australia), 51
Tatmadaw (Burmese military), 115, 118–19, 124–39, 157, 163, 170
Thailand, 8, 16, 117, 119, 134
thakins, 122, 141n34
Thanlyin, 53; *see also* Syriam
Than Tun, 123
Thatcher, Margaret, 185
Thein Sein, 125
Thembu people (South Africa), 14, 24, 31, 96–100, 156
Third Reich, 4, 10, 51–3, 63, 67, 70–1, 73–4
threat-response model, 163–71
Tiananmen square, 162
Tibet, 126
Tocqueville, Alexis de, 9
Tokyo (Japan), 123, 152
torture, vi, 10, 12, 68, 74, 76, 99, 104
totalitarianism, 5, 51–4
Toynbee, Arnold, 154
transformation, 6, 43, 50, 70, 116, 134–9, 163–76
Transkei (South Africa), 13, 15, 88, 96–7, 100
Transvaal (South Africa), 37, 52, 90–4, 96, 106–7
Traun river (Austria), 63
Trinity College, Dublin, 11, 37–8, 158
troika commissions (EU), 186
Trump, Donald (US president), viii, 152, 170, 179–82, 185–6
Truth and Reconciliation Commission (South Africa), 103–4
Turin (Italy), 179
Turkey, 3, 6, 177
Tutu, Desmond (archbishop), 89, 103, 115

uitlanders, 90
Ulster, 36
Umkhonto we Sizwe (Spear of the Nation or MK), 98–9
Umtata (South Africa), 36
Union of Myanmar Economic Holdings (UMEH), 129
United Nations (UN), 94, 138, 178
United States, vii, 3, 7, 21, 37–45, 62–73, 98, 126, 131
United Wa State Army (Burma), 136
U Nu, 124–5, 127
Uppatasanti pagoda (Burma), 188
Upper Burma, 120–1; *see also* Burma
utopia, 45, 106, 117, 156, 165, 184

Vaal river (South Africa), 92
Venice (Italy), 12
Verwoerd, Hendrik, 88
Vichy France, 67
Vienna (Austria), 2, 8–9, 14, 37, 51, 61–78, 151–9, 176
Vietnam, 21, 134
Vikings, 7
Voltaire, 6
Voortrekkers, 88, 91–2, 106, 165; *see also* Boers, Afrikaners
Vorster, John, 87–8

Wachau (Austria), 64
Wandsworth prison (London), 10
Washington (USA), viii, 4, 134, 170, 185–6
Waterkloof Air Force base (South Africa), 88
Waterloo (battle), 39
Whitehall, 35
Wicklow (Ireland), 37
Wilde, Oscar, 32–51; *family*: brother (Willie Wilde), 36–7, 41–2, 48; children, 42; father (Sir William Wilde), 36–7; mother (Lady Jane Wilde, also known as Speranza), 36, 43–4, 48; wife (Constance), 42, 48; *life and career*: American tour 1882, 39; at Magdalen College Oxford, 38–9; at Trinity College Dublin, 37; childhood and early youth, 36–7; life before marriage, 42; pursuing respectability, 41–2; pushing the boundaries, 43–5; reputation, 50–1; supporting Parnell, 42–3; trial, prison and exile, 47–50; West End success, 45–7; *works*: *Ave Imperatrix*, 40; *Decay of Lying, The*, 65; *De Profundis*, 10, 48–50, 74, 164–5; *Duchess of Padua, The* (or *Guido Ferranti*), 40, 45; *Ideal Husband, An*, 46; *Importance of Being Earnest, The* 11, 43, 46–7, 50; *Lady Windermere's Fan*, 17, 33, 39, 45–6, 73; *Picture of Dorian Gray, The* 17, 21, 34, 42, 44 48, 65, 78–9, 159; *Salome*, 42, 44, 65; *Soul of Man under Socialism, The*, ii, v, 17, 34, 65, 165, 169; *Woman of No Importance, A*, 46; *Vera, Or the Nihilists*, 40, 47
William III (William of Orange), 35
Win Htein, 136, 140
Winter Palace (St. Petersburg), 9

Wirathu, 12
Witwatersrand (South Africa), 92, 97

Xhosa, 90–1, 96–7, 103, 121

Yangon, vii, 2, 11, 20, 33, 117–143n91, 156; *see also* Rangoon
Yeats, William Butler, 34, 48, 50

Yugoslavia, 183
Yunnan, 120, 135

Zaw Zaw, 129, 142n75
Zuma, Jacob, 88–9, 100, 105, 10–9
Zulu people, 37–8, 91–2, 102
Zurich (Switzerland), 15, 69
Zwingli, Huldrich, 15